Lois Shawver, PhD

And the Flag Was Still There: Straight People, Gay People, and Sexuality in the U.S. Military

Pre-publication REVIEWS, COMMENTARIES, EVALUATIONS . . .

"This is a first-rate account of the gays-in-the-military issue. . . . Extensive documentation makes clear that the author's arguments have validity. A conscientious reader would have to conclude that the arguments favoring the integration of gays and lesbians into the military must be taken seriously. The author's exposition of the etiquette of disregard neutralizes the claims that modesty and privacy norms are unchangeable."

Theodore R. Sarbin, PhD
Emeritus Professor of Psychology and Criminology, University of Santa Cruz

More pre-publication
REVIEWS, COMMENTARIES, EVALUATIONS . . .

"The book is provocative. . . . Its strengths lie in its grounding in the real world of interpersonal interaction, its insightful use of social and behavioral science knowledge, its clear and persuasive logic, and its ability to speak directly to the issues that are at the heart of homosexual and heterosexual fears, anxieties, and biases. . . . This is the kind of book that, while written against the backdrop of the 'don't ask, don't tell' policy of the U.S. forces, can be read and used to advantage by the general public or by planners, educators, and others. As a careful, well-researched, and pragmatic examination of the key issues involved in homosexuality and military service, it provides an antidote to ideologically based views on both sides of the issue."

Franklin C. Pinch, PhD
Colonel (Retired),
Military Sociologist

"For anyone interested in the issue of gays in the military, this book is must reading. Dr. Shawver tackles this complex and emotional subject in an understandable manner and makes a clear, persuasive, and scholarly case for lifting the ban in the U.S. military."

Lawrence J. Korb
Former Assistant Secretary
of Defense

Harrington Park Press
An Imprint of The Haworth Press, Inc.

NOTES FOR PROFESSIONAL LIBRARIANS AND LIBRARY USERS

This is an original book title published by Harrington Park Press, an imprint of The Haworth Press, Inc. Unless otherwise noted in specific chapters with attribution, materials in this book have not been previously published elsewhere in any format or language.

CONSERVATION AND PRESERVATION NOTES

All books published by The Haworth Press, Inc. and its imprints are printed on certified ph neutral, acid free book grade paper. This paper meets the minimum requirements of American National Standard for Information Sciences–Permanence of Paper for Printed Material, ANSI Z39.48-1984.

And the Flag Was Still There

Straight People, Gay People, and Sexuality in the U.S. Military

HAWORTH Gay and Lesbian Studies
John P. De Cecco, PhD
Editor in Chief

New, Recent, and Forthcoming Titles:

Gay Relationships edited by John De Cecco

Perverts by Official Order: The Campaign Against Homosexuals by the United States Navy by Lawrence R. Murphy

Bad Boys and Tough Tattoos: A Social History of the Tattoo with Gangs, Sailors, and Street-Corner Punks by Samuel M. Steward

Growing Up Gay in the South: Race, Gender, and Journeys of the Spirit by James T. Sears

Homosexuality and Sexuality: Dialogues of the Sexual Revolution, Volume I by Lawrence D. Mass

Homosexuality as Behavior and Identity: Dialogues of the Sexual Revolution, Volume II by Lawrence D. Mass

Sexuality and Eroticism Among Males in Moslem Societies edited by Arno Schmitt and Jehoeda Sofer

Understanding the Male Hustler by Samuel M. Steward

Men Who Beat the Men Who Love Them: Battered Gay Men and Domestic Violence by David Island and Patrick Letellier

The Golden Boy by James Melson

The Second Plague of Europe: AIDS Prevention and Sexual Transmission Among Men in Western Europe by Michael Pollak

Barrack Buddies and Soldier Lovers: Dialogues with Gay Young Men in the U.S. Military by Steven Zeeland

Outing: Shattering the Conspiracy of Silence by Warren Johansson and William A. Percy

The Bisexual Option by Fritz Klein

One-Handed Histories: The Eroto-Politics of Gay Male Video Pornography by John R. Burger

Sailors and Sexual Identity: Crossing the Line Between "Straight" and "Gay" in the U.S. Navy by Steven Zeeland

And the Flag Was Still There: Straight People, Gay People, and Sexuality in the U.S. Military by Lois Shawver

And the Flag Was Still There

Straight People, Gay People, and Sexuality in the U.S. Military

Lois Shawver, PhD

Harrington Park Press
An Imprint of The Haworth Press, Inc.
New York • London • Norwood (Australia)

Published by

Harrington Park Press, an imprint of The Haworth Press, Inc., 10 Alice Street, Binghamton, NY 13904-1580

Library of Congress Cataloging-in-Publication Data

Shawver, Lois. And the flag was still there: Straight people, gay people, and sexuality in the U.S. military.

p. cm.

Includes bibliographical references and index.

ISBN 1-56023-851-8 (alk. paper).

1. United States–Armed Forces–Gays. 2. Sex discrimination–United States. 3. Homosexuality–United States–Psychological aspects. I. Title.

UB418.G38S58 1994

355'.008'–dc20 94-31507

CIP

ABOUT THE AUTHOR

Lois Shawver, PhD, is a clinical psychologist and has worked as a psychotherapist for twenty years. She teaches psychotherapy and related courses to graduate psychology students at the California School of Professional Psychology in Alameda, California. Dr. Shawver has published articles on a broad range of topics and has served as an expert witness in many court cases on the issue of bodily modesty. She served as an expert in the Canadian review of their ban on homosexuals in the military and was influential in the lifting of that ban in October 1992. Dr. Shawver is also serving as an expert in a number of pending cases in the United States.

CONTENTS

Foreword

I know about the struggle of gays in the military from personal experience, having been discharged from the military for being a lesbian after 26 years of service as an army nurse. I have since been reinstated to my former position as a Colonel in the Washington State Army National Guard, where I continue to serve today.

In every society there are groups considered outcasts, disfavored minorities, and undesirables. At times, these citizens are sometimes even called demonic–deserving hate, persecution, and death. It takes inordinate perseverance and personal sacrifice for the persecuted to survive. Sometimes they assimilate into mainstream society and "pass," thereby escaping societally approved persecution or even genocide. In so doing, they may physically survive, but their very being–their soul, their essence–is denied.

For the past few years, homosexuality, as it exists in American society, and homosexuals in the military have caused a raging social, political, and personal debate. Homosexuals are coming out of the closet, no longer willing to have their very existence denied. Fewer are willing to be silent any longer, or to be defined through false stereotypes created by others.

Now, even the threat and the fact of persecution will not prevent us from seeking our rights as full citizens. Part of that refusal to be silenced extends into the military, where gays and lesbians have been persecuted for more than 50 years. Thousands have been denied their very livelihood as they were and are stripped of their rank and branded unfit, unsuitable, and dishonorable by the military. Thousands have been interrogated, brainwashed, imprisoned, intimidated, and ultimately discharged from the military, not because of misconduct, but because of who they were–homosexuals in the military.

The history of the United States abounds with examples of persecution, of groups ostracized for being different and thereby forced to retreat out of fear for their lives. The status of previously persecuted groups, such as religious and racial minorities, Native Americans, women, and people with disabilities, has gradually changed as prevailing social views have changed. But changes occur only as people stand up to be counted and say "I am worth something; I am of equal worth." And as they stand up first as individuals and later collectively, others in society see, learn, and take up the call for justice. Sometimes the changes in society occur because they must in order for the society to survive. However, no social change can occur without the majority within the society believing that the change should take place. We are now at such a crossroad.

The unfounded fear of homosexuals and of homosexuality is tragic, for it speaks of fragile egos and the need of some people to undermine and negate others. It is easy to be prejudiced against something we do not know or understand. It is easy to project our value system onto others and declare them wrong, bad, or unfit. But such a value system undermines the good that each of us has in us; it undermines the fact that we are all created within the spirit of a greater power to serve on earth for just a short time.

Each of us has some basic tasks to accomplish while we are here. Our first task is to come to know ourselves as individuals, as sexual beings, as rich, loving, creating, caring, and responsible members of society. Our second task is to recognize that not everyone is the same and life still can be wonderful, good, and safe. We must realize that acknowledging and accepting differences in others does not negate anyone else. Our third task is to overcome unfounded fear by learning about those who are different–not becoming different ourselves, but reaching an understanding of those who are unlike ourselves.

This last task is most difficult because we are raised in the comfort of what we know and are often taught that all else is wrong, sinful, or evil. We learn to protect ourselves from everything that is different. We become ever more fearful, and more imprisoned in our own ignorance. Yet the very task of learning about that which is different will remove irrational fears, free us from judgment, and provide inner peace.

The irrational fear of homosexuals serving in the military is based upon unfounded stereotypes, hatred, and ignorance. The fear expressed by military leaders that homosexuals in the military would undermine morale and disrupt the mission totally belies the fact that there are thousands of gays and lesbians serving in the military today. These dedicated men and women are every bit as capable as their heterosexual colleagues. The very nature of the military is such that if service members undermine the mission, disrupt their unit, or are unable to perform their tasks, they are not promoted and therefore not retained in the military. In other words, if homosexuals serving in the military were a problem, *they would not be there now.*

In recent years, as more and more gays and lesbians have revealed their identities and spoken out against injustice and prejudice, the issue of homosexuality has been forced into the arena of public debate in our society, some of which has been good and some hurtful and irrational. It is becoming more obvious that gays and lesbians exist as productive members of society and the military. Nevertheless, it has been a painful process to try to overcome some of the ignorance and stereotyping that is so ingrained in our culture. The cost of speaking out while serving in the military is one's career. The debate in the country and in Congress continually returns to the issue of personal privacy, which is denied to individuals serving in the military. The debate centers around the false stereotype and that homosexuals cannot control their social or sexual behavior, and are responsible for diseases and child abuse. The reality, of course, is that these unacceptable behaviors do not represent the actions of homosexuals but rather of a minority of misguided individuals from all backgrounds within society.

There is no rational basis for defending the military's policy of trying to keep homosexuals from serving. To date the only reason justified by experience has been the discomfort of heterosexuals and the collective "wisdom" of military leaders (who themselves have their own anti-gay prejudice). There is no evidence of any homosexuals serving in the military undermining one of its missions. That is undoubtedly not their reason for choosing to serve their country. Certainly, if you cannot do the job, you do not belong in uniform; performance, and not prejudice, must be the determining factor.

And the Flag Was Still There methodically strips away the myths surrounding homosexuality in the military. It delves into the underpinnings of prejudice and human behavior as we adapt through the "etiquette of disregard." The difficulty is to objectify the fear and the prejudice sufficiently to enable fresh opinions and beliefs to be formed. This book examines each argument presented by the military regarding why homosexuals should not or cannot serve in the military. When the underpinnings of each argument are disclosed, irrational fear and ingrained military prejudice is all that remains. There is no rational justification for banning homosexuals from serving in the military. To attempt to do so is to perpetuate a lie, perpetuate a prejudice, and condemn to silence thousands serving in the military today. *And the Flag Was Still There* exposes the fallacy of the "don't ask, don't tell" law and highlights the shame of today's military: We defend the rights of others around the world and deny our own.

Margarethe Cammermeyer, PhD, RN

Preface

It was just a little over three years ago when I got a surprising call from George Logan of the department of Personnel Policy in the Canadian military. I was sitting in my home office when he called me and invited to submit testimony in a big case on the issue of whether there should be gays in the Canadian military.

Why me? I wondered. I had never published either on gays or on the military. And my image was a long way from a gay activist. My husband and daughters thought so, too.

The Canadian military had chosen me for two reasons, George Logan explained. First, everyone who had a name in homosexual scholarship refused the work because they did not want to work for a military that seemed bent on rationalizing this unfortunate ban. Second, although I had not worked as an expert on homosexuality or the military, I was established as an expert on the issue of bodily modesty. I had testified in a dozen or so trials in the United States and in Canada on the issue of whether women officers violated the rights of male prisoners by working in jails and prisons. I had published in that field and I knew that literature, they said, and the issue of bodily modesty was going to be a key issue in this new debate on whether there should be gays in the military.

"Really?" I responded.

The key question, I was told, would be whether the privacy rights of heterosexuals are violated by having to share quarters and undress in the presence of homosexuals. The concern was that gays would leer at straights and violate them emotionally if not physically. The idea was that if it is a violation of women to have to undress in the presence of men, so it seems likely to be a similar violation of men. Because modesty was a key issue, they explained, I was invited to submit my opinion.

At this point I was eager. My research on bodily modesty had convinced me that it was central to the American sense of sexuality.

My work as a psychotherapist for the last 25 years had convinced me that fear of homosexuality undermines many people's sexual adjustment, heterosexuals as well as homosexuals. I had never put these two interests together but I felt equipped to do so. The well-known gay activists might not be willing to work for the Canadian military, but I would.

I accepted the offer. Perhaps, they were surprised when a few months later I submitted documents testifying that homosexuals would not be likely to leer at heterosexuals or violate their modesty traditions. Regardless, I believe my testimony was part of the reason the Canadians decided not to pursue their case in court and that instead, in November of 1992 they dropped their ban against homosexuals in the military. I understand my predictions that the issue would become a nonissue have been borne out.

It was not so many months after I submitted testimony to the Canadians that I became aware that a similar issue was simmering in the United States military, and I began to market my new expertise by making contact with those who could provide me with a forum to voice my views. After reading some of my material, John De Cecco, editor for this book program, kindly invited me to write this book.

Since then I made a diligent study of the topic of gays in the military. I have read everything I could find on the topic, became acquainted with attorneys working on these cases, and met and discussed the issues with researchers and authors, as well as many gay people and military people. I have submitted testimony in many cases that are being processed through the United States court system, and I look forward to testifying in others. During this time I have become increasingly confident that it is time for the United States to drop our military ban against homosexuals. It hurts too many of our people to pretend that homosexuality does not exist, to condemn it and treat it as something that can be stamped out like a bad habit. The homosexuals among us are our children, our parents, our favorite aunts and uncles, if not ourselves. Moreover, as I will argue in this book, the inconvenience and embarrassment that intimidates heterosexuals about homosexuality is based on groundless fears and superstitions.

In this book, I will try to explain why we can and should gracefully accommodate the reality of the many deserving gays and lesbians in our society. Writing the book has been a pleasure. The literature in the field is mushrooming and I had a wealth of new books and articles to anchor my analysis, much of it subsequent to the testimony I submitted in Canada.

Moreover, I was fortunate to develop many useful contacts. For example, Victoria Hudson put me in touch with Randy Shilts, and although I never spoke with him before he died, his assistant Linda Alban was invaluable in my search for names and phone numbers of people to interview and she provided me with scarce documents. I was also assisted by several attorneys, particularly Mary Newcomb, Kathleen Gilberd, Christopher Sipes, and many others. Al Klassen, senior author of the important book *Sex and Morality* was kind enough to review Chapter 6 for me. This book is also greatly improved by all the time that the many people I interviewed afforded me as well as the time supplied by many others whose stories were not included because of limits of space and time.

I was fortunate to have a consummate writer's consultant, Roy Carlisle, who has a talent for enhancing literary artistry with a sensitive balance of criticism and encouragement. It is also my good fortune to have a thoughtful and accomplished husband, Douglas Kurdys, who not only has a PhD in clinical psychology, in English literature, and is a practicing attorney, but who earned a number one ranking in northern California tennis for his age bracket while I was writing this book. His masculine perspective on life helps to keep my feminine consciousness balanced. I want to thank my friend Professor Paula Voos who read and commented on several versions of each chapter while working on her own book on collective bargaining, jetting off to serve on an important national commission or while stirring her family's dinner with a child tugging on her apron strings. And I am grateful to Ruth Weatherford, a teacher and very successful lesbian psychologist and psychotherapist whose reading grounded and reassured me and sometimes helped me understand, and also for the reading provided by Joan Roth whose comments were methodical and thought provoking. I appreciate the reading and flattering assessment of Theodore Sarbin, whose writing inspired me during graduate school. I want to thank my daughters Natasha Shawver and Marina Shawver, as well as their father, my first husband, Ernest Shawver, Jr., all of whom contributed substantially to this process in a variety of useful and important ways. Finally, I thank John De Cecco, whose theoretical ideas are a such a pleasure to study. I have also enjoyed a rewarding working relationship with my publisher and the Haworth staff who supported my project even when they realized just how many footnotes and references there would be.

But as important as all the above people were in helping me produce the best book that I can, it is all useless unless people pick up a book on this topic and dare to read it. Perhaps, the most credit goes to the heterosexual reader who has never felt a whiff of homosexual concern. This is a book that will challenge all the traditional folklore about homosexuality. Our society has given us a false mythology about the nature of what it means to be gay or lesbian and it takes a special type of reader to be willing to rethink these issues. But I am especially pleased to have readers who struggle with private homosexual interests and concerns. As a psychotherapist, I hope this book provides them with a perspective for evaluating their concerns and weaving them into a healthy place in their lives. I also want to thank my gay and lesbian readers for accepting me as a scholar in an area of scholarship that can either help or hurt their concern for advocacy. I believe we must do more than market a new "gays are beautiful" image. Our society has wounded the typical homosexual with a cultural shame. The story that needs to be told now should not hide this unpleasant dimension of what it means to achieve a homosexual identity in our culture. The story here is not merely about the courageous gay who claims that identity. It is also about closets and secrets and about our society finding a way for the many people who feel a compelling homosexual desire to live their lives out of shadows. This kind of desire is far too common to require that it be relegated to the closets of a secret perversion. Only by recognizing what is wrong with the way our society treats homosexuality can we begin to speak about what has been an unspeakable truth for so long, and only then will we design constructive policy.

Chapter 1

Why the Military Would Ban Homosexuals

It was April, 1993 and a great crowd of well-behaved people had marched on Washington. The TV cameras shot pictures from above showing swarms of marchers moving slowly down Pennsylvania Avenue. A camera moved down and caught their animated faces. So that is what gay people looked like. Mostly they looked like ordinary people. They seemed festive, but well behaved. They were celebrating the eve of an executive order to lift the ban against people like themselves in the American military.

The crowd moved toward a stage where singers and comedians took turns at the mike. Giant speakers sent their voices echoing through the spring air. Tall, muscular young men, and chubby boys with rolling bellies, sat without shirts under the gentle heat of the spring sun. They were flanked by pretty young girls and white-haired old ladies, people in wheel chairs, people with white, brown, black, and yellow skin, eating hot dogs and drinking in the promise of acceptance. They were becoming America's accepted children, enjoying the feeling of being adopted. Somewhere mothers and fathers watched and could see that they were not sexual freaks, that there were other good people who were gay. There was optimism in the air. It was just a matter of time, so they all thought, and the ban would be lifted. The President would get a briefing from his men, Congress would listen to the opponents, and then there would be an executive order that would put the matter to rest. Promises had been made. The world was changing, and it would include them.

And then, on July 15, the ban was lifted, but in its place was a new ban, with a new name, "Don't ask, don't tell"; a new ban that, when read between the lines, looked almost exactly like the old one.

The new ban said you could be gay in the military, as long as you never let it be known. Well, under the old one a soldier could always be gay as long as it was never known. And under both bans, you could be asked but need not tell. And under both bans, if you did tell that you were gay it would be grounds for discharge. So the gays had thought they would win this battle, but when the smoke had cleared, the military had clearly won.

And this new ban, the new "Don't ask, don't tell" ban, snuffed out all the commotion, all the publicity. The gay people stepped back into their closets. The talk shows stopped talking about gay rights. The newspapers stopped carrying front page stories. The forces that had whipped it into a front page issue had lost steam.

But although things seemed quiet, out across the land, in courthouses everywhere, attorneys began gathering the files that had lain dormant in the back storage rooms for some months. These were the cases of proud young soldiers who had, in the last year, announced that they were gay and taken their cases to court. These were all soldiers with sterling records, and toothpaste smiles. They had spoken on talk shows and said, without shame or stridency, that they were gay and proud, saying things like, "I didn't know I was gay when I joined the military. Admitting it is the only honest thing to do."

These cases had sat on the dockets for months now, awaiting the lifting of the ban, waiting to vanish as the ban became history. But now they were started up again. The attorneys dusted off the files and the slow relentless motor of the judicial system began to click away. Sooner or later these cases would come to court. Decisions would be made here, and there, and then appealed, moving the sluggish beast, finally, into a constitutional issue that promised to plop itself onto the awesome docket of the Supreme Court. There, the newly chosen justices, Clarence Thomas and Ruth Bader Ginsberg, and all the rest will tell us if the military ban against homosexuals is consistent with the intent of the Constitution of the United States. This group of carefully selected jurists will have to weigh the evidence and decide.

And we should weigh the evidence and decide, too. Should homosexuality be conceived of as a transgression like any other transgression? Should homosexuals be discharged to protect the sensibilities of those who do not like them? Or is the ban a hypocritical policy that ignores homosexuals when it is convenient[1] and asks them to lie and pretend they are heterosexual?[2] Does the military, which dismisses numbers of women far out of proportion to the numbers who are actually in the military, use it to harass women soldiers into having heterosexual sex?[3] Is the ban used to harass and frighten men into submission? Or is it that in preventing these gay people from enlisting in the military profession we are denying them their basic rights as envisioned in our Declaration of Independence?[4]

On a practical level, in the 1980s alone, the United States military spent 500 million dollars on the training of soldiers who would later be discharged as homosexual. This does not include the salaries for the people investigating what can be very insubstantial charges.[5] No one believes that this effort actually eliminated all, or even a substantial portion, of homosexuals, or homosexuality, from the forces. Is this 500 million dollars well spent? Is there a better way for America to deal with the issue of homosexuality in the military?

WHY THE MILITARY WANTS TO BAN HOMOSEXUALS

Before we can consider whether there is a better way, we have to ask why the military wants to ban homosexuals.

When the ban was first implemented 50 years ago, a group of psychiatrists came up with a list of five categories of mental illness that soldiers should be screened for. Later, the military added homosexuality to this list.[6] And so homosexuality was treated as a form of mental illness. By the middle 1970s, however, both the American Psychiatric Association and the American Psychological Association had formally declared that they believed homosexuality should not be considered a mental illness.[7] Today the military also recognizes that homosexuality is not a mental illness.[8]

Today the military, therefore, is in an odd position. It originally justified its ban on the grounds that homosexuals are mentally ill, and yet, today, everyone agrees that they are not. And so, one might ask, how does the military justify its exclusion policy? The answer is, with great difficulty.

The Stated Reasons for the Ban

Today, the military holds that we should ban homosexuals from its ranks even if we accept homosexuals in the broader society, because the military, so they say, is a special case. If there are homosexuals in the military, they will demoralize the troops and if the troops are demoralized they will fight less well.

In its basic form, their argument goes something like this:

> Military personnel often have to dress and toilet in close quarters. Just as it is a privacy invasion for men to observe women undress so it is a privacy invasion for homosexuals to observe heterosexuals in states of undress. The experience of such a privacy invasion, the sense that others present might find one's body sexually exciting, can be expected to diminish morale and thus reduce the effectiveness of combat units. Even having to interact socially with homosexuals will diminish morale. Since the primary business of the military is warfighting, a policy which diminishes the effectiveness of the combat units is unacceptable.[9]

It is, therefore, an argument about privacy, or modesty, in situations of undress, and about morale.

The Underlying Reasons and Questions

Although the military's stated reasons for banning homosexuals needs to be taken seriously, and we will analyze them seriously in this book, it seems likely that their stated reasons are only part of the story as to why they would ban homosexuals. The energy that is often apparent in their arguments against homosexuals is remarkable and out of proportion to the evidence available to substantiate their views.

First, concern with privacy hardly seems sufficient to explain military leaders or recruits indicating that they would be willing to quit if the ban was lifted. The military has typically been unconcerned with soldier privacy in spite of the fact that it is aware that there are homosexuals in their ranks. Although recent facilities have introduced many safe and inexpensive ways to improve privacy protection for soldiers in latrines and other private areas, a recent RAND report tells us that the military is lax in upgrading the privacy protections in older facilities.[10]

Second, moral outrage seems unlikely to be sufficient to cause the military's drive to ban homosexuals. Research shows, for example, that the Navy discharges a disproportionate number of homosexuals,[11] yet the Tailhook scandal, during the same time period, makes the zeal in weeding out homosexuals seem hypocritical. The Tailhook scandal resulted from 117 officers sexually harassing 90 victims, seven of which were men, at the Tailhook Pilot's Convention in Las Vegas in 1991. The Navy initially downplayed the incident, and the investigation was taken over by Congress. There was such substantial evidence that the Navy had blocked a thorough investigation into the facts, that it eventually resulted in the resignation of the Secretary of the Navy, Lawrence Garrett.[12] And if the Secretary of the Navy would block investigation of a morally outrageous incident (which even included homosexual transgressions) it seems unlikely that the enthusiasm the Navy evidenced during this period for discharging homosexuals was a simple result of moral outrage.

A part of the reason for the ban, surely, has to do with the military's image of itself. This is the institution that in not so many years past sold itself to the civilian world by saying it could make men out of boys. And many frustrated parents have shipped their sons off to military school so the discipline could set them straight. In our society, the military has played the role of the institution capable of turning undisciplined, careless, rebellious lads into industrious, fearless, right-thinking men. Surely it is understandable that an institution that understands itself as turning boys into men would hesitate at the thought of turning a blind eye to whether or not the men they had produced had come to prefer the sexual company of other men over that of women.[13] This has little to do, however, with whether the military can function effectively without the ban. It has to do with the military's concern that open acceptance of homosexuals will damage its masculine image.

But still, could it work? Could a person's sexual preference be as irrelevant to his or her military performance as a person's religious preference? America is a country that idealizes tolerance. Catholics and Protestants may have their differences, but, to our way of thinking, this does not justify their killing each other or even threatening each other. Perhaps more than any society in history, we believe in the right to live and let live. We do not outlaw those who worship different gods, or allow those who endorse one set of religious convictions to require others to conform to them. In such a society, is it not possible for a fundamentalist Christian soldier who finds homosexuality personally abhorrent to be as tolerant toward his homosexual neighbor as he or she might be toward one who worships a different god?

If it can work, and if the homosexual can fight along with the heterosexual without any disruption in the effectiveness of the combat unit, then we cannot ban homosexuals from the military without violating the basic rights that have inspired the very foundation of our government.

HOW DO WE DECIDE ABOUT THE BAN?

The question as to whether homosexuals can fit into the military, as our military is evolving, is a psychological question. Beware of ready-made answers from either the military or religious leaders. The question is psychological because it is a question of the psychology of soldiers accepting homosexuals. And the question is: Can soldiers accept homosexuals sufficiently for our military to be effective?

The Military Experience Cannot Tell if Removing the Ban Would Work

Our military commanders are not in a position to be knowledgeable about whether self-disclosed homosexuals could be accepted satisfactorily by military personnel. We can presume that these commanders, through their long, individual, distinguished careers have given little thought to what it means for a person to be a homosexual, or to what kind of people homosexuals are. They did not have courses on this topic, and if they did read about homosexuals, it was from the pages of writings by psychiatrists, psychologists, and sociologists. If they thought about it in the routine of their daily experience it was, presumably, because the unpleasant reality forced itself to be dealt with. Individual servicemen and women would be suspected, investigated, identified as homosexual, and then discharged. Just like that. It was a clean process, really, not one in which commanders would have the time to study what the effects would be if these homosexuals had not been summarily removed. So, keep in mind, if the military brass declares that it would be destructive to lift the ban, theirs is not likely to be an opinion based on the experience of observing recognized homosexuals working and living with heterosexuals on military bases. The military brass is likely to be quite uninformed about homosexuality and how disclosed homosexuals would conduct themselves.

Biblical Interpretation Is not Relevant

Do not trust Biblical arguments against homosexuals as relevant to the question as to whether there should be homosexuals in the military. Our country is founded on the belief in separation of church and state. If we were to allow Biblical interpretation to guide political policy then we would deny the religious freedom of those who interpret the Bible differently–for even among those who endorse the Christian Bible as the sacred authority there are many who believe that homosexuality is not immoral.[14] Even among Roman Catholics, 34 percent believe that homosexual behavior is not sinful.[15] And we must respect not only the beliefs of Christians who feel that homosexuality is morally acceptable, but we need to respect and tolerate those other Americans whose moral conscience is not grounded in Christian Biblical interpretation.

A REASON TO THINK IT MIGHT WORK

Because our country protects the civil rights of groups with varying beliefs and values, as well as the rights of those of different cultural background and genetic makeup, we need to drop the military ban against homosexuals if we cannot justify it on the grounds that it will damage our national defense.

And, importantly, there *is* evidence that a military without a ban can work because it does work in other countries. The fact that it works in other countries does not prove it will work in the United States, of course, but the fact that it is working in Canada strongly suggests that it *might* work in the United States.

There are many ways in which the Canadians are very much like the Americans. One can cross the border into Toronto, for example, or Vancouver, and it has the look and feel of an American city. And many in the Canadian military believed that homosexuals would disrupt morale, just as many believe that in the United States.

In fact, from 1989 through 1992 the Canadians engaged in a heated debate over the issue of homosexuals in their military much as the United States is doing now. There were several court cases. The Canadian military did studies, and listened to experts tell them that removing the ban would destroy cohesion and demoralize the troops. They listened to prophecies of disaster, of violent rebellions and wholesale resignations, and then, just as a big case was coming to trial, in October of 1992, they dropped their case and dropped the ban. A careful review of the evidence had led them to decide that they could not defend the ban, for in the final analysis, the evidence suggested that dropping the ban would not be disruptive of military goals.

The advocates of the ban predicted disaster, but nothing happened.[16] There were no riots, no massive walkouts, no filed grievances, no gay bashing, no demonstrations. Everything carried on with little evidence that there had been a change. The public outcry that had been predicted just fizzled into thin air.

Our own military has dismissed this evidence on the grounds that few homosexuals disclose their identity after the bans in other countries are lifted. But this is no reason to keep the ban. In fact, it is only one more piece of evidence that we do not need, and should not have legal prohibitions against homosexual disclosures. The fact that hoards of homosexuals do not declare their homosexuality recklessly testifies that they will be circumspect and manage their identities cautiously. It is testimony to the fact that we do not need legal prohibitions against them.[17] Gay advocates do not expect the removal of the ban to make it possible for them to be emotionally accepted completely by everyone.[18] Even if all prohibitive rules are lifted, gays will inevitably be required to manage the disclosure of their identities with caution and concern.[19]

And if homosexuals do not disrupt the workings of the military, do not diminish its capacity for fighting wars, we should not have the ban. The ban costs money. It involves the government in policing the private and sexual practices of consenting adults. It can be used selectively to harass and abuse soldiers–heterosexual soldiers as well as homosexual soldiers. And, most important, unless homosexuality disrupts the working of the military, the ban violates the human rights of a group of American citizens.

RECOGNIZING OUR CULTURAL CONTEXT

Born as we are on one tiny spot on a big diverse planet, in our own little wrinkle of time, we lose sight of the way our values and customs reflect our unique cultural context. And so it seems odd to us when we learn how different cultures have done things differently, how, for example, warriors in the seventeenth century fought their courageous battles wearing decorative battle clothes, or how the Chinese bound the feet of their noblewomen, crippling them so badly that they could not walk, or how the men in certain Eskimo cultures show their hospitality by extending the sexual services of their wives to male visitors.

Such foreign traditions amaze us because we see immediately that these people absorbed a culture very different from our own. We are surprised because the culture we have absorbed since infancy presents itself to us as if it contains the universal truths.

But all cultural truths are fickle. They fade as we cross the border into other countries, and even when we sit tight on the same spot, cultural truths fade over time. What was beautiful yesterday is no longer beautiful. And what feels right changes too. The vigilante justice of the cowboys, and the Salem persecution of witches, no longer seem valid. We no longer try to marry off our teenage daughters, or bequeath our estates only to our eldest sons. Over and over we learn that what feels stable and universal in our cultural traditions is mostly illusion.

Still, it is natural, perhaps, for all of us, to cherish the cultural fashion of our particular youth. We are fascinated with remnants of the eras we remember, old photographs, old cars, old songs. The future seems less well formed, more alien. And we will be older in it in a way that is hard to fathom. It is hard to let the past fade away. We can think of a million reasons to keep things the way they were.

But it is dangerous to cling to our own past blindly. The world we bequeath to our children will inevitably be a different world, with different traditions, different memories. And that is as it should be. We should not blindly perpetuate our traditions for we have not found the secret key to human happiness. Our divorce courts are full. Our prisons are full, and the counselors in schools and county offices have far too many cases to help. It is only fair that we let the rules evolve, that we do not cling to the rules we played by just because they were the rules we inherited. And the strongest among us will join our children to help them envision a better future. For all that any of us can do is to recognize the changes that are happening and try to shape their process a little, and in productive ways.

Our culture is now changing in ways that more easily accommodate homosexuals. The masculine soldier of our grandfather's army is in many ways an anachronism in today's army. And although there are some who will feel discomfort with their inclusion, our culture does not accommodate unfounded prejudice. Just as southern whites were required to send their children to integrated schools, so heterosexuals should be required to tolerate homosexuals if their objection is founded merely in prejudice.

Today, heterosexuals are gradually becoming more informed about homosexuality, and this information will lessen the sense that homosexuals are radically different from the rest of us. Nearly half of us today know a homosexual, and those of us who do know homosexuals are more likely than the rest of us to accept them.[20] As we become acquainted with more of them, it will be hard to hang onto the myth that homosexuals are identifiable by appearance, that the men have unbearded and feminine faces[21] and that the women are masculine and unattractive.[22]

If the ban is dropped, it will be, in part, because we have learned to value the right of people to be different, and have come to insist that our government not interfere lightly with the discreet sexual practices between consenting adults, be they heterosexual or homosexual. It will be because we have come closer to our national ideals which require us to respect differences in values, religions, and backgrounds.

But dropping the ban also means that we are beginning to heal a cultural wound that has ached in the American consciousness for almost a century now. About a century ago, we began to be afraid of male homosexuality. It took a while, culturally, for the fear to settle in, for us to worry when our sons looked too girlish, to cut their hair short as soon as possible and throw away the fancy clothes we used to admire on them as infants, to whisper in fear when our sons looked too delicate. Today this wound is still not healed. We still worry. If we are concerned with lesbianism, it is mostly because we fear lesbians will damage the masculine confidence of men.

This wound causes deep damage to heterosexual romantic relationships, preventing men and women from understanding each other, giving them different expectations, and generally providing us all with a recipe for romantic disaster. Our fear of homosexuality traps us in a romantic predicament that makes a mockery of love. We are so concerned to live up to our cultural expectations of how real men and women should be and perform, that we lose the sense of caring for each other's differences.

Healing this wound will take some time, but learning to live with the gays and lesbians will diminish our fear of homosexuality in ourselves, our children, our lovers.

SUMMARY OF THE BOOK

This book concludes that the military's objection to homosexuals is rooted in a fading set of images we have all known–images about the nature of men and women, and images about the military.

The military's argument for the ban begins with their contention that our practice of segregating the toilet and showering of men and women should justify segregated toileting of homosexuals and heterosexuals. But the data to be reviewed will show that this is a bad analogy. Separate rest rooms and dressing rooms for men and women increases heterosexual allure more than it decreases it.

There are better ways to diminish an awkward sexual excitement than to segregate people, for there is an etiquette, used in all cultures, that works remarkably effectively to diminish sexual excitement. It is the same etiquette that a doctor uses to minimize the erotic potential of a medical exam, and the same etiquette that an artist might use to minimize the erotic potential of drawing a nude model. This etiquette minimizes sexual excitement in a wide variety of contexts in our own culture and it does so in militaries around the world. It will suffice to minimize the sense of privacy invasion that heterosexuals would otherwise feel with people who identify themselves as gay or lesbian.

The heterosexual's fear that homosexuals will violate them is based largely on myths we all learn by word of mouth. Because homosexuality has been a taboo topic we are all, homosexuals and heterosexuals alike, uninformed about it. We will look at some of these myths, ask how much truth they contain, and try to dispel the fears that are based on fictions.

We will study the typical process people go through when they decide they are homosexual in our condemning culture, and what we learn here will give us reason to think that homosexuals are unlikely to violate heterosexuals. They seek the approval and acceptance of their gay identity within the heterosexual community. They are a part of our society, and want a place in it, not to take it from the rest of us.

Our study will also show us how ineffective cultural condemnation is in stamping out homosexuality. When we try to stamp it out, as we have tried, it does psychologically unhealthy things not only to homosexuals but to our culture as a whole. Afraid of looking unmasculine, or unfeminine, we posture behind showcase heterosexual relationships with those whose purpose is to demonstrate to the world our heterosexual success rather than provide us with the basis of love and support. We deny people of our gender the physical touches and tender words that are tokens of our deepest respect and affection. We sacrifice meaningful caring in order to avoid being vulnerable. The data we will look at will tell us that the psychological damage has been especially destructive for men in our culture.

Moreover, we set up a legalistic system in the military that specifically damages particular people who are called homosexual and who are wrongly demeaned by a system that sanctions and punishes them for it. When we look at how it works, we will find it objectionable. To toss out a token few, the military must damage those few badly and create a climate of fear for all.

There was a time, perhaps, not so many years ago, that these fictions of gender may have served an important role in the world, at least as we understood the dangers then. It was a time when we thought we needed to inspire young men with the glory of masculine imagery in order to have them battle for us to their death.

Somehow, perhaps, this masculine war imagery created a psychologically entangled concern with antihomosexuality in America. And America has been more reluctant, as a result, than most countries to lift the ban. We are more afraid of homosexuality than most countries.

But the fact that we are less threatened by war in this new era may help us re-evaluate our excessive anxiety about homosexuality. For this is a new era. We are the only superpower in a world that no longer has a nuclear arms race. Oh, there is always some danger of war, but the danger is so much less now that we can no longer afford to insure ourselves against it at all psychological costs. We can count on the fact that our military will be primarily concerned in this new world with a peacemaking role. We will be trying to minimize suffering, not protecting ourselves from annihilation.

What we need now is the image of the good soldier, able to protect and guard people not so much from evil enemies that he or she will annihilate, but from the mischief of political rivalries, clan warfare, civil riots, civil dissent, and even natural disasters. Our new soldier will be heroic not because he protects so many, but because he, or she, protects so many while destroying so few. It is the imagery of peacekeeping, of humanitarian intervention, not of one nation against another nation, but of a union of united nations protecting themselves against their own internal mischief.

This new heroic imagery for this new era will honor and protect human diversity, people of many religions and values, people of many beliefs, against those who would abuse and limit their freedom to follow their own beliefs and values. And we must begin by allowing this sort of freedom within our own ranks, by allowing those whose sexual feelings are predominantly homosexual to define themselves, if they choose, as being homosexual.

But before we can draw the conclusion that our society is ready to lift the ban against gays, we need to review the evidence that will tell us that heterosexuals will be able to accept them, that self-identified gays will not feel like an important invasion of heterosexual privacy, that gays will not destroy military morale, and that all the other evils that we have imagined are only ungrounded fears.

Chapter 2

The Question of Heterosexual Modesty

Those who oppose homosexuals in the military sometimes argue that homosexuals invade the privacy of heterosexuals when they must undress and toilet together. People who argue in this way are struck by the fact that we segregate the toilet of men and women, and argue that we do so to protect the modesty of people by shielding them from the sexual arousal caused by observing each other in such intimate situations. If this is justification for segregating the sexes, so the argument goes, it is sufficient reason to segregate homosexuals from heterosexuals. We cannot really provide separate dressing and toileting for homosexuals and heterosexuals, so it is justification for banning homosexuals from the military.[1]

The problem with the argument is that it is built on our folklore's faulty picture of why we segregate the toileting of the sexes. The argument assumes the folklore picture that we segregate their toileting to prevent people from becoming sexually aroused by the sight of each other's nakedness. A deeper investigation of these traditions, however, reveals this hidden irony: The traditions that are supposed to suppress sexual excitement actually seem to enhance excitement while causing many people to feel anxious and demeaned by sexual feelings.

Before we ban homosexuals from the military to protect the modesty of heterosexuals, we need to study the meaning and significance of modesty between heterosexual men and women, and then ask ourselves, in the light of our findings, if the analogy applies. Should heterosexuals be as modest before homosexuals as men and women in our culture are before each other?

THE MYSTERY OF MODESTY

A remarkable fact about the human experience is that we are all born absolutely unashamed of our bodies, and that somehow during early childhood, our experience of what it means to have a naked body that excretes waste begins to change. Finally, we become, in our minds, the clothed persona who wear denims or silks, neckties or earrings, and lose touch with our essential nakedness.

But, psychologically, it is no easy task for a human creature to lose touch with its nakedness. It is not as though we could toilet and dress ourselves once and for all and forget that the real person is hidden under these layers of fashion draped across our bodies. We have to construct ourselves this way each day, several times a day, combing our hair, wiping off stains, flushing away evidence of our physical humanness behind closed doors, in special private rooms or stalls that we build at great expense everywhere, in order to present this illusion of a fully dressed and well-groomed persona.

It is not that we have no regrets about having to create and re-create our self presentation in this way, but mostly our regrets focus on the stubbornness of our bodies to mold as completely as we would like into the image we want to present. It is hard to get them into the right shape, to make the right statement to the world as to who we really are. It is hard, but we are pretty good at it.

And we have to be good. Dressing and presenting ourselves in the right image is serious business. If we do it very poorly, we will be rejected by all. We will not find employers to hire us or partners to love us. Occasionally, perhaps, a foolish person, seeing the predicament of our self-construction, has tried to venture out into the peopled world undressed, only to be carted away and covered. We would stop only to create a file on such a person, writing a few notes about exhibitionism or self-hate.

Our predicament is that our cultural upbringing requires us to shape our appearance by continuously cutting our hair, cleaning our teeth, even watching what we eat so we can continue to wear the clothes that hang in our closets, just to present ourselves in our usual public image. And if a haircutting and a diet isn't sufficient to give us a winning image, we can go to a cosmetologist who will coif our hair into a new look. And there are pads and corsets available to shape the appearance of our body underneath, and if that, too, is not sufficient, we can call on the services of a cosmetic surgeon to suck and tuck and stuff our bodies into more perfect contours before we drape ourselves with new garments selected under the guidance of the huge American fashion industry, all because we require our bodies to look great, even sexy. Anything less will not work in the American way of life.

But the grief our customs cause us may be much more severe than the difficulty we have zipping up our jeans. For the way we suppress awareness of our nakedness has something to do with what is sexually exciting, and what is not, and that reaches into the deepest parts of who we are. It relates to why homosexuals are banned from the military, but it relates more broadly, to why lovers everywhere fight with each other, and all of us dream of someone more wonderful and beautiful wrapping our simple nakedness in their love, forever and ever. Until then, we will hide behind our clothes and behind all the mysterious traditions of Western modesty.

Now, the task is to unravel the mystery of our modesty traditions in an attempt to understand them, their prevalence, their history, and their role in shaping our lives with an eye toward seeing if these issues are relevant in the case of heterosexuals toileting in the presence of homosexuals.

First, we need to look at how modesty varies in different cultures and the way people in our own culture develop modesty sensitivities. Then we will need to look at how modesty relates to sexual feelings in the heterosexual culture, and how we manage the embarrassment of modesty. Finally, we will ask how this relates to heterosexual modesty before homosexuals in situations of toileting and undress.

THE PRUDISHNESS OF AMERICANS

Modesty traditions vary greatly from culture to culture. The adult women of the Moslem world cover not only their entire body, but also their faces, while the adult women of New Guinea go almost completely unclothed without embarrassment.[2]

Within Western cultures, northern Americans tend to be more modest than people from other European backgrounds, and this shows up in modesty research. For example, in 1981 Ronald and Juliette Goldman asked children from Australia, England, Sweden, the USA, and Canada: "Suppose we all lived in a nice warm place or climate, should we need to wear clothes?" The modest American children were the ones most likely to say "yes."[3]

But we Americans are much less prudish than we used to be. In the Victorian era, just a century ago, it was scandalous for a woman to expose her ankle, and authorities thought little girls should be made to feel ashamed of their bodies. One book, popular enough to go through 22 editions, told its readers:

> One of the first things that a mother seeks to instill into the mind of her little girl, is a feeling of shame which centers about the pelvic organs and their functions. This feeling, together with shyness, bashfulness, timidity, etc., develops a modesty which constitutes one of the chief, if not the greatest, of feminine charms. The mother is paving the way for her daughter's future happiness, for this commendable virtue not only acts as a shield and protection to the girl, but, by giving play to the imagination, provides for the happiness of her future lover.[4]

During Victorian times, people were so prudish in English-speaking countries that they sometimes put pinafores around tables and chairs to hide the legs (all legs were obscene) and placed books by male and female authors on different shelves.[5] Literature from Shakespeare to the Bible was routinely purged of all "indecent language,"[6] and marriage manuals taught that married people should engage in sexual intercourse only occasionally and only to promote conception.[7]

The Victorian standards of modesty faded with the change of fashion.[8] During the twenties and thirties of this century, the so-called flapper period, young women shocked their mothers by cutting off their long dresses above their knees and kicking up their heels in public in the new dance craze, the Charleston.

Is it just that each generation is becoming less modest than the last? Historians think otherwise. The historical evidence is that the Victorians were a particularly modest group. [9] In fact, "Between the late seventeenth century and the very beginning of the nineteenth, exceptional freedom was provided for the popular expression of sexuality." [10] And it seems that although we are becoming less constricted by modesty concerns,[11] we are still more concerned with modesty than most of our pre-Victorian ancestors.

THE DEVELOPMENT OF MODESTY IN AMERICAN CHILDREN

Times have changed, but we still teach our children modesty habits. Children are taught modesty habits much as they are taught table manners. Little girls are scolded and ridiculed when they expose their panties and little boys are are not allowed to drop their pants in the middle of the kindergarten room. These are rules that well-behaved children must learn. Of course, this does not mean that children initially *feel* embarrassed, or even that they ever feel embarrassed, but they are taught that they *should* feel embarrassed if their behavior is immodest, and, whatever else, they must behave as though they *do* feel embarrassed.[12]

And gradually, children do. In our culture modesty behaviors begin to appear in little girls between four and six, and in little boys between five and eight, and modesty increases for both sexes, each year, at least until the age of ten. According to one study, for example, between the ages of two and five, the bathroom door is closed 64 percent of the time. It is closed 86 percent by age group six to nine, 96 percent of the time by children ten to 13, and virtually 100 percent of the time by children 14 to 17. Other measures of modesty, such as how often a sibling is denied access to the rest room when the sibling knocks, show similar increases in modesty concerns with age.[13]

The child who masters our society's modesty traditions must do more than learn to be inhibited. The child must learn to be more modest in some situations than in others and more modest with some people than with others.

Specifically, we require our children to be more modest with the opposite sex than with the same sex, and children do, in fact, become more modest with the opposite sex. Studies suggest that young children are about half as modest in the presence of a self-sex sibling when compared to an opposite sex sibling. However, modesty discomfort also varies with age and familiarity with the observer. In Western culture, modesty is generally more severe around nonfamily members and especially around nonfamily adults. Also the well-trained child learns that it is not just a matter of covering strategic parts of the body. It is a matter of dressing appropriately, not presenting oneself to nonfamily adults in the living room, for example, wearing pajamas or underwear.[14] All of this is a part of modesty tradition in our society that we teach our children.

WHAT OUR MODESTY MYTHS TELL US

All cultures pass along traditions by using myths–stories that contain hidden rules as to how we should behave.

In our culture, we pass along our modesty myths with scandals of people who reveal their bodies shamelessly, or stories of how people respond or think they would respond upon seeing nakedness. These myths tell us that nakedness is universally erotic. But although nakedness can be erotic, the little truth that is there blinds us to a much greater element of fiction.

The truth is that observing the opposite sex undressed can be sexually arousing if we arrange the observation to make it so, but in most cases it is not erotic to observe nakedness and toileting of the opposite sex. The reasons for our sexual modesty have more to do with our sense of maintaining an attractive social image than they do with preventing others from feeling an overwhelming sexual arousal. We do not give the old man in the hospital a modesty shield, for example, to prevent visitors from becoming sexually aroused, but to protect the old man's sense of dignity.

Still, our myths tell us that we separate the sexes simply to prevent sexual arousal. When we are children these myths are couched in children's language. They are the reasons children learn they must shut the bathroom door, so people of the opposite sex will not see them.

And the stories continue into adulthood literature with stories of the scandal of bodily exposure, the embarrassment and the humor.[15] These myths inform us over and over in many ways that the adult male and female body cannot be observed undressed without it being sexually arousing. Our myths say that men are especially vulnerable to this arousal and that women who let their bodies be seen by them easily are loose women. But in order to sustain this imagery we think of beautiful women exposing their bodies in situations contrived to be sexually alluring.

THE REAL EFFECT OF MODESTY TRADITIONS

What we fail to see is that the excessive modesty in American culture makes nakedness seem sexier and more lower class. Our myths have eroticized nakedness and made the erotic a symbol of social inferiority. And because these myths are everywhere, we think this is the natural state of things, that men and women everywhere have these sorts of modesty feelings.

How Modesty Makes Nakedness Sexy

Because of our myths we can be amazed that the native women of foreign lands can expose their breasts without the men being overstimulated by the eroticism of the situation, but everywhere that modesty traditions are less severe, the naked body is seen as less erotic.[16]

For example, the Japanese, traditionally, have tended to be much less modest about their bodies than Americans. Thirty or 40 years ago, in fact, it was very common for men and women to share the same public rest rooms without even having enclosed stalls, and at that time public baths for both men and women were common. Westerners were often amazed that the Japanese did not think of these experiences as sexual.[17] Even today the Japanese are much less concerned with modesty than Americans, but, today, Japan is gradually absorbing American modesty traditions, and research shows that there has been a simultaneous increase in sexual activity and interest in Japan.[18]

This seems to demonstrate how the modesty myths work: when people routinely hide their bodies and create a sense of romantic ceremony about exposing their bodies, they create an erotic anticipation as to how sexually alluring the naked body will be. This anticipation increases the sexiness of nakedness.

How Modesty Makes Sex Seem Lower Class

The myths and tradition of modesty also imbue nakedness, and the exposure of the body and bodily functions, with the connotation of being wanton and lower class. This notion is grounded in our culture since at least the Victorian times.

Before the reign of Louis XIV, the Western world, aristocrats and peasants, had a manner that was very coarse by modern standards.[19] The notion of etiquette was introduced into society by the court of Louis XIV, but it was imitated by the peasants and business classes. Then, when the revolutionaries overthrew the aristocracies in America and France, the manners, which had acquired the connotation of aristocracy, were used to establish an aristocracy within the middle class. These self-made prudish aristocrats in the next century, the Victorians, argued that true nobility was a matter of decorum and manners.[20]

The Victorians even redefined the meaning of the words "ladies and gentlemen." These words no longer referred to people of inherited title, but, rather, to ordinary folk who were well versed in the arts of modesty and decorum. The word "noble" no longer referred to members of an inherited aristocracy but to a person with refined and elevated sensitivities. Nothing was more noble, the Victorians said, than to be modest and polite.[21]

And so the people of the Victorian middle class began to compete with each other to be more and more polite. And the more polite and prudish they became, the more status they had in Victorian culture. It meant that the Victorians became more prudish, as far as we know, than any people before them from Western or European cultures. Decorum and manners were glorified and elevated to new and remarkable heights.[22]

It was during this period, too, that personal privacy began to be possible. Hallways were introduced into private homes, which meant you did not need to march through someone else's bedroom to get to the kitchen.[23] And lavatories in the home, without hot water of course, were just coming into being. Toilet paper was newly available.[24] For many reasons, it became more possible for families to hide toileting and dressing from each other more completely. And so the Victorians became Victorian, that is, prudish and devoted to the appearance of asexual propriety. This new privacy and modesty served the function of making the modest person appear more cultured, more upper class.

The appearance of asexual propriety was partly created by enforcing chastity for middle-class young women.[25] A woman's virginity before marriage was a status symbol. And as the belief developed that only lower class women were interested in sex, it became increasingly important to women, and their parents, that women not be interested in sex. As a result, many of the wives in this period were sexually damaged by inhibition, the birthrate plummeted,[26] and gradually the idea became popular that normal women did not like sex.[27]

Victorian men were not nearly so restricted. It was understood that normal men were lustful and prone to illicit sex in a way that was almost noncontrollable.[28] It was understood that women were the ones who controlled men's unruly impulses–or they controlled men as well as they could (if they were ladies).

Nevertheless, outside marriage, there developed a large pornographic underground serving the needs of frustrated Victorian men. Victorian pornography became an industry,[29] and sex began to have two layers, the proper, modest layer with refined women who were often emotionally damaged and unavailable for sex, and an illicit layer that was hidden in the world of outcast women.

Steven Marcis tells us about the development of the modern pornography industry during this period:

> The sexual character or roles attributed to both men and women changed; sexual manners and habits altered; indeed the whole style of sexual life was considerably modified. Among the principal tendencies in this process was a steadily increasing pressure to split sexuality off from the rest of life. By a variety of social means which correspond to the psychological processes of isolation, distancing, denial, and even repression, a separate and insulated sphere in which sexuality was to be confined was brought into existence. Yet even as sexuality was isolated, it continued to develop and change–that is to say, human consciousness of sexuality continued to change and increase. Indeed the isolation was both the precondition of and the vehicle through which such development occurred. The growth of pornography was one of the results of these processes . . . .[30]

The reverse side, of course, of having made modesty and propriety a symbol of refinement and status, is that nakedness and sexuality became symbols of the lower class.[31]

The Anxiety Stemming from Being Modest

But although modesty may make nakedness more sexy this does not imply that it increases sexual pleasure. Our modesty traditions also make people anxious.[32] The American culture is burdened by the pretense of modesty, and by the pretense that the average man is aroused by the sight of the average woman and thus must not look at her nakedness. It is true that men are often aroused in this way, but less true than our mythology suggests.

This modesty pretense causes anxiety in three different ways in our culture, and, it causes disappointment and grief in two more. First, the modest people, particularly more traditional women, are made anxious by the thought of exposing their nakedness because doing so can cost them status. Second, our modesty traditions pretend that all women's bodies look sexually alluring, like the images in *Playboy*, and our culture is burdened by the fact that this is a pretense. Third, men who do not respond sexually to the image of the women they love, or to women in general, are made to feel inadequate and anxious.

With regard to the first source of anxiety, the feeling of being demeaned when seen naked, our fashion tastes have been cultivated so that everyone seems to look better to us with clothes, and the kind of clothes, of course, can greatly increase the status of the wearer.[33]

Second, the culture that eroticizes women's bodies in this way also sets women up to feel physically inadequate, and increasingly inadequate as they grow older, to sustain the sexual response of their lovers. And, by making them anxious about exposing their bodies, their training inhibits their sexual response.[34]

Then, third, trying to pretend that all women's bodies are, or should be, erotically stimulating to all men, causes us to feel that only the most beautiful women make good sexual partners. Since there are only a few such women, most men are not likely to have one, and hence they feel shortchanged and anxious about being inadequate. The culture that advertises this as the norm is bound to make many men feel guilty that they need to imagine such a woman, or look at such a woman, in order to have the kind of sexual response that they have learned is normal for men.

And, finally, even the women who are physically attractive enough to serve the *Playboy* role, which titillates many American men's sexual response, are themselves disappointed to learn that by exaggerating men's sexual response to her by having a body which she can present alluringly she does not move men to be concerned with her sexual pleasure as well–and so she may come to feel that the sexual encounter is not very satisfying for her, or that she is not very sexually adequate.

OUR MODESTY FOLKLORE AND HOMOSEXUALITY

Toileting in gender-segregated privacy, men and women hide their nakedness behind closed doors. They present themselves fully packaged to each other. This makes it possible to present nakedness as part of an erotic script. It would be hard to have the eroticism of a strip tease in a nudist colony. The parts of each other's bodies we see routinely become less sexual in our minds. And so it is hard for a modern man to fathom how his great-grandfather might have been aroused by the sight of a woman's ankle slipping out from under the layers of her long skirt.

The effects of modesty, therefore, enhance the sexual appeal of the modest person, but the mythology of modesty does not reveal this effect. The mythology of modesty that we use to explain our traditions paints a false picture of why we are modest.

This mythology creeps its way into the statements of those who would ban homosexuals. For example, Colin Powell has said,

> To introduce a group of individuals who–proud, brave, loyal, good Americans–but who favor a homosexual life-style, and put them in with heterosexuals who would prefer not to have somebody of the same sex find them sexually attractive, put them in close proximity, ask them to share the most private of their facilities together, the bedroom, the barracks, latrines, the showers, I think that's a very difficult problem to give the military.[35]

But the fact that it is accepted mythology does not mean that it is true.[36] Just as mythology used to tell children that the stork brought their baby brothers and sisters, or that the stages of the moon caused lunacy, or that people who sail off over the horizon will fall off the edge of the earth, so the mythology we tell ourselves today about modesty is also false.

Modesty is an artificial timidity that allows us to present romantic images to those who do not see us undraped. We use it to enhance our status, to create curiosity, and to make our nakedness seem sexy. It is a cultural aphrodisiac.

It would seem odd, therefore, if we chose to enhance the modesty that homosexuals and heterosexuals have in each other's presence, because banning homosexuals from situations of privacy will only enhance homosexual allure.

SUMMARY

We Americans are a prudish people who cloak our modesty traditions in romantic folklore–a folklore that, on reflection, contains important illusions. These myths tell us that we must segregate the sexes to control the strong erotic urges between the sexes. Our analysis here, however, indicates that the gender segregation of toileting serves more to foster sex appeal between the sexes than to diminish it.

There are, however, standard ways of diminishing the erotic potential of nakedness. These techniques are woven into all cultures, even our own, in those contexts in which we wish to diminish sex appeal. To understand how we typically diminish our sexual arousal, we need to study how people in our society manage their nakedness with an etiquette of disregard.

Chapter 3

Nakedness and the Etiquette of Disregard

Legend has it that Lady Godiva, a beautiful English countess in the eleventh century, was distraught because her husband had levied heavy taxes on the common folk of Coventry. And so she pleaded with him to lower taxes until he finally agreed, but only if she would ride through the town naked. The lady consented, but when her ride was announced to the townfolk they were also told they would be required to stay inside behind shut doors and windows. And everyone did: Everyone, that is, but the errant subject, Peeping Tom, who peered through the crack of the window just as Lady Godiva was supposed to approach. He got what he deserved, though, because at the instant she was to come into view, Peeping Tom was struck blind, and so no one saw Lady Godiva naked.

Perhaps, most people are not physically blinded when someone nude comes into view, but something like that often happens. There is a desire to avert one's eyes, to look the other way, or if one is required to look, to look minimally and to not really see, to be casual about it, to disregard the shock of nudity. For nudity, for most people, in most contexts, is psychologically blinding.

And it is not just nudity that is blinding. We are blinded by anything that is potentially embarrassing. It is because we have all been trained in the etiquette of disregard, which requires us not to stare when the person we would stare at might be embarrassed. We are hesitant to look or comment even when the amount of physical exposure is trivial, even when it is more symbolic than real; once it becomes registered in our minds as something one should disregard we have a hard time treating it any other way.

For example, sometime in 1992, a talk show host stood giving his comic monologue that had started his famous show for the previous

30 years. Only this time there was something different. This time, it was plainly visible that Johnny had forgotten to zip up his pants. It was not that people could see anything through the zipper. But it was easy to see his pants were unzipped. Three or four minutes later the cameramen seemed to recognize the problem and the camera zoomed on Johnny's face.

Later, after a commercial, sitting behind his table, he laughed, red-faced, and joked about it. Why didn't someone tell him? "Hey, Johnny, your pants are unzipped!" It was just a comedy show. And Johnny would not have been above dropping his pants to get a laugh in the right kind of routine. Why didn't people call out and embarrass him? Make a joke of it?

People did not comment on it because having unzipped pants is symbolic of an embarrassing exposure. Dropping one's pants is comical, but there was no doubt this was an unintended event. People did not tell Johnny because they wanted to treat him with an *etiquette of disregard*, with a preprogrammed social politeness that requires everyone to act as though nothing of interest is happening.

The etiquette of disregard protects us in all sorts of situations. We use it whenever we feel it would be impolite to stare, to protect people with a deformity, or a disability, from curious looks. It would likely protect a naked lady running from a burning building, but certainly a woman having a baby in a cab, and perhaps even a nursing mother in the back of the bus. This etiquette protects people routinely from curious stares in public rest rooms, locker rooms, department store dressing rooms, saunas, and a variety of other private situations that are shared by people of the same or opposite gender.

It also protects heterosexuals from leering stares from the typical gay. Just as there is an unwritten rule that men do not address a woman with their eyes glued to her breasts, so the rule is that in bathrooms and showers everyone, straight and gay alike, should not stare.

And if they should not stare, they certainly should not leer with erotic interest. And erotic interest can fade in the mood of this etiquette. It is hard to carry off the pretense of disregard while indulging in private erotic excitement.

One gay soldier describes it this way: "Taking a shower with all the other guys [in boot camp] was just like in high school and I do not remember ever being attracted to anyone in the showers or being aware of anyone looking at me." And another gay soldier says, "I don't remember ever getting sexually aroused when in a shower or latrine situation unless I wanted to. In other words, just taking a shower or using the bathroom in and of itself was never sexually stimulating."

Nevertheless, many in the military anticipate such staring and leering from homosexuals. For example, a straight Lieutenant Colonel argues against gays in the military on the grounds that they would ogle heterosexuals, and he says:

> . . . the Army must . . . consider the privacy rights of the heterosexual soldier forced to share a room and latrine with an acknowledged homosexual. The thought of someone becoming sexually aroused watching you dress or shower is disconcerting. Sexual advances and the fear of such advances under these circumstances will damage morale.[1]

Is this a realistic concern? After all, even if homosexuals do not stare at straights in public rest rooms, they do sometimes make homosexual contacts with other gays in these settings. The etiquette of disregard is powerful, but homosexuals do not always conform to this etiquette with each other. Why would they conform to it with heterosexuals?

The straight soldier who has never really known a homosexual, other than, perhaps, someone rumored to be gay, can only imagine what showering with a gay would be like on the basis of the rumors and jokes told about *faggots* daily, jokes that portray gays as eager to violate him sexually. And if gays are like that, such a soldier might reason, the military showers and latrines would provide all the setting that was needed, on one lonely afternoon when nobody else was around, for forced copulation to happen. And why wouldn't gays be like that? After all, this soldier thinks to himself, he would, himself, find it exciting to shower with women. His own sexual drive would make him completely dangerous to women. So it would seem natural, to such a soldier, that gays would crudely and eagerly want to violate him. To accept gays in the military, in that way of thinking, is to accept being violated by gays. Reasoning this way, the gay becomes the straight soldier's bogeyman.

But are these realistic concerns? Or would we, as the head of a gay veterans group recently said, ". . . not hear the explosion of Mardi Gras celebration but a sigh of relief from thousands of men and women."[2]

The answer to that question depends on whether gays would conform to the etiquette of disregard. We know that some gay people do cruise public rest rooms and locker rooms and make contacts with other gays. Can they, or would they, try to make contact with straights and draw them into that way of life? Would they even impose their behavior on those who would prefer not to see it? Or would they continue, as they seem to be doing, to hide that behavior from heterosexuals with the etiquette of disregard?

First, we need to ask if people who can find each other sexually attractive sometimes look at each other's nakedness with disregard. Can men and women disregard each other's nakedness, for example? We are inclined to think that there are no settings in which men can stare at undressed women, but this is not so. And we need to look, too, at the disregard that is presently practiced by everyone in single sex privacy settings, like public rest rooms.

Part of the answer, too, will come from asking when and why people violate this etiquette, as background for deciding if homosexuals are like the rest of us.

Our conclusion will be more informed than that of the soldier who has never known a gay and has only heard about gays from his commander who calls them faggots. Of course, our study of these issues will not leave us so informed that we will know, in every case, how a particular gay person will be. Our purposes, however, do not require that. If we have reason to think gays will be largely conforming to the etiquette of disregard, then we have no more reason to exclude them than we have to avoid walking across the street just because some psychotic motorist might decide to run us down. We can never create policy to protect us all from everything, with certainty.

What we want from our analysis is a more informed understanding of how things are likely to be. And that kind of analysis needs to begin, as always, with a careful review of the most relevant facts we can find.

WHERE DO WE FIND THE ETIQUETTE OF DISREGARD?

When and where do Americans practice the etiquette of disregard? For the most part, people in our society dress and toilet behind closed doors. But there are several situations in which people undress and toilet together, sometimes with those of the opposite sex, and sometimes with the self-sex, and in all of these situations, modesty is protected by a routine disregard of the sexuality of exposed people.

Conforming to the etiquette of disregard, we minimize observation to what is required by the task at hand. We make no mention of any sexual connotation of the exposure, and to behave toward the subject as though the subject were not in any way an object of sexual interest.

There are four routine situations in our society in which this etiquette protects people from embarrassment: medical situations, nudist camps, art classes, and public rest rooms. In the first three situations, the gender of the observed and observer is not controlled. In the last the gender is controlled, but there is strong evidence that in all these cases the same etiquette is in effect.

Disregard in Medical Settings

Even in the doctor's office, people take off their tops or expose a buttock for an injection by a nurse or a doctor, often of the opposite sex, and for the medical person to show anything but disregard for the sexuality of the patient's body would be scandalous.

Hospitals are even more of a strain on people's customary attempts to keep themselves covered. Short gowns that tie in the back with the backside exposed are legendary. And people unaccustomed to hospital levels of modesty can be surprised to learn that they are expected to submit to having their clothing pulled down often by young people of the opposite sex, for such procedures as having their genital areas shaved or having catheters inserted in their urethras. What is surprising is that this treatment can be received, not without embarrassment completely, perhaps, but with much less embarrassment than is anticipated. People submit to procedures they anticipate will mortify them only to learn how little embarrassment they actually feel. This is because the medical personnel have learned to treat them with an etiquette of disregard.

Perhaps nowhere in medicine, however, is modesty more routinely tested than it is in the gynecologist's office. Here young women who have been trained to be modest before older men, are required to submit to an examination in which, often, an older man inspects their genitals with his eyes and hands. The first examination generally takes place in early adolescence and often prior to a young woman's having been examined even cursorily by a lover. Yet we find that women adapt quickly to this experience and typically decide that it makes no difference whether the doctor is a male or female.

How do young women endure this embarrassment? They endure it because the doctors practice an etiquette of disregard, chatting casually with patients during the examination, even joking about irrelevant topics while they probe their patient's vaginas. They might even discuss the procedure, but if so, they do so with a detached and professional style.[3]

And if gynecological exams are not embarrassing enough, there are the exams of proctologists. These would be unbearable for the typically prudish American were the medical people untrained, or unwilling, to conform to an etiquette of disregard.

Today, most of us learn to expect the physician to minimize our embarrassment by a kind of disregard, and so we are willing to endure routine exams. In the more prudish Victorian times, many people, especially women, were not willing. Our great-grandmothers often preferred to die rather than to tolerate such a procedure,[4] but if they chose death, it is likely because they underestimated how much modesty comfort they could have felt if embarrassment had been minimized with the etiquette of disregard.

Disregard in Nudist Camps

Since we sometimes have the illusion that clothes are the primary protector of modesty, it comes as a surprise that most people find it much easier to join a nudist beach than they imagined. What they soon discover is that they are treated with the etiquette of disregard. They find that people are focused on their activities, not their bodies, that they do not stare at each other with erotic interest or curiosity.[5] And not being stared at, people begin to feel more confident and natural.

Americans are often surprised by the casual and nonsexual approach the nudist has to nudity.[6] In a world in which undress with the opposite sex is thought of in terms of topless bars, stripteases and wet T-shirt competitions, it is hard to fathom beaches full of naked people, adults and children, comfortably involved in nonerotic activities. But when nudity is everywhere, people are less preoccupied with erotic fantasies about it,[7] and sex, unexaggerated by our forbidden sexual curiosities, is free to grow and evolve around intimacy and affection.

Because we Americans have learned to think of nudity as sexual, we are surprised to learn that most of the participants in nudist camps are not sexually promiscuous. In fact, they are less sexually experienced, usually, than nonnudists and are less likely to engage in sex that would be considered a transgression in nonnudist society than are nonnudists.[8]

Disregard in Art Classes

Although art students are typically made anxious by the idea that they will draw nude models, they too seem to adapt quickly and find the process much less embarrassing than they anticipate. They simply go to class and discover that someone is willing to stand before a whole class of people who will look at the model with no apparent awareness of the possibility of sexually enjoying the view.

And artists must, of course, observe the model in some detail. They are studying the way the parts of the body fit together, the way the muscles drape over the bone, the way the skin reflects the light. But they manage any initial embarrassment by disregarding the model as a sexual person, someone with whom one could interact, (until, at least, the model puts on a robe during a break) and they do this whether the model is of the same or the opposite sex.[9]

This shows us one of the primary features of this etiquette of disregard. Those who conform to it observe the exposed person only to the degree necessary for the task at hand. It is understood that the artist's model will want to put on a robe when the artists are not working.

And notice that the disregard etiquette allows the artist to look at the subject in some detail, while disregarding the sexual potential of the situation. Disregard is accomplished by simply staying in a frame of mind which minimizes the erotic.

Disregard in Public Rest Rooms

Cultural myths tell us that if we segregate the sexes for toileting there is no embarrassment, but the evidence suggests otherwise, for people regularly guard against embarrassment in these settings by conforming to an etiquette of disregard. For example, the data suggests that men and women feel some embarrassment using public urinals, and they show this embarrassment by a delay in the time it takes them to begin urinating.[10]

Men manage their embarrassment at open urinals by selecting one, if at all possible, so that they have at least one vacant urinal between themselves and others.[11] And, although women's rest rooms are typically less open, more likely to have stalls which more completely enclose them, when they are open, they, too, use an etiquette of disregard to ease modesty embarrassment.[12]

THE FLEXIBILITY OF OUR MODESTY CONCERNS

Sometimes people are embarrassed to undress or toilet before others and some people are more easily embarrassed than others. Why is this? Isn't it possible that some people's modesty is so deeply a part of who they are that they will always find bodily exposure embarrassing?

It is true that some aspects of a personality are much less flexible than others. A person's intelligence, for example, is much less flexible than a person's mood. Among the less changeable dimensions of a personality, too, are a person's deeply rooted values, or attitudes. Values and attitudes can be woven into an enduring philosophy of life. And so, to evaluate the flexibility of modesty, we need

to ask the nature of this dimension of personalities. Is it rooted in people's moral value system? That is, is modesty an attitude? Or is it merely a habit? Or even the casual expression of a fashion? For whereas habits are hard to change, they are not nearly so enduring as values, and, on the other hand, fashions are more changeable than habits. Fashions change, effortlessly, with the season, however brief or long.

Is Modesty a Value, Habit, or Fashion?

Let us look, then, to see if modesty is an attitude (which, by definition, reflects a value and is important to us), a habit (which we often want to change but which has some resistance to change), or a fashion (which is dictated by popular opinion and is important only so long as those whose opinion we value say it is).[13]

Is modesty an attitude? If so it is rooted in concepts and persuasive arguments about what is good or bad. A modest woman who felt it would be wrong to go to a gynecologist, would be avoiding doing so because of her values or attitudes. It might even be the case that she would not be embarrassed by the experience, but that she would feel it would be wrong and that if she did so she would feel self-critical.[14] By definition, we like our attitudes and we endorse our behaviors which reflect our attitudes.[15]

If modesty is a habit, on the other hand, then it is devoid of reason, for we are often unhappy with our habits. They do not reflect our values. People who have developed a habit, say, of clearing their throat, or tapping their fingers, are not prepared to tell you why it is good to do these things. Such things may be difficult to change, but they can be changed, generally, with self-practice and when we change them we do so without violation of our inner values.

Like habits, fashions are devoid of reason. But fashions change with the season and the context according to what authorities, or other people, define as good or appropriate for a particular place or time. It is the fashion to wear much more abbreviated clothes on the beach than in the business office. It is not that it is immoral to wear a bathing suit to a business meeting. (Why would it be more *immoral* in a business office than on the beach?) It is just inappropriate or highly unfashionable to do so.

Because our modesty is different in different contexts (the beach, business office, hospital room, art class) it is probably best thought of as a fashion sensitivity. That means, we would expect most people to adapt to less private toileting and undress without embarrassment, if other people seemed to feel it was appropriate and to engage in it without signs of curiosity, interest, or self-consciousness. And that is what studies suggest people do.[16] Nevertheless there are probably some habit elements in modesty. People habitually put on the clothes they have hanging in the closet and have to think about where they put their swim clothes when the occasion arises, and may, when they first put them on, feel a little exposed.

To say that modesty is probably best thought of as a fashion, does not mean to say there are no poignant feelings associated with it. People can be very self-conscious and embarrassed about violating fashions. But if we can all imagine being embarrassed by being naked, or wearing revealing clothes, we can all, also, imagine being self-conscious and embarrassed by wearing extremely silly clothes that are highly unfashionable. Both of these experiences might make us, in the right context, highly self-conscious and uncomfortable.

But the fact that the amount of covering we need to feel comfortable is highly dependent on the context tells us that modesty today is largely a fashion and, as such, our feelings about it are highly flexible and can change with the change of fashion.

Evidence for the Flexibility of Modesty

On the other hand, aren't there some people who are more modest than most? Whose childhood traditions have so accustomed them to hiding their bodies that they do not adapt to the fashion?

Even people with a high degree of bodily modesty are generally able to adapt and modify this trait if they conform to the custom of the context. Even when modesty reaches neurotic proportions, it is cured more easily than most other kinds of neurotic problems.

For example, paruresis, the difficulty in urinating in the presence of another person, is a modesty problem. Most people who suffer from it, experience it in a mild degree,[17] but it can reach neurotic proportions as when the victim of this disorder is unable to frequent public places because of the inability to urinate in public rest rooms. It is often one symptom among many in people with pronounced sexual problems[18] or for people with a history of having been sexually abused.[19]

Yet this inconvenient form of bodily modesty is one of the most treatable of psychological problems. There is almost a 100 percent success rate in from five to 20 brief treatment sessions even for unusually severe cases.[20] The usual treatment of choice is a desensitization procedure in which the the patient might be asked to visualize urinating in a pubic setting, then really to urinate while people are in the next room, and then while they are at some distance in the same room and, finally, while they are in close proximity.

Paruresis is more frequently studied than other forms of bathroom modesty because paruresis can be so disabling. However, the more standard form of bathroom modesty (simple psychological discomfort with no loss of ability to urinate) also seems to adapt quickly with experience.[21] And, as we have noted, women adapt quickly to gynecological exams and almost everyone who tries it adapts quickly to nude beaches.[22]

The Contagion of Modesty Embarrassment

Like other fashions, modesty embarrassment is contagious. When observers disregard the sexuality of a situation, embarrassment is lessened, but also, when the person with the undressed body behaves with little evidence of embarrassment, with disregard, the observer is likely to treat it with disregard as well.

Consider the case of the straight soldier who explained how he feels about a gay soldier seeing him in the shower. He said, "I have had a few incidents with gay soldiers in the showers and latrines staring at me, nothing compromising. It never bothers me since I just don't care who sees me. I figure we are all adults and can behave like adults. . . . I am not worried about a person being gay or straight. I think I can look at it as if a gay person came up to me and made a comment about the way I looked, I would have to take it as a compliment. All I have to do is say no and thanks anyway . . . ."

This works in other contexts as well. Not only does the doctor put the patient at ease with an etiquette of disregard, but the patient, by participating in the irrelevant small talk, helps to create the context which makes the situation less embarrassing to experience.

VIOLATIONS OF THE ETIQUETTE OF DISREGARD

Sex, as we know it, would not be possible if everyone always conformed to the etiquette of disregard. People with sexual inhibitions, in fact, may need special help in moving from a disregard of the erotic into an erotic mindset that makes sexual functioning possible. But in most contexts in which people are undressed or toileting, the rule is that they treat each other's sexuality with disregard.

Whether it is satisfying to slip into an erotic regard of another person's body, however, depends typically on whether the observer feels permission to do so. The relevant permission is generally communicated by the sexual object, but the felt permission can also be a culture of other observers, as, for example, in the case of male adolescents feeling permission from their friends to stare with erotic eyes at women without concern for the woman's permission. When this behavior is transported into the adult world it is a form of harassment.

It is a different matter when the observer does not have the support of other observers who approve. People who allow themselves to be aroused by other people's bodies, dressed or undressed, without any support or approval are likely to find themselves diagnosed as voyeurs by psychologists, at least if this observation is extensive and uncontrolled. When, and if, such observers are noticed by the observed, they are likely to cause anxiety.

The degree of offense, however, depends on how seriously the voyeuristic observation is indulged, and, if the observer shows some signs of conforming to the etiquette of disregard, of being embarrassed at having been noticed to be erotically regarding the other, it might be taken as a compliment. Thus, a man who was embarrassed to be noticed peeking down a woman's blouse would cause less anxiety than a man following a woman and observing her, erotically, at length.

HOMOSEXUAL VIOLATION OF DISREGARD WITH HETEROSEXUALS

These rules, which require us to treat each other with an etiquette of disregard, apply to homosexuals as well as heterosexuals. The question is not whether homosexuals will find heterosexuals sexually alluring. It is whether they will violate this etiquette, and turn privacy situations with heterosexuals into erotic settings. And the question is not whether an unusual homosexual will occasionally violate these rules.[23] Perhaps many heterosexuals violate these rules occasionally, but they behave as though they believe in the rules, and only voyeurs will flagrantly violate the rules without the permission of either the person observed or a support group.

The question heterosexuals need to have answered is how likely it is that homosexuals will cause them discomfort by flagrant violation of the etiquette of disregard, by allowing their minds to slip, in more than the most trivial way, into an erotic state, and, especially, by thinking of this erotic regard of the exposed heterosexuals as acceptable.

Evidence that Homosexuals Honor Etiquette of Disregard

Do homosexuals violate the etiquette of disregard with heterosexuals? Most homosexuals do not, at least in any flagrant way. Most homosexuals are not easy to identify,[24] but if they leered at heterosexuals in private places, they would be more noticed by heterosexuals.

If they were allowed to reveal that they are homosexual, would they stop conforming to the etiquette of disregard? The answer has to do with the gay person's ability to make contact with other homosexuals. One closet homosexual man declined an invitation by an attractive man to have a drink after class at a straight bar. Asked if he was interested in pursuing the straight man, the homosexual responded:

> If he had told me he was gay I would have been interested, but I've never seen much point in chasing straight men who aren't interested, when there are so many equally good-looking gay men at the bars who are interested. I've always considered myself a fairly logical and practical person, so why waste my time and efforts on someone who is not interested?

The evidence tells us that homosexuals will conform to the etiquette of disregard even if they are allowed to reveal their identity.

After all, homosexuals have much fewer sanctions against revealing their identity in civilian life than they do in the military.[25] Yet in civilian life, too, they conform to the etiquette of disregard. And the evidence suggests that they do so because they want acceptance from heterosexuals.[26] Furthermore, the research available indicates that gay people are just as embarrassed by eroticism in public situations with heterosexuals as heterosexuals are.[27]

Perhaps the most telling evidence for the homosexual's sense of importance attached to being acceptable to heterosexuals in the shower is told by a gay soldier describing the only time he can remember developing an erection in the presence of someone he presumed to be a heterosexual.

> There was an instance where I wasn't able to be nonchalant in the shower with another guy and I did get an erection. It was particularly embarrassing and I worried about his reaction for several days.
>
> I was a member of a . . . task force . . . and we were called out to go . . . play war. I had been awake for over 36 hours reading tech manuals and working on electronic equipment, and I was so punchy I was slightly giddy. The unit I was with was given special permission to use the officers' showers because they had hot and cold water, as opposed to the grunts which only had cold water. Ooooo-rahhhhh.
>
> The showers were inside this big green tent and the floor was gravel, covered with wooden pallets. You walked into the tent and around a partition and there were benches to sit and undress–no privacy–and then around another partition were the showers. Just two opposing rows of nozzles, probably four to a side.
>
> I walked around the second partition and my eyes met a very attractive and very well-built guy. He and I were the only ones there, I was mesmerized by him–I just froze in the doorway and watched him. I don't know how long I stood there, but all of a sudden I realized I had an erection and that he was rinsing off and looking right at me. My towel was over my shoulder and my hands were at my side, so he would've had to have been blind not to notice my "condition." I walked to the

> farthest side of the shower and glanced at him as I started to get wet. He was glaring at me very hard like he was going to say something and then he looked away. I avoided looking at him until he left. I spent a lot of time waiting to be sure he was gone, at least it seemed that way, but when I rounded the partition, there he sat, nude, drying his toes. I avoided looking at him again, and as we dressed he started a plain ol' conversation with me about the military exercise we were on and asking me questions about Hawaii and the base where I was stationed. I was nervous and felt that my voice was shaking as I answered. He left before I did and he told me that he'd catch me later.
>
> I was s-c-a-r-e-d t-o d-e-a-t-h. His initial passive-aggressive reaction and his subsequent chatty friendliness was contradictory. I was afraid he was going to say something to someone and he was just being nice to be deceptive. I saw him the next day and he looked right at me but didn't say a word as we passed, and that further increased my anxiety. Nothing came of it that I know of, but it was a frightening experience.

With the social sanctions we have against homosexuality, it would be a foolish homosexual who would not be apprehensive about being seen as flirtatious by a condemning heterosexual.

That social sanctions, not laws, are the powerful deterrents against gay people making advances is also indicated by the finding that when laws against homosexuality (e.g., solicitation) are removed, there is no apparent increase in that behavior.[28]

How Homosexual Contacts Are Made

Nevertheless, many male homosexuals do make sexual contact with other homosexuals in public settings. How do they do this without violating the etiquette of disregard with heterosexuals?

Most often the contact is made in a setting in which homosexuals are known to congregate. When that is not so, they must be able to discern whether someone is, or is not, a homosexual. Since the appearance and typical behavior of most homosexuals is indistinguishable from that of heterosexuals, this is done by a graduated series of interactions that allows identification to be made. Notice how careful this soldier is. This kind of care is required if a homosexual is to identify another homosexual in a context that is not clearly meant for gays.

A gay soldier explains how this is done. He says,

> As I said before, gays learn to recognize one another; it's the hungry look in the eyes. One of us would start up a conversation, and then talk for a while. Then, when the heat in the sauna started to become unbearable, it was out to the shower. If my new friend followed me, then that was a good sign. If he went to a shower close by, then the game of peek-a-boo would usually begin. Standing there under a cold shower, rubbing down any sore muscles, letting the water run down over my body, and watching the other man do the same thing. Gradually, the peeking turned into more obvious looks. Then back into the sauna for round two.

Still, the process is not complete. The soldier continues his account, showing how increasing evidence is gathered with infinite patience, always making certain that, although this was a public setting, no one observed this interaction.

> If they followed me back, then that was a good indication that we were going to find something even more interesting to talk about. But never never never would any flirtation occur in the presence of others. This was really taking a risk at this point. So caution was the name of the game.

Then the interaction would be moved discreetly, and still ambiguously, into a more private exchange only to become more guarded, again, if others came into earshot.

> Only when we were alone could we begin to ask each other questions that would verify what we were both thinking. Usually, the conversation started with a compliment on "What good shape you're in, how often do you come in here?" "How many situps do you do to get such a flat stomach?" "Your legs are really strong, do you run?" or something similar. The reply was something equally complimentary, and now we could

> look each other over more slowly and deliberately, while we continued talking. If someone came in, then the conversation would turn to something safe, like sports or what was going on at the clubs, or how good a beer would taste. Then out to the showers, same routine.

It would still, however, be possible to abandon this process, to recognize that the other person was merely being friendly, so the identification process continues still:

> Depending on what intuition said, it was back to the sauna, or ask him out for a beer or if he wanted to go do something. If he wanted to spend more time together, then we would do that, and it could turn into a sexual encounter. I generally checked them out pretty carefully, and was quite confident that they were interested in me before I would risk going any further with them. I've had several friends investigated by . . . [military's force for investigating homosexuals]. It was no picnic, and those . . . don't stop until they succeed in destroying your life. So discretion was very important.

Even when making homosexual contacts in public settings, gay men are careful to honor the heterosexual's etiquette of disregard. They work around it cautiously, making sure each move is reciprocated, before assuming the other person is homosexual.

SUMMARY

When heterosexuals predict that homosexuals will invade their privacy, they are likely to be making these predictions on the basis of little information. Most people who are apprehensive about homosexuals have never met one, and most have never showered with a person whom they knew to be homosexual. The prevalence of stories about faggots take on the quality of a bogeyman story with no basis in reality, only a basis in our modesty myths.

The evidence, when we actually look at it, tells us that homosexuals are likely to conform with considerable care to the heterosexual etiquette of disregard. Homosexuals in our society live, for the most part, a very closeted existence, and they shower and toilet with heterosexuals without revealing their presence. This implies that they are capable of showering and toileting with undressed heterosexuals without their control being overwhelmed, and, if they can do this without telling us that they are gay, they can do it while disclosing that they are gay as well.

Although it is true that gay men sometimes recognize other gay men and have furtive encounters in public rest rooms, when straight people are around these settings gay men practice the etiquette of disregard and this makes their sexuality invisible to non-gays. This is not difficult for them to do.

One gay soldier tells of trying to explain this to a straight roommate who could not understand how gay men could shower and undress all the time with men and not feel driven to distraction by the sexuality of the experience. The gay soldier told this story:

> I had a straight roommate . . . who was OK with me being gay . . . . Anyway, he could never understand how we (gay guys) could shower with other men and not get all excited. When we would play racquetball and shower afterwards at the gym, he'd turn the shower on and run through it on his way by (not much of an exaggeration). I finally had to drag him along to the nude beach on the North Shore to help make my point. The point being that whenever you're all nude, there's no mystery and no spark for the fire, as it were, and that "intent" is also important on the part of all parties involved. He told me he was able to appreciate the body of a nude female without getting sexually excited, but he couldn't understand that from a gay standpoint. I still don't understand his viewpoint. . . . We argued many evenings about what was the real turn-on, if it was conjured in the mind or just the mere visual stimulation. Anyway, I had made my point and he finally understood what I was getting at.[29]

The belief that homosexuals will be driven to distraction and violate heterosexuals in the shower is just a consequence of our heterosexual modesty myths, which lead us wrongly to think that people who can be sexually attracted to each other cannot manage situations of nakedness together.

The fact that homosexuals do manage situations of nakedness without evidencing their homosexuality, is wrongly taken by heterosexuals to mean that no one present is homosexual. Homosexuals are among us everywhere, and their invisibility is testimony to the ease with which they, too, can and do conform to the pervasive etiquette of disregard.

Chapter 4

Why Some People Dislike Gays

Three 12-year-old boys in their underwear are cutting up in their junior high school locker room. A smaller 12-year-old, Allen, is sitting one bench over feeling left out. He is putting on his gym socks and trying not to watch the fun. Then someone notices him. "Look there's Allison!" one rowdy youngster giggles. "He's a fairy, aren't you Allie boy . . .?"

"No, I'm not."

"Don't you know what a fairy is? Only fairies wouldn't know that. I think you're a fairy."

"No, I'm not."

"I bet you are, 'cause you don't like girls, do you? You think girls are dumb, don't you?"

It is in ways like this that people in our culture learn about homosexuality. This and as they look at the graffiti on the rest room walls:

> Roses are red
> Violets are blue,
> I kiss the boys
> and the boys kiss me, too.

"Do you think girls come in here sometimes?" one boy asks another.

"Nah, it's just some queer writing that stuff."

"What's a queer?"

"You know, a guy who likes to do it with other guys. Yuk."

"Do what with other guys?"

"You know, kiss 'em and stuff. Real sicko stuff."

Or maybe in football practice one kid calls another a "homo."

"What's a homo?" that kid asks another after school.

"It's a guy that wants to be a girl. You know, like Stevie. I think he's a homo."

"Stevie?"

"Yeah. Look at the way he walks sometime. He walks like a girl. He does it on purpose. He likes to pretend he's a girl."

Then two 15-year-old boys who have already learned the basic words are sitting on the grass one summer, smoking cigarettes. One says to the other. "I heard that Coach Jenkins is a queer. Have you heard that?"

"You're kidding. Coach Jenkins?"

"I hear he likes to get in boys' pants."

"Wow! He better watch it. Some guy'll bust him in the jaw."

"I think guys like that belong in prison, but you gotta stay away from him. I hear he can make guys like it."

"Really? Can you do that?"

"You better believe you can. That's how a guy gets to be a queer. Some dude touches you and makes you want it. I hear it happens in prison all the time."

It is in ways like this that people in our culture learn about homosexuals. Our information comes from the whispered gossip of uninformed children. For the official culture does not teach little children about homosexuality. And adolescent sex-education courses typically omit mention of it, too.[1] There are no movies about homosexuality for children and adolescents, no stories or comics to inform them, nor gossipy conversation about them from the adults at the dinner table.

And when they are adults, they are not likely to find much better information on the subject. There are few accounts of them on television, few books and most of those buried in the back shelves of bookstores. College courses do not mention them.

Our images of homosexuals were most likely acquired in junior high when our hormones are pumping new sexual feelings through our bodies, but when all sexual acts still seem a little shocking, when the thought of our parents having ever had sex seemed disgusting. It is about this time that we acquire our main concepts about homosexuals, from the childish rumors whispered to us on the sly and the mysterious messages scrawled on the back of rest room doors.[2]

Because homosexuals are not officially talked about, at least until we are much older, homosexuals become shadow people in our society, people we hear about in whispered tones, or joke about with people who will laugh, but seldom know in the flesh and blood as struggling human beings who brush their teeth and walk their dogs like the rest of society. They remain in our minds the people who do the things that are scrawled on bathroom walls. That is what defines them.

The images of homosexuals that get laid down in our young minds are, nevertheless, more or less standard, and there are five myths that we are likely to have heard, with an emphasis sometimes on one, sometimes another.

Before we can be open to the facts that have become available about homosexuals, facts unavailable to us as children, we need to examine these old myths, and try to see the extent to which they are true. And so we will take these myths seriously and try to evaluate their validity. Then, in the context of an examination of these myths, we will try to survey the general feelings that Americans exposed to these myths have about homosexuals in our culture.

FIVE HOMOSEXUAL MYTHS

There are five myths[3] that seem to lay the foundation of the way most people who have never known homosexuals think of them.

First, there is the myth that homosexuality is unnatural, that homosexuals want to be the opposite gender, something that they are not, something unnatural. Second, there is the myth that homosexuals are mentally ill, that homosexual desire is a kind of sickness, like a desire to smoke opium, or to wash one's hands excessively. Third, there is the belief that homosexuals are predators, that they will attack heterosexuals, or seduce them, and turn them into homosexuals. Fourth, there is the myth that homosexuals do what they do because they have an uncontrollably strong sex drive. And, finally, there is the myth that homosexuality is a matter of free choice.

All five myths are based in rumor and yet, society has reason to wonder if they are true, if only because of the prevalence of this mythology and the dearth of other information about gays. And so we will examine each myth, and see if there are any data to suggest they are true. We will find that there is a little truth in some of the myths, but that they greatly oversimplify the picture and frighten heterosexuals unnecessarily.

Homosexuality Is Unnatural

People persuaded by the homosexual myths often believe gay men are like women and lesbians are like men. For example, in May 1993, when Congressman Ron Dellums began House Hearings on the topic of homosexuals in the military, a ranking minority member, Floyd Spence, a South Carolina Republican who had been in the house for more than 20 years, commented, "I'm used to men being men and women being women. I can't understand all this mixed-up stuff, frankly."[4]

Floyd Spence was voicing our myth that homosexuality is unnatural. This myth says that all adults should fit simply in our Norman Rockwell concepts of men being men as our culture defines them, cutting their hair short, wearing the pants, and women being women. Since the vast majority of people try to make themselves look like this, even if they privately wonder if they really fit the mold, it is easy to think that everyone is like these simple concepts, through and through.

It is likely, in fact, that Spence has never known a homosexual,[5] never noticed or read anything about homosexuals, and never talked with anyone about them, or even thought about them to any great extent. What little he knows about them, probably came to him through the grapevine of rumors that informs us all when we are adolescents.

Not having well-informed concepts of homosexuals available to him, it's reasonable that he tries to understand them on the model of something he knows. Gay men are like women, he reasons, and lesbians are like men. It is the myth that there are two natural categories of people, men, as they should be, and women, as they should be. It is confusing because homosexuals do not fit in these simple categories.

For our gender myths tell us that the natural human being is one who is male or female like our gender myths say they should be, even though what we call the maleness of men and the femaleness of women is partly a result of trimming our images down, cutting our hair in a gendered way, donning the clothes of our gender, of shaping and molding ourselves. To say that this is the natural state, just because we have grown accustomed to it, is like saying that the way a poodle looks when we clip it so that it has a ball on the end of its tail is its true natural state. We become so accustomed to these images that we mistake them for nature. And to look at the homosexual and say he or she is unnatural is like looking at an unconventionally clipped poodle, or even an unclipped poodle, and seeing that as unnatural.

There is, however, a little of Floyd Spence in all of us, even among homosexuals. We are used to seeing people clipped and shaped into the traditional images of men and women. What bothers us about homosexuals, when we are thinking this way, is not just that they have sex with each other, but that they jar our picture of the natural way men and women should relate to each other. The picture of two men holding hands, or staring into each other's eyes, is alien to our image of how things should be, according to the concepts that we have had since we were children. It is not so much that homosexuality is "unethical." It is that it just does not seem natural. It is like using avocados to make ice cream (as the Filipinos do). It does not seem right.

But is there any truth to this myth that gay men are like women and lesbians are like men? There is a subgroup of homosexuals for which it is a bit true, but not for most. Most homosexual men do not act or look like women, and most lesbians do not act or look like men.[6] In fact, it is their superficial resemblance to heterosexuals that allows them to hide their homosexuality so successfully.[7]

How can homosexuals form couples without one of them playing the role of the opposite gender? Many homosexual couples base their relationships on a model of "best friends" with the added element of romance,[8] and most homosexual couples do not have distinct sex typing in which one plays the role of a man and one plays the role of a woman.[9]

Even the sexual act need not mimic traditional male-female roles. Homosexuals, like heterosexuals, can caress in ways that lead to orgasm, without assuming gender specific roles, or they can alternate between passive and more assertive roles the way heterosexual men and women sometimes do. The myth that homosexuals are unnatural, that the men are like women and the women are like men, is mostly untrue.

Homosexuals Are Mentally Ill

People who have been persuaded by our homosexual myths often see gays as sick.[10] Gays have not always been seen as sick. The preferred nineteenth-century model for understanding homosexuality was that it was a form of degeneracy, or a regression back to a primitive and unevolved human state.[11] And Freud thought of homosexuality as a natural variation of normal human sexuality.[12]

During the 1940s, however, several psychiatrists argued that homosexuals were sick. Sandor Rado, for example, claimed they were sick because, so he argued, they were afraid of the opposite sex.[13]

Irving Bieber popularized the notion that homosexuals were made sick by overly protective mothers and fathers who were overly distant, [14] and argued that this was evidence that homosexuality was a mental illness.

There was a dramatic shift of professional opinion on this subject in the early 1970s. Studies during this period indicated that Bieber's theory of how parents cause homosexuality is wrong.[15] Several authors made a convincing case that homosexuality was much more common among both humans and animals than most people had believed.[16] New research indicated that homosexuals were not more likely to have neurotic symptoms than other groups.[17] And gay people themselves began to speak out and convince psychologists and psychiatrists that they could lead healthy lives if society would let them.[18]

As a result, in the mid-1970s both the American Psychiatric Association and the American Psychological Association voted in resolutions declaring that they believed homosexuality was not a form of mental illness.[19]

And so the view that homosexuality is a mental disease has become a footnote in the history of medicine, for today there is consensus that homosexuality is not a mental illness.[20] The belief that it was a mental illness lasted less than half a century. Today it is thought of as a natural condition, like left-handedness.

Homosexuals as Predators

The third myth is that homosexuals are predators[21] who convert their prey into homosexuals.[22] This myth is based mostly on stories about male sexual aggressions in prison.

There is some truth to the predator myth in prisons.[23] Antiquated prisons are often set up in such a way that it is difficult for the guards to control unruly inmates and it is tempting for them to rely on a few seemingly well-behaved prisoners to keep the peace.[24] While these seemingly well-behaved prisoners present a good face to the guards, they can dominate and control the traditional prison by raping and threatening to rape other prisoners.[25] The evidence is that these rapes are largely done by heterosexual prisoners who use the threat of rape as a control device to get the other prisoners to carry contraband for them, give them their food or other treats, or generally do their dirty work. [26]

Would these homosexual rapes be likely in the military? No. The homosexual rape that occurs in prisons is very different from homosexual sex outside of prisons.[27] To confuse the two is as mistaken as to treat all men as rapists. Presumably this homosexual rape does happen much less in the modern, more progressive prison.[28] Like all rape, it is not a sexual act so much as an act of domination. In prison it is committed by convicted criminals, and we know that lesbians and gay men are no more likely than straight people to be criminal.[29]

Homosexuals Are Promiscuous

Another myth we should examine is the myth of the promiscuous gay man. There is some evidence that it is true that gay men have more anonymous sexual encounters than other men or than women, lesbian or straight.[29] This is a fact that is taken by some to mean that male homosexuals have an overwhelming sex drive.[30] It is as if they are so driven by homosexual desire that they cannot control themselves.

But one forgets that gay men often have such anonymous sex as an adaptation to a society that makes it difficult for them to have more committed relationships. Only when the stigma against male sexuality, or the suspicion, even, about close male friendships, is diminished will we be able to judge if promiscuity is inherent in some male homosexuals.

In the meantime, there are many gay men who find anonymous sex unsatisfactory. One such promiscuous gay man said the following about it:

> After the event, I wonder what the hell I was doing; it was not satisfying. It was too fast, too scary, and now I feel shameful to boot. . . . I think that . . . a lot of gays . . . could bring more intimacy into our relationships if we shared our experiences without being shamed or humiliated, and worked our way out of this addiction as a community. We need to be recognized as people, with the same rights, needs, and wants as everyone else. Education and coming out are the only ways that people will understand that we are more than sexual.

The new gay liberation movement tends to see such promiscuous behavior as symptomatic of gays living in a culture that forbids more satisfying relationships.[32] John De Cecco explains what the committed gay relationship means to the modern gay community.

> In the gay community it [the gay relationship] has become a symbol of self-acceptance of one's homosexuality, an index of psychological health, of self-esteem. The gay relationship is almost the political sell of the gay liberation movement; it is viewed as the unification of the sexual and the emotional that comes from being gay and proud. It politically stands in defiance of the heterosexual marriage, as if to proclaim, "Anything you can do I can do better." At the same time, in emphasizing durability as its essential feature, it is at least a partial endorsement of marriage as the model of intimate relationships. That two men who have sex together can love each other has come to symbolize the ultimate detoxification of homosexuality and justifies the addition of the gay relationship to the pantheon of human achievements.[33]

There is a growing sense that gay men want such committed relationships, not just fleeting encounters, and there is a growing body of literature exploring how those relationships can be fostered.[34] The men most likely to engage in anonymous homosexual sex are men who do not think of themselves as gay.[35]

Homosexuality Is a Free Choice

The final myth about homosexuality is that homosexuality is a matter of free choice. For example, one straight person considering the validity of this myth of free choice said,

> . . . People are queer because they don't have respect for themselves. They just feel like doing things that the rest of us don't believe in and so they do it. If I did everything that seemed interesting to me to do, believe me, I'd do some pretty bad things.

People who buy this myth do not realize how hard some gay people want to be straight. Jess Jessop was such a gay person struggling to overcome his homosexuality. He explained, "I had spent most of my twenty-two years . . . trying to conceal my homosexuality and prove my masculinity. . . . My very decision to join the Navy was in part motivated by a desire to demonstrate my manhood to myself and to the world. Surely no one would call me queer if I was defending my country. . . ."

And Jess did defend his country. He pumped bullets into the face of a Viet Cong, and jumped through combat fire to try to rescue fellow soldiers. But the inner feeling of being a homosexual never left him. When he was recommended for the Silver Star, he was so full of shame that he declined it and took a dishonorable discharge instead.

Jess said, "All these successes in a very masculine environment should have made me feel better about myself. But I knew that deep down inside I was still queer and that no matter what level of excellence I might achieve, if anyone ever learned my deep dark secret, I'd be disgraced and drummed out of the Navy. There was never a day when the thought didn't cross my mind, when I didn't feel like the world's greatest fraud. Each day the dishonesty of living a lie produced a little more self-hate.[36]

"If homosexuality is a matter of choice, then homosexuals have chosen a life style that the majority of people in *our* society find disgusting." Jess continued, "It is not surprising that people who make such choices . . . are discriminated against. They have, after all, separated themselves from society."[37]

Homosexuality, like most everything else in life, is a complicated issue of choices and lack of choices. It is not a black and white issue. If the discussion on free choice is meaningful, one has to consider what the options are, and whether or not the possibility of success is reasonable to count on.

All choices are not equally reasonable to make, even if the outcome is generally favorable. Compare for example, the difference between choosing to run into a burning building to save a cat, with choosing to buy a magazine in a supermarket. Even if both were good things to choose, a reasonable person would not always choose to save the cat.

And, although there are some homosexuals who can and do choose not to have homosexual sex, the evidence suggests that homosexuals cannot choose to stop feeling homosexual feelings. The primary choice for homosexuals is between living a life in which their homosexuality is a secret shame that haunts all experience, or in which they learn to recognize the sense of dignity they will feel if they can own up to and disclose their homosexuality.

WHO DISLIKES HOMOSEXUALS?

Based on several polls in 1992 and 1993, nearly half of Americans feel negative about homosexuals,[38] and disapprove, specifically, of having homosexuals in the military.[39] On the other hand, nearly that many Americans accept homosexuals, approve of them, and want policy to protect them.[40] What is the difference between these two groups?

First, people dislike gays because they do not know much about them. Not knowing much about gays, they can only accept the cultural myths about them which put gays in a bad light. There is also evidence that most of the dislike of homosexuals is straight men disliking gay men. Most people are not very opposed to lesbians, and women are more accepting of gay men than men are.

The Uninformed

Research tells us that many people believe our homosexual myths[41] and that those who do so are more disapproving of gays.[42]

People are more comfortable with homosexuality when they have learned something about it other than the myths. Only about half of Americans are aware of knowing either a lesbian or a gay man,[43] and those who are aware of knowing someone gay are much more likely to support gay rights than those who do not.[44] One can also become more educated about gays by reading a book or taking a course on the topic, and the data show that such activities also result in less negative feelings about gays.[45]

Men's Dislike of Gay Men

Both men and women are relatively tolerant of lesbians, but a fair number of men are very condemning of male homosexuality.[46] We know that the men who are most opposed to gay men are themselves highly masculine. They prefer those homosexuals who do not make their homosexuality obvious,[47] are highly bothered by the way homosexual men seem to challenge traditional male-female sex roles,[48] and work harder than more liberal men to present public evidence of their own masculinity.[49]

Furthermore, the evidence suggests that these highly masculine, antihomosexual men are distant in all their relationships, be they with men or women. They not only try to avoid homosexuals as friends but also anyone who might look homosexual to others.[50] They are also likely to be distant and guarded in their interaction with heterosexual men and women as well, and feel an emotion-charged antipathy towards homosexual men when they can find no way to avoid them.[51]

At its extreme, this antipathy shows evidence of being a true phobia. When phobic people are confronted with the object that frightens them, they typically have an increased heart rate and blood vessel constriction, and this is commonly seen as diagnostic of phobias.[52] And research shows that many men who are intolerant of homosexuals respond to pictures of male homosexual sexual interaction with the same physiological responses that spider phobics have when they are shown spiders. More tolerant heterosexuals do not have these physiological responses.[53]

Highly intolerant, or homophobic men, are even guarded against any man who befriends homosexuals. Unlike more tolerant men, men highly negative toward gays are inclined to see those men who befriend homosexuals as a little bit homosexual themselves.[54]

Women's Feelings about Lesbianism

Women are less disapproving of homosexuality in general than men are,[55] and they also seem to worry less about it among their friends. This greater comfort may result from the fact that society seems to scrutinize men's behavior for signs of homosexuality with much more vigilance than it does women's.[56] For example, a woman can take a job in a man's world much less awkwardly than a man can stay home and mind the children while his wife works.[57]

Women's greater acceptance of homosexuality may also be related to the fact that they are more likely to know a lesbian than men are to know a gay male.[58] Women who work outside the home are more likely to know both a gay man and a gay woman than a man is.[59]

Nevertheless, the same people who introduced men to the fear of homosexuality early in this century, introduced into the feminine psychology a fear of lesbianism. If women are relatively comfortable with lesbians today, they are still much less comfortable with affection between women than were their great-grandmothers of the early Victorian era.

Before the turn of the century, women often devoted their lives to each other in what was called a "Boston Marriage."[60] It was common for women to feel and express considerable romantic attraction for each other, especially when they lived together as they might in a dorm of a woman's college. We do not know how often this attraction was played out with explicit sexual interaction, but the Victorians, with their list of sexual perversions, began to suspect girlish closeness was sexual and so they acted to alarm young girls and warn them of lesbianism.

And so, at the end of the Victorian period, physician "Mrs. Mary Wood-Allen, M.D." published a well-received book for young women. She warned of the dangers of overly close friendships with other girls. She said:

> Girls are apt at certain periods of their lives to be rather gushing creatures. They form most sentimental attachments for each other. They go about with their arms around each other, they loll against each other, and sit with clasped hands by the hour. They fondle and kiss until beholders are fairly nauseated, and in a few weeks, perhaps, they do not speak as they pass each other, and their caresses are lavished on others. Such friendships are not only silly, they are even dangerous. They are a weakening of moral fiber, a waste of mawkish sentimentality. They may be even worse. Such friendship may degenerate even into a species of self-abuse that is most deplorable.
>
> When girls are so sentimentally fond of each other that they are like silly lovers when together, and weep over each other's absence in uncontrollable agony, the conditions are serious enough for the consultation of a physician. It is an abnormal state of affairs, and if probed thoroughly might be found to be a sort of perversion, a sex mania, needing immediate and perhaps severe measures.[61]

This kind of alarm that women's closeness will represent lesbianism was more present 20 years ago than it is today.[62] The feminist movement seems to have made the spectre of lesbianism less ominous. Today, when a woman is suspected or known to be a lesbian she is less disdained than a man who is thought be gay.[63]

SUMMARY

In our culture we grow up thinking men and women are all heterosexual and it is surprising to learn that there are homosexuals. When we do learn about them, our lessons do not come to us through the conventional media but, instead, through unofficial sources as unreliable as whispered rumors and graffiti. Because of this, we are often very misinformed about homosexuality. And, since the myths about homosexuals are largely negative, many people, especially those who have never met homosexuals, dislike them. This seems to be especially true for men.

This leads us to an important conclusion: People who are given more accurate information about gays, either through educational sources or by meeting gays, are likely to be more comfortable with them than those without such information. We should be reluctant, therefore, to accept the surveys of soldiers who tell us that they would have trouble living with gays. They are often basing their predictions on false notions about gays, that would change if gays were integrated into the military.

Chapter 5

The Problem with Don't Ask, Don't Tell

A tall, skinny young man in jeans comes to a therapist's office for the first time. He sits stiffly in a soft chair meant for comfort.

"What leads you to come see me?" the therapist asks him.

The patient stares at his hands, fidgets then looks up, shakes his head and starts to talk. "I think I might be gay," he says. He sighs and looks back down at his hands.

"What makes you think that?"

"Well, I'm 20 years old and I just don't think I've ever been attracted to a girl. I mean I like girls, but the thought of having sex with them just doesn't appeal to me."

"And what about guys?"

"I think I have always been attracted to guys," he sighs again, looks up, glances around the room. "I remember being attracted to other guys when I was in the fifth grade. I know I have got to be gay, but I just don't want to accept it."

"Have you ever had sex with a guy?"

"Not exactly."

"What do you mean?"

"I mean when I was 16 this guy was staying over at my house and I, well, we masturbated together. We didn't touch each other. We just masturbated and watched." He sighs again. "But I know. I just know. I remember once," he muses, "there was this jock in P.E. I was 13 or so. I just missed a basket, and this guy yelled out at me that I was a faggot. It stabbed at my heart like a knife," he sighed again, "because I knew it was true."

"So how do you feel about that?"

"I hate it. This just screws everything up. My dad," he shakes his head, "will never understand this."

"Are you sure?"

He laughs and rolls his eyes, "Believe me. This is something he'll never understand."

"But how do you feel about being gay?"

"Me, too. I don't believe in this. I want to be straight. I want to find the right girl who can love me. I want to have a family, put my sons in Little League, buy my daughters pretty dresses. . . . But if I'm gay I guess I can't do that."

"So you think you're gay?"

"I came to you to find that out."

"Well," the therapist says, "in a way you get to choose. You can be a straight person who has a secret homosexual longing that eats at you, or you get to call yourself gay and try to find a way to live your life as a gay man."

"Isn't it possible that I'll fall in love with a woman?"

"One never knows for sure, but I've never seen it. You could test it out for a few years if you like. Maybe try to have sex with a woman."

"It just seems so repulsive to me. It seems like it would be unfair to the woman. I'd hate somebody marrying me that felt like that about me."

The therapist nods understandingly.

"And how would I live life as a gay man? I don't think I have ever known another guy that was gay. I hear about them in the news, but I have never met one."

"Well, we can talk about that. Once you meet a few you learn how to meet others, if that's what you want to do. You can try to be straight, though."

Looking suddenly stressed, the young man says, "I just can't believe this is happening to me. I don't want to be gay! I don't have any respect for faggots."

And so the session goes. It is hard for this patient, but it is harder for most. Most people struggling with these issues do not have a therapist to turn to. And most people have more difficulty than this patient in telling a therapist about homosexual concerns.

But this is a real story and it took several years for this man to identify comfortably as gay. His father and mother also entered therapy, for a while, to help them come to terms with the fact that they had a gay son. But a few years later he made his choice with their blessing. Now, he lives with another man and thinks of himself as gay.

Most people in our culture do considerable soul-searching before they call themselves gay. The attractions and longing are not enough to convince them, at least for a long time.

In the beginning, the gay person simply enjoys the pleasure of homosexual feeling. Then something happens for many in this culture, to cause a kind of psychological wound of shame. That wound tells them not only that gay sex is fun, but that they are different, that they are homosexual. For a while, after that wound, they cover and hide their shame, telling no one except, sometimes, anonymous or secretive lovers. Then, after a while, they understand that they are caught in this trap of shame and that there is only one way out. They must start to tell. This telling is a kind of confession. It is not easy, and it must be done over and over, often with painful rejection. But, in the end, after a period of forced confessions, it is possible to learn to manage a gay identity with grace and comfort. When this happens, gay people live lives in which their homosexuality is secondary to the process of doing things, loving real people, and growing.

Many people have homosexual feelings in our culture and do not call themselves homosexual, and many more worry privately that they should be called homosexual. Only those who have gone one step further, who are trying to heal their shame, or who have healed that shame, will tell a heterosexual, "I'm gay." The problem with the military's new policy of "Don't ask, don't tell" is that it eliminates mature gay people who could fit comfortably into its institutional structure while keeping less mature people who are struggling neurotically with secret homosexual feelings, and it fosters the formation of neurotic guilt along with anonymous sexual encounters and, sometimes, aggressive behaviors and loveless heterosexual marriages that are designed to hide what the military says cannot be told.

THREE MEN WHO FORMED THEIR HOMOSEXUAL IDENTITY IN THE MILITARY

It is a curious fact that a person can feel homosexual feelings, feel obsessed with such feelings, even, and not be able to say, or even know, that he or she is gay. But that is the way the human psyche works. We often do not know ourselves.

The true stories of three soldiers[1] will help us see how this can happen, how gay people must often struggle in a private soul-searching quest before they can inform us that they are gay.

Notice how light and innocent their initial homosexual feelings and actions are. They were just childish experiences or feelings that were smiled on by others. Eventually these homosexual feelings became increasingly important, and somehow they were converted into a poignant shame, a shame that could only be healed eventually by repeated and courageous confessions.

And as you read through these stories, you might recall the controversy as to whether homosexuality is genetic. It is only a controversy. The data is far from conclusive. Ask yourself if it matters. Whatever causes homosexual feelings, they come initially without being deliberately beckoned. They come, in fact, in children, who have never heard of homosexuality, who do not even know what it means.

Example of Homosexual Identity Formation in World War II

In the 1930s when Edward was a cute little dark-haired boy in short pants, he went to a prep school for the well-to-do. At nights after the lights were out, there were occasional thunderstorms, and the boys would scramble together under the blanket. Filled with excitement they sometimes hugged each other, and sometimes touched, and it was there, under the blankets in a thunderstorm, that Edward first remembers feeling homosexual desire.

Then later, when he looked the part of a proper adolescent, with carefully combed hair and sweater vests over his shirts, Edward and his school chums wandered, sometimes, out to the far back corner of the schoolyard. There they would pull out their hidden cigarettes and, having grown up in each other's clutches during the storms, they would also, sometimes, touch. These touches led, eventually, to orgasms. It was naughty, but no one thought it meant anything. They all had girlfriends. They would all someday marry.

And as a young adult, Edward did marry. He married Martha, a pretty, demure woman, also from this higher social strata. They had little sex, but this did not lead Edward to think that he was gay–for it was Martha, they both thought, who did not like sex. Women, so it seemed, were often like that. Nevertheless, Edward and Martha enjoyed each other. Theirs was a positive relationship.

Then one day as they sat in easy chairs listening to the static sounds from their big, wooden radio, a news report jolted them with alarming words that the Japanese had bombed Pearl Harbor. In that moment, the world they had known threatened to collapse. The secure feeling of being an American dissolved.

Two days later Edward was joining the great wave of young men flocking to recruiting offices, joining the Army. This affluent young man from prep school was ready to fight with his life in a world war that threatened to destroy everything he had ever known.

When Edward went to boot camp to become a soldier he was only a little surprised to find that here, as in prep school, men could be sexual together. And Edward, of course, participated. It was easy, and it did not imply that he, or any of them, so it seemed, was homosexual.

Then there was a war to fight, and Edward was advanced to sergeant. He could no longer fraternize with his men. There was only one secretive homosexual act over the next year.

But after that year had passed, on a day when enemy fire was flashing everywhere, Edward's driver maneuvered their jeep over the rocky countryside. Suddenly their vehicle was tossed in the air by enemy fire. The overturned jeep was on top of them. The driver was dead and Edward lay unconscious and wounded in a way that would always cause him to limp.

Up until this point, Edward had thought of himself as sexually more or less ordinary, like the many other males he had for decades now touched and been touched by, but while he lay in the hospital, he developed a homosexual identity. The doctor one day was making his rounds and he stopped at Edward's bed. On this particular day, in addition to his back injury, Edward was bothered by an itchy rash on his arms. He showed the rough skin to the doctor who turned his arms this way and that and asked, "How long has it been since you had sex?"

"It's been years," Edward replied.

"Well, that's the reason." The doctor nodded and moved methodically on to the next patient.

It was at that moment that Edward suddenly believed that he was a homosexual. This was his homosexual identity crisis. He stared at the rash and felt that it was caused by the suppression of homosexual desire. There he was, 30 years old. When he reflected he knew he no longer felt heterosexual desire. He felt shame and fear as he contemplated the homosexual desire that would not lie quiet inside him.

It was not so many months later that Edward stood by the window in his own American living room. His pretty wife Martha sat demurely on the sofa with expectation on her face.

"I am a homosexual," he told her.

She looked stunned, and then concerned, and then sad. She shook her head. There was nothing to be done but to end the marriage. They both agreed. There was nothing else to do.

And so Edward began trying to cure his shame with confession, but his confessions, such as they were, were never enough for him, and his psychological wound of homosexual shame, like his physical wounds, would never completely heal. It heals sometimes for others, but not for Edward.

Today, Edward is a 76-year-old man. He goes to the grocery store in a suit and tie, walking with his old war limp. He has not had a sexual encounter in 20 years. Even so, he is, psychologically, still a closeted homosexual for none of his drinking buddies at the officer's club know that Edward secretly thinks of himself as a homosexual.

Example of a Promiscuous Gay Soldier

Tony grew up a farm boy in the 1950s. He remembers watching the other boys in junior high, feeling flashes of attraction, having a crush on his P.E. teacher, but these experiences were innocent. He did not know at this age what a homosexual was. Still, he wanted to be like all the other boys.

And so he dated. He found a girlfriend. He took her for walks. He kissed her. Inside his heart he was filled with homosexual feelings, but he did not understand them, and there seemed nothing to do about them. And so he waited. Time passed, and still the heterosexual feelings did not come.

His first homosexual contact took place in college, in a toilet stall, when a man surprised him by showing him his erection and offering to pleasure Tony. The excitement loomed inside him, and it felt surprisingly easy to surrender to the opportunity. He had an orgasm quickly, and it was over. Then walking out of the rest room he was filled with homosexual shame.

One month later he decided, for the first time, to have intercourse with a girl. To his surprise his body worked. He had hoped that this would cure him of homosexual desire, but his shame and desire would not fade.

And so, throughout that semester Tony carried on a double life. There were fleeting but passionate moments with anonymous men in rest rooms once a month and there was laborious, monotonous sex with the woman he was dating. With his head spinning in confusion, he flunked out of college and joined the military. He hoped the military could turn him into a man.

But as in college, it was easy to meet other men. He says, "We met each other all over the place, from working together, to waiting for the dentist, to sitting together during chow break, to getting drunk together, to going out to a movie or club together." And so, still trying to be heterosexual, he asked his girlfriend to marry him. She did not know about the homosexual sex, and she said yes. For the next eight years, Tony and his wife had occasional sex, and she never knew.

Tony describes this period of his life:

> Day after day, I would sit in men's rooms during lunch times waiting for sexual experiences. I met all kinds of men. Most of them also married. I learned that sex was separate from love. I learned that we could be sexual in secret with other men, and that there did not need to be intimacy. . . . [M]y shame increased . . . I was living a lie. I was a homosexual man. I wanted the physical contact with men. I needed men to be attracted to me, to be sexual with me, to want me.

But he did not imagine that he could find a fulfilling homosexual relationship. He continues:

> I knew better than to expect love or emotional support from these men, after all, the gay men that I knew were not in supportive love relationships, only brief sexual encounters. Besides, look at what the future as a gay man looked like. . . .

And then, for the first time, Tony fell in love with a man. It was a man he met at the gym. In the locker room, Tony introduced himself. They talked casually, and so, over the next few days they became friends. One day, while they were out walking, this new friend told Tony that he found Tony attractive, energetic, exciting, and Tony's heart pounded. Romantic subtleties crept into the conversation. Their words became bolder. Finally, when they were confident of each other's desires, they walked to a hotel, miles from the base, registered, and spent the night.

But Tony was married, and he wanted to be heterosexual. Moreover, Tony's wife did not know of his homosexuality, and Tony's new lover did not know of his wife. For two weeks he struggled with what to do. Finally he wrote his lover an anguished letter saying that he did not have the courage to live life as a homosexual.

He says, "I was so full of pain but I could not tell anyone. I hurt so badly for what the future looked like for me as a gay military man. I felt bad for all of the men and women who love members of their own sex. I abandoned and disowned my real self back then. I allowed this straight facade that I hid behind to ruin my chances for a loving, caring relationship with someone. I hated myself for years after that.

"The problem with the military," Tony explains, "is that we were never allowed to be together for long enough to have a long-term relationship. We always had to say goodbye to one another. That was the saddest part, because it turned us into sex objects, rather than long-term friends or partners. There was no incentive for long-term relationships because there was no hope of staying together. Just the thrill and passion of the moment and a short freedom from the pain and loneliness that was our fate as outcasts from society, perverts, or whatever ugly name that society or the military shamed on us."

After he broke up with his lover, Tony changed inside. He tried to have sex with men in the rest room stalls, again, but it felt empty.

When, at last, he met another man and fell in love, this time, somehow, he found the courage to live life as a gay man.

That was 12 years ago. Today he lives with his lover, John. They own a home together, and have set up housekeeping.

Example of a Non-Promiscuous Gay Soldier

John was about 13 when he had his first homosexual experience. It was out at the swimming creek with the older boys. All the boys were naked and one of them noticed that John had an erection. So the boys laughingly guided John through sex. And there were other times that this group of boys encouraged John to act on his feelings. Some of the boys seemed a little interested in homosexuality themselves to John, and his difference was only slightly noticeable to him. And so, John expected to turn out like everyone else, and he began his process of waiting for the right girl. In the meantime, he decided to join the Navy. It seemed more fun than going to college.

There was no sex in the military barracks for John, but, like Tony, he found sexual encounters in civilian rest rooms. It happened a few times. But, mostly he continued in the stage of innocence, waiting for a girl to come along who interested him.

Then one day, sitting in his own room, watching television, he heard Anita Bryant, the beauty queen who preached fundamentalist Christianity in the 1970s. She was complaining about homosexuality. John says, "I saw her on the news and heard her thumping her Bible and that was all it took. I scrambled to read the passages in the Book of Romans and Proverbs, and saw it for myself–'Thou shalt not lay with a man as with a woman.' It was too much for me to comprehend and I started dousing myself with marijuana and booze. . . . Her campaign is what codified my thinking. Before that I didn't look in the mirror and see myself as a homosexual. I knew what homosexual meant, and I was having occasional sex with men, but I didn't connect the two."

And so, it was at this point that John became wounded with homosexual shame. After this, there was a difference in his self-image, his outlook. He became depressed, and started trying to suppress his gay feelings and to lie. He describes this period, "The more I believed that being gay was bad and that I should try to avoid it, the more the thoughts flooded in and the more horny I became." Things seemed terrible.

Then, one day, John saw a tall handsome man staring at a statue in a park. John walked up to him. They started to talk, and John's heart skipped a beat. He said of the experience, "When he smiled at me, in that instant, I thought, this has to be *the* guy, and two minutes into our conversation I knew I never wanted to be without his company from this point forward. I also had an incredible desire to touch him, not sexually, just touch him physically. I wanted to climb up his sweater and be right next to him touching his skin. This is making me cry."

Before long, they got an apartment far away from the base. John hid his homosexuality from his unit, but he and his lover lived discreetly together for almost two years. By this time, John thought of himself as a gay man in a monogamous relationship, but he was in hiding and still in shame.

Then, suddenly his gay partner was transferred. There was no way to avoid separation, no way to explain their problem to their commanders. John says, " I took him to his plane and waited in line with him as he boarded. I couldn't say anything to him because I had a lump in my throat and I was on the verge of tears. . . . I sat in the car and cried for a long time after he took off."

On the base, John continued to lie to hide his sexuality, but the desire to confess, to heal the wound of shame within him, began to grow.

During this time John was friends with a young heterosexual couple who often invited him over for a homecooked meal. Then, after dinner they would all sit for long hours and talk into the night. John considered both of them to be his best friends. And, so, when the need to confess grew inside him, it was this couple that he wanted to tell. And one night, as they were talking after dinner, he simply said it, "I'm homosexual." He was crushed as he saw their faces wash with horror.

They decided to help him go straight, introduced him to women, encouraged him to have sex in their guest room. Like Tony, John was able to perform heterosexually, but it did not diminish his increasingly intense attraction to men. His homosexual desire haunted him, and soon he was again having fleeting, anonymous sex. But this brush with promiscuity was brief for John.

Soon John met Tony, whose story has already been told here, and they both decided they could live more honest and contented lives if they accepted their homosexuality. John divorced his wife. The two of them left the military and set up housekeeping. And now, they have lived together as a couple for 12 years. They have several dogs that they take to shows. John does the yardwork. Tony keeps up the house. They go on vacations. They share their bank accounts, and they continue to love and struggle with the problems of life.

WHAT IT MEANS TO FORM A GAY IDENTITY

Like all of us, Edward, Tony, and John, learned about homosexuality from our cultural myths, but these myths had seemed to refer to others. When they felt homosexual feelings inside themselves, they did not automatically assume that they were one of the homosexuals. When it dawned on them, finally, that they were gay they felt wounded by the cultural condemnation we place on gays, and they struggled inside themselves to hide what they felt and, hopefully, extinguish their gayness–but it did not work.

Finally, when their struggles were failing, when the feelings and attractions were growing even stronger, they somehow began to want to cure themselves through acts of confession. They told their wives, their friends, of their homosexual predicament, all in the hopes of finding a life of self-acceptance.

Edward has never succeeded at this, and Tony and John are still struggling, but they are much closer. Today they are accepted by their parents and family, and many friends. The wound caused by this culturally imposed shame is beginning to heal.

THE STAGES OF FORMING A HOMOSEXUAL IDENTITY

In our culture, there seem to be four stages in the formation of a healthy homosexual identity in which a person who feels considerable homosexual feelings can live gracefully as a homosexual.

In the beginning is the stage of innocence. In some cultures that do not view homosexuality with disdain, and for some people in our own society, this is the only stage of homosexuality.

But often the stage of innocence is ended with a psychological wound that makes the person ashamed of his or her homosexuality. This is the stage of shame. While it continues, people hide their homosexuality. It ends with a recognition that the trap of shame can only be ended by courageous confession. Gradually, these confessions become less and less difficult, and finally, this leads to a stage of self-acceptance as a gay person.[2]

These stages are not inherent to homosexuality. They are merely the way men and women can sometimes heal themselves from the wounds our culture causes them.

The process is quite similar for women as it is for men, although it may be changing. Today, there is less opprobrium or fear among women about being homosexual, and many seem to be able to engage in it longer in the stage of innocence.[3] Some today move back and forth between men and women as sex partners without having to define what it all means. Eventually, lesbian women, and gay men, too, if we let them, may show us new ways to form a homosexual identity.[4] The evidence is that this will not increase the proportion who engage in homosexuality.[5] For now, though, many American men and women who continue to be wounded in this way will try to heal themselves with confession.

The Stage of Innocence

Homosexuality begins in the stage of innocence. The child's body feels homosexual feelings. These sexual feelings seem innocent and natural and occur, often enough, alongside heterosexual feelings.[6] There is no evidence that these homosexual feelings are unique to future homosexuals, although perhaps future homosexuals experience them with greater intensity.

In these early years, the child is not likely to know anyone who is called a homosexual. The world seems full of ordinary people. No one considers the possibility of homosexuality for anyone.[7] There is no information available or even any sense of needing information.[8]

Then, often in junior high school, negative terms begin to appear, often in childish phrases. John describes his memory of this:

> I remember the kids in the lunch room joking that they were drinking "homo" milk (homogenized). I spent some time in the Junior High library digging in the foot-thick dictionary looking up words having to do with sex, and homosexual was one of them.[9]

But regardless of how strong the child's homosexual feelings are, or whether the child engages in homosexual acts, merely learning this word does not mean to the child that he or she is a homosexual–for in the stage of innocence, these things do not imply to a child that he or she is gay.

Perhaps the key to this stage of innocence is that it does not cause the person to feel different from others. Other people seem to feel these things, more or less, even though they are never talked about. It is not surprising that people in this stage do not recognize they are different. After all, our culture hides the distinctiveness of all of our sexual desires, leaving us wondering if we are secretly like the others.

The Stage of Shame

The stage of innocence ends when a person is wounded with homosexual shame. The stage of shame is typically initiated by a feeling of realization. When John, for example, watched Anita Bryant on television, he had a feeling of realizing that he was homosexual, and it caused this wound of shame. When Edward's doctor explained his rash by saying it meant he had not had enough sex, this somehow initiated the stage of homosexual shame.

The stage of shame brings hiding. Suddenly, all that was innocent and fun must be hidden, often in acts that are fleeting and anonymous. While they are hiding, homosexually wounded people worry less about the feelings of sexual longing than the crushes and romantic attachments that grow inside them during this lonely period.[10] In the privacy of this hidden experience, people search their souls and study the unspeakable truth inside them, and wonder what it all means.

It is interesting to reflect on the fact that this time of shame and hiding is possible only because most closeted homosexuals pass easily as heterosexuals.[11] But while they go unrecognized, the sense of dishonesty and danger grows.[12] There is even a growing fear, if they are found out, that they could be physically hurt by angry, rejecting heterosexuals.[13]

There are several ways that gay people create the mask that hides them. There are lies, of course. But there are also marriages, as Tony's, to help perfect the heterosexual image.[14] The gays that marry like this have the most pressing desire to be accepted as straight.[15] Such marriages may remove them from suspicion, but it does not mean that they become more heterosexual.[16] The research suggests, in fact, if anything, that such a marriage further increases homosexuality.[17]

In this stage of shame and hiding, there are techniques for satisfying homosexual desire inconspicuously, of having homosexual sex quickly so that no one will notice, as Tony did in his many sexual encounters.[18] And, there are, often enough, still efforts to change, as John tried, when he had sex with women.[19]

But throughout this period of shame, the normal friendship pattern is disrupted. People in homosexual relationships cannot disclose the daily process of their lives.[20] They cannot even talk about what they do on weekends with their colleagues, and people who have not yet found romantic partners, live lonely lives that are empty to share.

Families are broken. Youths in this period of shame may run away from home and take up prostitution or crime to support themselves rather than tell their parents that they are gay.[21]

But do not think that closeted homosexuals always show shame by hanging their heads in the corner. The best cover for adolescents struggling with shameful homosexual feelings is "an attitude." "This defiance grows out of a feeling that one should feel shame. It is a resisting of the shame."[22]

Society wounds young homosexuals with the feelings of shame and leaves them struggling on their own to heal this wound. And there in the closet of this lonely place they grow increasingly in need of healing this wound with confessions.[23]

The Stage of Confession

The confession feels like the only way to heal the anguish of shame. It merely takes courage. As well as we can tell, about half of homosexuals disclose their identity to their friends and coworkers.[24] When they begin to disclose they tend to choose heterosexuals they judge will be accepting of their homosexuality.[25] It is a gesture of friendship and trust[26] and sometimes of daring.

An important part of disclosing homosexuality is confessing to parents. This confession is often required for gays to find a way to stay close to their parents. John described how it was to tell his parents.

> My mom was sobbing and sniveling and she rushed into the bedroom. I sat on the sofa and waited for a bit for them to come out. By the time they came out, I had lost any patience for my mother's situation. I saw it as one grand attempt to make me feel so badly that I couldn't possibly admit to her that I was gay. As usual, she was totally consumed with *her* problem–how could I do this to her, what was she going to tell the ladies at the church? (a real question she posed to me).

The gay person who goes through the stage of confession goes through many experiences telling and shocking parents, friends, and colleagues.[27]

But gradually, these confessions begin to heal the shame. Why, after all, should a homosexual feel shame? In a world in which everyone struggles to find how to live, to get along with lovers and family, to find sexual contentment? Why should the homosexual be seen as different? And, gradually, with the confessions, and with life, self-acceptance comes.

The Stage of Self-Acceptance

The confessions themselves are a training ground and they yield important benefits. Eventually the homosexual can tell who will be judgmental, and can gravitate to the people who will be accepting.[28] Finally, the telling is less a confession, and more a disclosure. And, finally, the homosexual knows others with similar feelings and learns to trust that there are straight people who can be trusted. And when the psychological wound is healed other things in life can become important.

This final stage of self-acceptance is hard won. Many people never achieve it. Edward who drinks with his buddies at the officers' club has never achieved it. He is still stuck in the stage of shame with only fleeting excursions into dangerous confessions.

Knowing how necessary and painful confession is for those who have been wounded with homosexual shame, many in the gay community urge others to work through their confessions to achieve a stage of self-acceptance.[29] For when a person accepts being gay there are new possibilities. One gay person can find another, and it is possible to love and create enduring relationships with others willing and able to reciprocate feelings.[30] It is also possible, at last, to establish a support system of gays and straights that helps the gay person navigate the rejecting heterosexual world without being repeatedly crushed by rejection.[31]

And, finally, the lonely alienated feeling of being different begins to fade and be replaced with the day-to-day life of relationships, homosexual and otherwise. Being homosexual stops feeling as central to the person's sense of self.[32] Anxiety and depression lift, and people get on with the business of caring about others and trying to be as good, as healthy, as whole, in every way, as they can be.[33] This is what homosexuals, like heterosexuals, want.

SUMMARY

There are two things wrong with "Don't ask, don't tell" as a policy. First, it encourages the neurotic closeting of homosexuality and related miseries such as unhappy marriages. Second, it causes the military to eliminate the wrong people, the gay people who are most mature, who know themselves best and who are most able to make homosexuality less central to their lives, people most capable of being trusted and being trustworthy. Telling people who they are is part of the process that makes it possible for gays to heal the wound of shame our society inflicts on them and for straights and gays to live together in mutual respect.

But bans against homosexuals, especially bans such as "Don't ask, don't tell," which specifically restrict the telling, undermine this healthy process and trap gays in an experience of shame and straights in a bubble of illusion.

And the ban is not needed. Even without such a ban, homosexuals in the military will disclose minimally and in discreet ways.[34] Heterosexuals will be protected from embarrassment with an etiquette of disregard which, will be adhered to if homosexuality becomes an open issue. Homosexuals, especially mature homosexuals in a stage of self-acceptance, are generally sensitive to and want to avoid heterosexual disapproval.

Using a ban to get rid of homosexuals is like using soap to wash off freckles. Homosexuality will not wash off of human nature. It begins before people understand what it is and takes root in the human psyche long before it is recognized. We cannot destroy it without destroying the natural development of our sexuality that takes place in childhood.

Chapter 6

How Many Homosexuals Are There Really?

In the late spring in 1993, with the big march of gays on Washington just a few weeks away, a new study was announced in the popular media that showed, purportedly, that only 1 percent of American men were homosexual.[1] This was a remarkable claim. Until this study, the popular mythology had us all believing that 10 percent of people in the United States were homosexual, and the 1 percent reported by this study was a lot lower. Moreover, the word was that this 1 percent study was a much better study than the previous 10 percent study.

Voices of all persuasions responded to this new report by saying that it meant that the homosexual population was so small that it was trivial and noninfluential.[2] Whereas Bill Clinton may have been persuaded to support the homosexual community when he thought that 10 percent of the people were gay, he would be less interested, so people thought, if only 1 percent of the people were gay.

The underlying problem was that this new study defined the word "homosexual"[3] in a very odd way. In this 1 percent study, two men who regularly kissed, embraced, caressed, and mutually masturbated each other and other men to orgasm would not be considered engaging in homosexual activity. In fact, in the Guttmacher study, two men who regularly had anal and oral intercourse with a variety of men would not be considered "homosexual" if they had had one heterosexual contact in the previous ten years.[4] Much homosexuality can be hidden behind definitions like this that make the numbers of homosexuals look unrealistically small. According to this definition, for much of their lives, neither Edward, Tony, nor John were homosexual.[5]

In the military, however, these behaviors do count as homosexual. There are no studies that count homosexuals with the military's definition of the term, but as we reason about it in this chapter it will seem that the Kinsey report is much more realistic than the 1 percent Guttmacher study.

For, although the definitions in this research are fuzzy and in disagreement, a picture of reality has begun to emerge from this new data. This research tells us that our cultural concepts of homosexuality are all wrong. First, the widespread belief that some people are truly homosexual and others are not is simplification of reality. People are a complex blend of sexualities, not merely homosexual or heterosexual. Second, more standard definitions of homosexuality give us estimates of at least 5 percent and as much as 18 or 20 percent. And if we used the military's definition of homosexuality, the counts would surely be higher still.

THE MYTH OF THE TRUE HOMOSEXUAL

When the teenage boy in the locker room whispers about the gym teacher, "Hey, I think Mr. Kenton is a queer," he does not talk or think in relative terms about subtle degrees of Mr. Kenton being gay–for the popular culture it is a black or white issue, either homosexual or straight. This is the myth of the true homosexual.

The myth of the true homosexual says that a group of people who are 100 percent homosexual exists. The challenge is to detect them. And so our culture tried. The psychiatrists and psychologists tried to do it by inventing tests, and the man (or woman) in the street tried to identify them by finding their own clues. But none of these methods of detecting true homosexuals has worked.

The problem is that homosexuality is not as black or white as our mythology suggests. Our traditional concepts are confused by the research findings and leave us talking in terms of the homosexuality of heterosexuals, and the heterosexuality of homosexuals. The only way out of this confusion is to invent new concepts about homosexuality that can help us understand.

The Medical Profession and the True Homosexual Myth

Belief in the "true homosexual" (regardless of sexual feeling and activity) began about 50 years ago. Before that, homosexuality was just something some people did that others either tolerated or condemned depending on how bad, or how important, homosexual sex struck them as being. Mostly it struck people as just a bad habit like belching at the table. There was no more reason to call people who had homosexual sex "homosexuals" than we, today, would call people who belch at the table "table belchers." But, about 50 years ago, we all became convinced that there were "true homosexuals" aside from their feelings and behavior.

Belief in the existence of the "true homosexuals" began, it seems when military psychiatrists dealt with the problem that soldiers often lied about their homosexual activity by trying to see past the soldier's words, peer into their secret minds, and detect the people who were true homosexuals. They were not looking merely for people who engaged in homosexuality[6] or felt homosexual feelings. They were looking for true homosexuals.

These psychiatrists taught us to believe in the true homosexual. They did it in two stages. First, they told us a person could be a true homosexual while neither acting homosexual nor having homosexual thoughts. Such a person, they said, should be called a "latent homosexual."[7] Then they argued that a person could act like a homosexual and not be truly homosexual. This type of person they labeled a "pseudo-homosexual."[8] So the true homosexuals had something unique about their psyches other than mere feelings, thoughts, or behaviors that marked them as different. Only psychiatrists, and perhaps psychologists, it seemed could identify them.

Or maybe not even they could. Numerous procedures for identifying true homosexuals were invented. For example, one psychological test that gained much attention had subjects draw a picture of a person (not telling them whether to draw a man or a woman). Men usually drew men and women usually drew women and it was believed by many that those who drew the opposite sex first were the true homosexuals.[9] Research has told us, however, that these tests cannot be trusted.

There is, today, no proven and reliable procedure that psychiatrists or psychologists can use to identify true homosexuals, however, and the concepts of pseudohomosexuality and latent homosexuality are no longer respected concepts.[10]

Nevertheless, people often do think of themselves as true homosexuals, or true heterosexuals, just as people sometimes think of themselves as true Christians, or true Americans. This identity is mostly a matter of self-image, although, as one might imagine, it can be confusing, in our culture, to have a self-image that says one thing, and feelings and thoughts that say another.

The Ordinary Person and the True Homosexual Myth

The myth of the true homosexual led ordinary people to believe we should be able to detect them. Stereotypes tell us what they look like, how they live. Sometimes people in the gay community cooperate, and behave or dress according to these stereotypes, but the evidence is that our clues for detecting homosexuals are not useful unless people want to be seen as homosexual.[11]

Typical clues ordinary people try to use to detect homosexuals are "apparent lifestyle" and "inappropriate masculinity or femininity." The idea is that people who are married to people of the opposite sex, especially if they have children, are not likely to be homosexual, and that feminine women or masculine men, were also not likely to be gay. But these are not good clues.

Apparent lifestyle is not a good clue. Lots of men who have wives and children have sex with other men without their wives, their friends, or their colleagues knowing,[12] and those who do tell on themselves do not disclose to everyone, especially not to people whom they expect to be judgmental.[13] Only a tiny portion of those married to women have wives who are aware of their homosexual activity.[14] Lesbians, too, are sometimes married heterosexually with or without the knowledge of their spouses.[15]

Homosexuals cannot be identified by their masculinity or femininity, either. Most men who identify as gay are as masculine as other men,[16] and there are many who angrily defy the effeminate stereotype by masculine posturing.[17] Besides, there are many heterosexual men who are feminine.[18] And, although privately some homosexuals may have a cross-gender masculinity or femininity, people whom the homosexual wants to fool are not likely to see this.[19] Studies on lesbians are similar to those on gay men. Although there are a few masculine lesbians, most lesbians seem to be about as feminine as other women.[20]

The Homosexuality of Heterosexuals

The notion of the true homosexual is especially troublesome when we realize how often people who think of themselves as straight have homosexual sex. We do not know what proportion of straight people have such sex, but it appears that about two-thirds of men who do engage in homosexuality think of themselves as basically heterosexual.[21]

Many of these people are in the stage of innocence. They have a million explanations to explain their homosexual activity. They will pass it off without concern, saying "I was just experimenting," "I was just horny," "It was just for variety," or " It's easier to get with guys,"[22] for something else must happen for a person to begin to see that this behavior means they should call themselves gay. And it is only in the last century or so that homosexual activity would ever lead people to call themselves gay. It is as though we had decided that everyone who runs to a bus is a runner.

There is something in our culture, especially our white and educated culture, that is teaching people that there is such a thing as a true homosexual. Perhaps people (especially white, educated men) who decide they are true homosexuals are people who feel particularly ashamed of secret homosexual interest or occasional homosexual behavior. White educated men in America may believe that other heterosexual men never have homosexual interest whereas men in many, perhaps most other cultures do perform a masculine role in homosexual relationships, frequently, without this implying that they are "homosexual." This is true, at least, for Mexicans and Mexican-American men,[23] Iranian men,[24] Pakistani men,[25] and Turkish men.[26] And American men who end up adopting a homosexual identity seem more likely to consider themselves homosexual if they have attended college.[27]

There are also psychological factors that predispose people to believe they are true homosexuals. We know, for example, that men who have homosexual experience as adolescents are more likely to grow up and think of themselves as being "a homosexual" than men whose homosexuality, even exclusive homosexuality, started after they were grown. Of men who are exclusively homosexual as adults, but had no homosexual contacts as adolescents, about half of them think of themselves as being straight. On the other hand, of those who are exclusively homosexual as adults and had a few homosexual experiences as adolescents, only about one-quarter think of themselves as straight.[28] People take their homosexual behavior less seriously, it seems, when it occurs only in adulthood.

But if one looks just at adult sexual activity, there seems to be "little coherent relationship between the amount and 'mix' of homosexual and heterosexual behavior in a person's biography and that person's choice to label himself or herself as bisexual, homosexual, or heterosexual."[29] The data tells us that more people have homosexual feelings than engage in homosexual behavior and more people engage in homosexual behavior than have a homosexual identity, that is, call themselves homosexual.[30]

And, although there is more data on male than female homosexuality (because of AIDS), there are many who hold that it is common for heterosexual women to experience homosexual desire.[31]

The Heterosexuality of Homosexuals

It is also the case that people who think of themselves as homosexual often have a heterosexual component in their personalities. It seems that as much as two-thirds or three-quarters of self-identified homosexuals are aware of heterosexual feelings.[32]

Women who call themselves lesbian often fantasize about men,[33] are attracted to men,[34] and have heterosexual sex with them[35] while preferring to make their relationships with women more central in their lives. Much the same is true of men who call themselves gay.[36]

And it seems that the majority of men who have male-male sexual contact in the United States also have female sexual contacts contemporaneous with or subsequent to sexual contact with male partners.[37]

Homosexuals with Little Sexual Desire

There is another reason to toss out the theory of the true homosexual. Many who call themselves "homosexual," who commit their lives to other gays, in fact, have little underlying homosexual passion.

Nonsexual homosexual commitment is not a new concept. In the nineteeth century women often committed themselves to each other for life in relationships called "Boston marriages." Boston marriages were a social benefit in a society that would otherwise leave the surplus of women in the lonely, ostracized role of "spinster." Most people today assume these relationships were not sexual in the modern sense of the term, that the women just planned their lives together.

Authors describe such relationships existing among women today.[38] Perhaps around a quarter of lesbian relationships have little or no sexual contact for up to five years[39] and other authors, too, comment that many lesbian couples do not focus their relationships on the sexual dimension.[40] Studies are inconsistent as to whether lesbians are generally more or less sexually responsive than other women.[41]

There are many cases, too, of men who live in committed homosexual relationships, yet have difficulty responding sexually to their partners (i.e., are impotent).[42] The frequency of low sexual desire in homosexual males is variously estimated between 1 and 38 percent.[43]

Nevertheless, it seems that most lesbians and gay males are as satisfied in their relationships as are heterosexual cohabiting or married couples.[44] The homosexual relationship, or way of life, does not require that the participants are particularly homosexually passionate, although they may be. And, since we do not require heterosexuals to be passionate in order to call them heterosexual, it seems appropriate that we accept the nonpassionate homosexual's self-definition as homosexual.

New Concepts of Homosexuality

Our myths and traditions lead us to imagine people as being purely homosexual or purely heterosexual, but this is a forced dichotomy. It is as though we insisted that people either loved chicken, or they loved cake. The truth is, a lot of people like both, and some people like neither. Forcing people into the homosexual category or the heterosexual category may be a little like insisting that everyone is really either a chicken-lover or a cake-lover and that they could not be both or neither.

Rather than think of people as purely homosexual or purely heterosexual, De Cecco and Shively suggest we think in terms of their two underlying, more or less separate, sexualities, people's heterosexuality and their homosexuality. Using this vocabulary, some people would have high levels of both kinds of sexuality, and some would be low in one or both. Some would have one form of sexuality missing altogether. This is the chicken-lover, cake-lover kind of concept. High interest in chicken has little to do with high interest in cake.

Sexuality in this sense is merely a potential. A person with a high level of heterosexuality would have a high potential for enjoying a sexual relationship with someone of the opposite sex. De Cecco and Shively also suggest that we think less in terms of sexualities and more in terms of relationships. Conceivably a person with a relatively high level of homosexuality might have a heterosexual relationship as the primary, or even only, sexual relationship.[45] In the stage of self-acceptance, at least, it is the relationship that is most important, not the transient feelings or fleeting encounters.

Our vocabulary for talking about homosexuality today presses us to speak of homosexuals as if they were a distinctly different kind of person. It is difficult to change a language that is so embedded in our culture, but these changes would allow us to understand homosexuality more thoroughly and to make better, less hypocritical policies.

But in the end, perhaps, it is less important what we call people than that we keep in mind what it all means. A "homosexual" is merely a self-concept, and it is made true by believing it to be true. Just as people can be Republicans because they believe themselves to be, they can be homosexual just by believing themselves to be.

RESEARCH ON PROPORTIONS WHO ENGAGE IN HOMOSEXUAL ACTIVITY

News articles that splash a headline saying 1 percent of people are gay, or 10 percent, or any percent, may make it seem that they have really counted true homosexuals, but the truth is, all they have really done is count the percentage of people who report having engaged in homosexual sex. A person who felt homosexual but did not have homosexual sex would not count. A person who had homosexual sex, but did not feel it, would. This is a way of side-stepping the definitional problem of what counts as a true homosexual. It makes the problems of counting "homosexuals" easier.

But it does not solve all the problems. If we want a realistic count of the numbers who engage in homosexual sex, we need a definition of homosexual sex that makes sense to us, that fits the way we typically use the concept. We also need to decide what to do about the fact that people are not always willing to tell an interviewer what sexual acts they have experienced.

Six Percent Admit to Homosexual Sex

What should we count as "homosexual sex?" In the Guttmacher study two men could kiss, caress, and mutually masturbate to orgasm and this would not be counted as a homosexual act. It is no wonder that they reported a smaller number of people having homosexual sex than other studies.

Most studies have a more credible definition of homosexual sex. Generally, it is either any behavior that causes the lovers to have orgasms[46] or subjects define it any way they want to merely by answering yes or no to a question like "Have you ever had sex with someone of the same sex?"[47]

A review of five such studies tells us that about 6 percent of men, nationwide, will admit to an interviewer that they have had homosexual sex since being an adult.[48] And we will use this as our base rate: 6 percent of men admit to having homosexual sex some time in their adult lives.

These studies tell us that about 30 percent of the men who had any kind of homosexual sex ever, also had homosexual sex in the previous year. This means, that about 1.8 percent of men admit to having had a homosexual experience in the past year.

Two or Three Times as Many Do not Tell

Now the question is: How do we correct for the fact that subjects do not always tell if they had homosexual sex? For if people do not want to confess to an interviewer their homosexual behavior, they can either shake their heads and refuse to answer the interviewer's presumptuous questions (who would blame them?) or they can simply stare at the interviewer and lie. And, because people who engage in homosexuality are often secretive we need to expect this to happen. It will not do to simply ignore the problem of subjects not telling us. All simple counts of people engaging in homosexuality are bound to be underestimates, and competent scholars admit to this underestimation.[49]

How much do subjects hold back? A lot of people refuse to respond to these surveys. An average of 25 to 30 percent refuse to respond.[50] The problem of subjects refusing to respond is a problem of all surveys, and, in fact, many feel it "threatens the inferential value of the survey method,"[51] but it is particularly a problem in sexual surveys[52] and even more so, it seems, when the questions are about anal intercourse,[53] as many of the questions in these surveys are.

One study has tried to evaluate homosexual activity among those who decline participation in surveys. This study indicates that large groups of nonresponding subjects results in serious underestimates of the proportion of men who engage in homosexual sex. Men who do not participate in surveys appear to be more than three times as likely to have engaged in homosexual sex as men who do participate.[54]

Surveys are also compromised by subjects lying. We know, for example, that the gender of the interviewer can have an affect on subjects lying.[55]

How can we correct for the dishonesty underestimate? There is one available study that gives us an estimate of this. Forty-five men were asked about homosexual experiences before and after being threatened with a polygraph. On the basis of this study, as well as we can tell, only about one-half to one-third of men who have had homosexual encounters actually disclose this to an interviewer when not pressured to do so.[56]

These studies are merely suggestive, but they provide us with a way to make an estimated guess about the effects of subjects not disclosing their homosexuality. It may be less accurate than we like, but it is better than pretending that subjects always disclose their homosexuality, and all we have to do is count the number of times they answer yes.

Nearly 6 Percent of Men Estimated Homosexually Active

Our base rate studies told us that 6 percent of men admit to homosexual sex at some time in their adult lives, and only 1.8 percent in the last year. How many men really have homosexual sex, including the proportion who do not admit to it?

We need to correct the base rate in two ways. First, we need to correct for the nonrespondents by assuming there are about three times as many who would say yes in the nonresponding group. If an average of 25 percent did not respond, and 6 percent of those who did respond said yes, then we would estimate that 18 percent of those who did not respond would say yes if we pursued them. This means we have 6 percent saying yes for 75 percent of the group, and 18 percent saying yes for the remainder. This gives us an average of 9 percent who would say yes if we had a response from everyone.

Now, we need to correct for those who are lying when they say no. Our best available study for estimating the proportion that lie tells us that we need to multiply the base rate by two or three to get this figure. This indicates that 18 to 27 percent of men have had homosexual sex sometime in their lives–one in five or even one in four.

How many men are currently having homosexual sex? The best data suggest we need to multiply the above figure by 0.3. This indicates that between 5.4 and 8.1 are currently homosexually active, or about 7 percent. This does not mean that they are currently exclusively homosexual.

So our best estimate is that about one in four or five men have had sex to the point of orgasm with another man, and about 7 percent, or about one in 14, have done so in the last year.[57] This puts the proportions at a somewhat lower level than estimated in a recent RAND report.[58]

Similar Proportions of Lesbian Activity

We also need to ask about the proportion of women who engage in lesbian behavior. However, not only is there less research on lesbians than gay men, but the research that exists has more problems. This is because female sexual contact forms a gradation from nonerotic to erotic that is more difficult to define than it is with men, and because lesbian behavior can be quite sexual without it being to the point of orgasm.[59]

Kinsey's data on women is probably, still, our best data today. It shows that the probability of a woman having orgasmic contact with another woman greatly increases with age. In the 1940s, when his research was done, women reported having only 4 percent lesbian contact at age 20, but 13 percent by their mid-40s.

The most obvious problem with the Kinsey data is that it is dated. A 1970 data sample suggested that women in that era had had about half the homosexual experience that men had.[60] Hite, on the other hand, reported 17 percent during the 1970s.[61] And a number of more modern observers are telling us that the women are engaging in lesbianism at increased rates today.[62]

It is hard to compare homosexuality between men and women. But in the past, only half as many women as men admitted to homosexuality. Today the numbers seem to be increasing, so it seems that the number of women engaging in lesbianism today is in the ballpark of the numbers of men engaging in homosexuality today.

THE MILITARY SITUATION

It is one thing to count homosexuals in the civilian world where the definitions are not set in policy and law. It is another thing to count them in the military. The military has its own definitions of homosexuality. They are encoded in the rules and laws that are used to discharge and punish people for homosexuality.

To estimate the number of homosexuals in the military, then, we need to calibrate the military definition with the research definition. Only if these two definitions correspond, at least roughly, will the percentages make any sense.

The Military Definition of Homosexuality

The military definition of homosexuality is contained in its laws and rules that prohibit and punish homosexuality.[63]

There are two separate sets of rules, or two military definitions of homosexuality.[64] One is an administrative directive which allows a military commander to discharge a soldier for homosexuality.[65] The other is military law which results in court-martial (a military trial that can result in prison time.)[66]

Most people's homosexuality is evaluated with the administrative discharge definition and that is extremely broad. It includes not only acts (kissing, mutual masturbation) intended to satisfy homosexual desire, but acts which seem to show a propensity or intent to engage in such acts at other times.[67]

The court-martial definition of homosexuality requires, on the other hand, sodomy, but the definition of sodomy is, particularly for women, quite vague.

On the Proportion of Soldiers Who Engage in Gay Sex

Research consistently shows that men who are veterans are more likely to have experienced homosexual sex than men who have never been in the military.[68] Another line of research shows that men who call themselves homosexual are at least as likely to have been in the military as other men.[69]

What makes homosexuality more likely to occur in the military than in civilian life is that what the military counts as "homosexual" is much broader than in civilian life. So, although homosexuals exist more or less in the same proportion in the military as they do in civilian life, or in somewhat greater numbers in the military, they surely exist in greater proportion in the military when we adjust for the military's very broad definition of a homosexual act.

Analysis of research on homosexuals who are veterans also tells us that only a token number of homosexuals actually get discharged from the military. Speaking very roughly, only about one in every 1,300 soldiers gets discharged for homosexuality, much less than 1 percent of the population of soldiers we can assume have a substantial interest in homosexuality.[70] We can speculate, further, that only an infinitesimal fraction of those with a secret homosexual interest get discharged.

And so we learn that a military ban against homosexuals does not really prevent homosexuality in the military. Moreover, when we discharge a few people as homosexual, and pretend that the rest are not, we are just creating the illusion that everyone who is not discharged is heterosexual. The truth, that we do not allow to be spoken, is that many young men and women struggle privately with their homosexuality without counsel. "[H]omosexuality occasionally becomes a disciplinary problem, [but it] . . . far more often remains a personal one and may be a source of deep unhappiness to more of our men than we suspect."[71]

SUMMARY

How many homosexuals there are depend on who you count as a homosexual. But however you define homosexual, there seems to be about as many in the military as in civilian life. Defining homosexuality fairly loosely to mean genital, homosexual sex, or sex to the point of orgasm, we estimated that about 12 to 18 percent of men, and perhaps a similar proportion of women, have engaged in homosexuality to some degree. However the the military defines homosexuality more broadly than this to include kissing, hand-holding, mutual masturbation, and other acts of physical affection. Therefore, it appears that the numbers that the military could conceivably count as homosexual, using their definition, is somewhat greater than the 12 or 18 percent we count in the civilian world using a narrower definition. Many of the people who would be counted would consider themselves heterosexual and live lives that suggest heterosexuality to others.

Chapter 7

How Would Homosexuals Affect Morale?

The room is just big enough to hold a blaring television and a dozen, padded, green vinyl chairs. It is six o'clock and six tired soldiers have settled here in their dayroom for the evening, slouched down in their seats. One sips a cola. Another nibbles popcorn.

"Not news!" the red-haired guy in the back hollers out. "Check out the sports channel!"

"Shut up, butthead," the tall skinny blond guy yells back. "I wanta see this."

A smooth TV interviewer announces, "And today, the Senate committee listened to a gay man . . . "

"Not another faggot story!" the red-haired guy shouts back.

"Shut up, butthead," a fat guy hollers, "or I'll deck you! They're going to try to make us live with these punks."

The announcer says, " . . . and elsewhere in the world . . . "

"See that, butthead? You did it again. Can't you keep your fuckin' mouth shut once in a while?" These are still endearments.

"What's the big deal? They aren't gonna let faggots in here. They wouldn't live ten minutes. Tommy over here would take 'em all out and shoot 'em. Right, Tommy?"

"Shut up, butthead."

"What's the matter? Don't you want to wipe out a faggot? What's the matter, cutie? Maybe you're a faggot, too? Huh? Huh?"

"Get outta here, butthead!" the soldier laughs. "You're the faggot I wanta wipe out."

Giggles and laughter twitter for a minute and then the blond guy asks, "Hey, got any more popcorn?"

These soldiers make it sound as though they know what homosexuals are like, and what it would be like to have them around. But they do not know. All the evidence shows that in spite of their expectations soldiers such as these would accept people who call themselves gay. Soldiers' expectations of disaster grow out of myth-based beliefs about homosexuals.

Gay soldiers will not change the social climate in dramatic ways. They are already there joking, often enough, with the others about gays. And if the behavior of gay soldiers in other countries is any example, the vast majority will not tell who they are until they judge accurately that they can do so without being provocative.

Things are likely to turn out better than soldiers would expect. But the soldiers' words make it sound as though they could not tolerate homosexuals, and the military takes this seriously because they think such a lack of acceptance would disrupt morale and cohesion. The military brass believes that good morale is central to our having a good fighting force and that removing the ban would compromise our country's ability to defend itself. It is an argument that gets our attention.

But there are many things wrong with this morale argument. In the first place, it is not really an argument. It is just an unrealistically simple slogan. Listen to it: "Homosexuals will disrupt morale and destroy the greatest army the world has ever known."

The military has been wrong about similar slogan-like arguments before. We could replace the word "homosexuals" in this slogan with "Negroes" and have the argument that was used to keep the military white. We could replace the word "homosexuals" with "women" and use the word that was used to try to keep the military all male. And we could replace the word "homosexuals" with "all volunteer army" and use the phrase the military used to keep the draft–but "Negroes," women, and an all volunteer army were accepted in spite of predictions of disaster, and they did not destroy our fighting force.[1]

For another thing, this slogan-like argument is wrong because it makes it seem as though there is nothing else involved, that good morale merely requires keeping homosexuals out. There are, however, many variables that affect morale: the quality of the leadership, for example, even things like better pay, or better tasting food can improve it. So many things affect morale that it is hard to single out the effect of homosexuals alone. Morale does not hinge on any single issue.

The slogan-like argument of the military is also wrong because it exaggerates the importance of morale. It is important to achieve a certain level of morale and cohesion, but very high levels can actually be disruptive, fostering insubordination and rebellion.

The argument is wrong, too, because the psychological atmosphere created by a ban damages morale by making men so guarded in their conversation that it prevents the natural development of friendship.

And, finally, the ban is wrong to the extent that it is merely a way of promoting traditional manly values. Such protests are based on old stereotypes of homosexuals. Homosexuals can be manly, and men and women who are gay can win our admiration. They can be ethical, committed, patriotic, respectful, and discreet. And any aspect of manliness that is contemptuous of those who simply speak the truth inside them is a psychological house of cards.

Dropping the ban will work. The evidence tells us this is so. Protests to the contrary are just the creaking of our grandfather's values as the old world makes room for the new.

MILITARY PREDICTIONS OF DISASTER UNFOUNDED

When the military tells us that lifting the ban against homosexuals will hurt morale and reduce the effectiveness of our military, we all form pictures in our heads of a troop of demoralized soldiers unable to summon the mental energy to fight.

But if we examine what the military means by the words "morale" and "cohesion," we will see that there are many ways to improve morale and that sometimes cohesion can be destructive. We will see that the argument for morale is often just a disguised argument for the importance of manly pride in the military, and of course, too much pride in heterosexual manliness, or heterosexual femininity, can create a kind of anxiety which, in the long run, does damage to morale, causing people to fret and worry about trivial homosexual interest. A society that tells people they should not experience even trivial homosexual interest, when in fact many people do, is inducing a neurotic anxiety in the general population that disrupts the sense of well-being and morale.

History of the Military Concept of Morale

Our ordinary concept of "morale" refers to a kind of positive enthusiasm. It is what gives soldiers their good spirit, their ability to keep going in difficult circumstances. It seems natural that the military would try to keep morale high. We want our soldiers to have good spirits in the face of tough and dirty work.

And so today we think it is good to promote military morale, but this is a recent concept. Until about WWI, the American consensus was that it was bad to promote soldier morale. Trying to enhance morale smacked of trying to indoctrinate soldiers or otherwise manipulate their psychology, make them believe propaganda or take over their minds.[2] Military effectiveness was supposed to be the natural result of discipline (applied sometimes with a flogging) and the manly virtues of courage, patriotism, loyalty, honor, and integrity.

Then military philosophy changed around the turn of the century when there began to be a slight and unofficial interest in improving morale.[3]

Starting in 1939, the military became increasingly involved in promoting military morale. In that year, the United States military began to experiment with a small Morale Division.[4] Over the next few years, the name of this division was repeatedly changed[5] and it was expanded to become a powerful agency directly under the Chiefs of Staff.

The technique developed to promote morale amounted to providing the soldier with entertainment, recreation programs, and other treats of civilian life to "keep his spirits up" as he went about the dirty business of combat.[6] WWII introduced the idea of providing the troops with entertainment programs in which celebrities flew to the center of battle and performed before great numbers of soldiers who would shortly have to fight, or by encouraging soldiers to put on their own theatricals with costumes and theatrical direction.[7] This was part of the war effort to improve morale, as was a program to ensure that the soldier got candy bars and the latest novels to read. And the WWII soldier was given something that no WWI soldier ever dreamed of: recreation time during duty hours.[8]

The troops may have developed a new kind of enthusiasm for a new military, but the older military minds protested the use of entertainment and recreation programs to bolster morale.[9] It seemed unfitting for the warrior, who should be disciplined and obedient, to be manipulated with sweets just to get him to fight.

But the proponents of building morale won the day. Morale was high, and the treats soldiers received were popular and perhaps effective, so they continued to be supplied. Not only was there recreation, entertainment, and sweets, but thousands of libraries were established to promote morale. Handicraft kits were delivered. Art contests were encouraged.[10] Service clubs were established everywhere with cafeterias, barbershops, reading and writing rooms, first aid rooms, and information bureaus.[11]

And so, although the old disciplinarian commanders still marched their troops until their blisters bled, the soldiers could escape from the misery with government treats and do so, in the service of their morale. So it was that the belief that morale was the most important thing of all in creating a fighting force became an increasingly popular philosophy among the troops.

History of the Concept of Cohesion

At the end of World War II, the old concept of morale faded into a new concept called "cohesion." It was not that the old concept was discarded, but "cohesion" seemed more conceptually sophisticated, better defined. Cohesion was a special kind of morale, and the most important kind.

The concept of cohesion trades on the metaphor of things sticking together cohesively. To be effective in a battle, so the cohesion argument goes, the soldiers need to stick together and support each other.[12] The word "bonding" often occurs when people talk of cohesion. Soldiers bond, they stick together, and the unit is cohesive.

This shift from morale to cohesion was inspired by a paper published at the end of WWII by Edward Shils and Morris Janowitz. This now classic article asked what gave the German Army its fighting strength and concluded the strength came from the extra tight relationship soldiers had with their buddies. Everything else being equal, the German soldier fought well as long as "he gave affection to and received affection from the other members of his squad and platoon."[13]

"Deserters," they explained, "were . . . men who had difficulty . . . [in] the acceptance of affection or in the giving of affection. They were men who had shown these same difficulties in civilian life, having had difficulties with friends, work associates, and their families, or having had criminal records."[14]

The new concept of cohesion held that soldiers fought for their buddies, not for the manly virtues of patriotism and honor, and not because they were highly disciplined. Loving thoughts about wife and children back home were not enough. The fear of being whipped or court-martialed was not enough. But close feelings with their buddies, were enough, the cohesion theory told us, to make men fight.[15]

So, suddenly, the challenge was one of promoting cohesion. And whereas morale could be purchased with a candy bar, cohesion could only be promoted by encouraging better relationships between the soldiers, better soldier bonding.

The Shils and Janowitz article was long and tedious, but through the years, the cohesion argument became slogan-like, and was used to promote various hidden agendas, for example, the exclusion of "Negroes," the exclusion of women, continued use of the draft, and now, antihomosexuality. We must promote these agendas, so the argument goes, or soldiers will not stick together cohesively and our ability to fight will be lost. Male bonding becomes a mysterious and magical ingredient that must be protected in a host of ways.

As Captain Paul Shemella puts it:

> The phenomenon of male bonding is impossible to explain. It has to be experienced. Declared homosexuals (and women, for that matter) do not bond with the men who fight our wars and do not belong in combat. Destroying unit cohesion is the fastest way to destroy fighting performance. There is no such thing as second place in a war.[16]

But military forces have predicted before that soldiers will have more difficulty than they do. Listen, for example, to Dwight Eisenhower arguing in 1948 that Negroes would destroy cohesion:

> I do believe that if we attempt . . . to force someone to like someone else, we are just going to get into trouble. . . . when you put [them] in the same organization and make [them] live together under the most intimate circumstances men of different races, we sometimes have trouble.[17]

These slogan-like arguments for morale and cohesion are merely a glib way of rationalizing discrimination and prejudice. Shils and Janowitz said our military needed cohesion, but they did not imply that the military requires racial purity or sexual orientation purity or any other kind of discrimination to achieve the necessary levels of cohesive bonding. Slogan-like cohesion arguments that are not grounded in solid and relevant research merely abuse the complex Shils and Janowitz argument for military cohesion.

And, as we shall see, the research that is available on morale and cohesion does not justify exclusion of homosexuals.

Cohesion Research

Cohesion is a researched concept, but the findings are not simple. Although research shows that military tasks are done a little better when the group is cohesive,[18] the effects are far from dramatic. It is not clear, for example, if soldiers work together better because they are bonded, or if they become more bonded because they are working together well.[19] Besides, soldiers can work together even when they are not highly bonded.[20] In fact, sometimes too much cohesion produces a bad effect, encouraging drug use, insubordination, and even mutiny.[21]

Moreover if we decide that we do want to improve cohesion in a particular troop, research tells us that it can be promoted in a variety of ways. We can, for example, promote cohesion by keeping soldiers together over a longer period of time,[22] by improving leadership,[23] and by having structured group discussions.[24] All these things have been shown to improve cohesion. Excluding homosexuals has not.

There is no data that shows that declared homosexuals reduce cohesion. When the military argues that homosexuals will destroy cohesion, they are basing this belief merely on an intuitive picture of what it would be like to remove the ban. Since they have not worked with self-declared homosexuals and have not researched it, they simply do not know. The ban against homosexuals has been removed in other countries without evidence of destroying unit cohesion. And gay soldiers who have been reinstated in the United States have not produced the morale disruption that some would predict. If anything, these facts indicate that gays would not diminish the ability of troops to fight effectively.

Manly Appeal vs. Cohesion

Although research does not provide us with evidence that homosexuals disrupt cohesion, experts often talk as if it does. Using the word "cohesion" may give their argument the ring of research, but these arguments are strictly intuitive, rooted, often enough, in a traditional belief in the importance of manly virtues. Lip service may be given to the importance of cohesion, but the meat of the argument is that soldiers need to feel manly and homosexuals make them question their manliness.[25]

Darryl Henderson provides us with an example of how experts use the manly virtues argument to exclude homosexuals while giving lip service to the importance of cohesion.

Notice, first, the way Henderson[26] argues for the importance of cohesion and then in the next quote suggests, without research evidence, that the way to achieve cohesion is to foster the romantic imagery of manliness by excluding homosexuals from battlefield units. First, he argues for cohesion. All he is saying here is "We need to foster the bonding of soldiers to each other." He says:

> The small group and its operating rules are extremely important in determining a unit's performance in battle. The individual soldier's loyalty to his small group and the group's expectation that he will comply with the group's expectations is the only force on the battlefield consistently strong enough to make a soldier advance under fire. Any influence or value that hinders or counteracts the bonding of the soldier with his unit is also an influence against cohesion and combat effectiveness. [27]

But Henderson's argument that homosexuals will disrupt cohesion is basically the argument from myth that we need to foster manliness. He speaks of a survey, but the survey was dismissed by the Canadians as invalid. These are merely Henderson's manly values speaking. He says:

> A soldier with strong heterosexual values could experience the most devastating personal rumors were he to willingly spend the night alone on a listening post with a known same-sex homosexual soldier. . . . It is well-documented that young soldiers fighting a war or training for war are attracted by the honor and romanticism of the experience and the associated opportunities to display the manliness or toughness important to young men. The survey results show that in any number of situations serious conflicts could result in units where prevalent norms based on manliness or toughness among young soldiers were organizationally mixed with the conflicting values of same-sex homosexuals.[28]

The conclusion that homosexuality will disrupt cohesion, therefore, is simply conjectural. It grows from the myth-based belief that heterosexual male soldiers will inevitably be so threatened by the presence of a homosexual in their midsts that they cannot fight effectively. But there is no data showing this is so.

On the other hand, there is reason to conclude that heterosexual soldiers can accept and live with homosexuals who are free to tell who they are because such gay soldiers can be expected to make these disclosures in ways that are respectful to heterosexual privacy.

Lesbian Baiting vs. Cohesion

Another negative effect that the ban against homosexuals has on morale results from lesbian baiting.[29] This is a technique male soldiers sometimes use to pressure women (heterosexual as well as lesbian) into providing sexual favors. "Write me an erotic letter," one commander tells a woman officer, "or we'll think you're a lesbian." "Have sex with me tonight and show me you're a real woman," says another.

In the not-so-distant past, it was possible for a woman to say "no" without it implying that she was sexually inadequate. But in today's military culture, when women are afraid of being discharged as a lesbian, it is harder to say "no." Do it for me," a commander can say, "or we will have to assume you're a dyke."

And even when a woman soldier does say "no," she can be raped. And in our military's current mixed-gender environment, the threat of being called lesbian can be used to intimidate her against reporting that rape. This intimidation carries a real punch, for women are much more likely to be discharged for homosexuality than are men.

The importance of lesbian baiting increases as women are increasingly integrated in the military environment, but the ban can be used to pressure men to perform heterosexually, too. "Why don't you have sex with her?" one can can say to another, and the man who is afraid he will be discharged for being gay may sometimes feel it necessary to prove that he is not.

WHY IT SEEMS THAT REMOVING THE BAN WILL WORK

Paradoxically, the antihomosexual climate caused by the ban may actually diminish morale. Because men's ability to accept nonerotic friendship from other men is diminished by a sense of homosexual danger, removing the ban should help them become more comfortable with each other, not less.

When the ban is lifted, heterosexuals will learn that most homosexuals will not disclose their identities. When they do, they will not do so to assault or seduce heterosexuals. Heterosexuals will feel more comfortable with the presence of homosexuals than they anticipate, and fear of homosexuals will be diminished.

This is the way it seems to have worked in other countries. Most important, when the ban was lifted in Canada in October 1992, it was found that the predictions of disaster did not pan out. This means that lifting the ban against homosexuals, by fostering heterosexual friendship among men, is likely to improve military morale.

The Sense of Homosexual Danger Is Unfounded

Our society has not only made it very dangerous to be a homosexual, it has even made it dangerous to look like one, associate with one, or to argue in their behalf. And the danger of being seen as a homosexual sympathizer is especially pronounced among men, especially among traditionally masculine men.

Men who feel the danger of appearing to be a homosexual sympathizer, will inevitably want to minimize the chance that this is so. This results in their reducing their contact with other men to competitions and challenges. Our society makes it so dangerous to be a male homosexual that men have become excessively guarded against appearing homosexual to other men and even against appearing to like homosexuals.[30]

It is no wonder, then, that many men find their same-sex friendships less satisfying than women do and that this is often manifested, especially in older men, by an increased loneliness.[31] As one psychiatrist stated it, ". . . most men do not have an intimate male friend of the kind they recall fondly from boyhood or youth."[32]

If men are afraid of doing or saying things that might make them look homosexual, it does not take much to give others this impression. As a society, we are quicker to assume that a man is homosexual if he deviates just a little from his male gender role, than we will judge a woman who deviates from hers. Men often think that emotional expression to other men implies homosexuality, and the men quickest to make that judgment are the men who express negative feelings about homosexuals.[33]

It is natural, then, since the spectre of male homosexuality in our culture is so damning for men, that many men will often be afraid to tell other men that they care, that they desire their company, that they sometimes long to let down their guard and cry with another man, to hug him and to be hugged in grief or celebration.

Men who are most negative about homosexuals feel especially guarded emotionally with other men. Such masculine men stand further from other heterosexual men,[34] and make a bigger effort to avoid touching them even when they know they are heterosexual.[35] They even avoid eye contact more.[36]

And men may be trying to avoid the appearance of homosexuality, too, just by acting disinterested in talking with other men, by not talking expressively, and by not revealing meaningfully to other men, for research shows that men do tend to talk less openly to their friends than women talk to theirs.[37] Masculine sex-typed men are even less disclosing than more feminine or androgynous men,[38] in spite of the fact that both men and women feel that self-disclosure makes a friendship more satisfying.[39]

Men have a harder time being emotionally supportive than women do and both men and women find less emotional support from men than they do from women.[40] One recent study concluded, ". . . the relationships of women with their women friends were especially strong and especially rewarding as compared to their friendships with men, and as compared to men's friendships with either women or men."[41]

If civilian, heterosexual men are so impressed by the danger of looking homosexual that they inhibit their friendships, that inhibition must surely be greatly increased in a military institution which relies on secret informants, coerced confessions, purloined mail, and endless investigations against people who are accused of being homosexual in a setting which sends people to prison for committing homosexual acts.

Removing the ban should promote, therefore, better relations among men because anything which lessens the psychological danger of looking homosexual so that heterosexual men can interact with each other with less guardedness against natural friendship, will surely enhance cohesion and morale.

Meeting a Homosexual Dispels the Sense of Homosexual Danger

The evidence suggests that even when the ban against homosexuals is lifted, most homosexuals will not disclose their identity easily.[42] But when they do disclose that they are gay, advocates for the ban expect disaster, bloodshed, and a loss of ability to fight wars. One retired Army colonel says:

> . . . [O]nce gays come out of the closet, they are perceived as a threat to manhood, and bloodshed results.
>
> The attempts of our leaders to halt the bloodshed will suppress the basic war-fighting instinct of our soldiers and result in an ineffective fighting force.[43]

Perhaps those who expect bloodshed imagine homosexuals disclosing their identities in defiant and provocative ways. But the evidence is that most homosexuals will not disclose their identities recklessly to people who are antihomosexual. When they do disclose who they are, we can expect them to be thoughtful and discreet. We can predict this because research demonstrates that when heterosexuals meet gays who disclose their identities, heterosexuals become more favorably disposed toward gays.[44]

Homosexuals can disclose their identity less provocatively than heterosexuals imagine. Consider the case of Fred.[45] He was sitting in a submarine with four other men in the undersea blue light, surrounded by equipment. He thought, "The worst they could do was kick me out of the service. I didn't come right out with it; I sort of worked it into the conversation." He knew each of the men, a chubby guy from Louisiana, a poor little rich kid with nappy hair, an ambitious son of an officer, and a kind of average guy from Minnesota. They were all friends. And one day, Fred worked the disclosure of his homosexuality into the conversation, right there as they sat working together in the blue light.

They were just talking about women. They asked Fred for a comment, and Fred shrugged and he told them. He said, "Hey, I'm gay." In describing the experience, Fred added:

> Submarine sailors have a mind of their own. They aren't totally ignorant. You tell them something like that and they can handle it. I was just putting it out there. I don't think they cared. If something is a little bit different, they like it just because it's different. They asked me a few questions, a little bit, but not too much. It was really very, very low key. I think they figured it wasn't a good idea to talk about something that could get me in trouble, and they had no problems keeping it quiet.

A disclosure that one is gay is not a sexual pass. Take the case of Frank and Bob.[46] They are in their middle forties today and they have been friends since they were ten. Both served full terms in the armed forces. After he left the military, Bob decided to tell all his friends he was gay, and he wrote Frank, who was still in the army, saying, "Frank, I'm a queer." Frank wrote back saying, "To say that your letter blew my mind would be the understatement of the century."[47] Today, 20 years later, Bob has been in a monogamous relationship with a man for 19 years, but he is still friends with Frank. Their relationship is completely nonsexual, but they are close. Since Frank's romantic partner does not like to hike, in fact, and Bob does, Bob and Frank go hiking together. And the evidence in other militaries suggests that homosexuals generally manage their identities, whether they disclose them or not, without alienating straights.

Removing the Ban Has Worked Elsewhere

When U.S. District Judge Terry J. Hatter, Jr., handed down his 1992 decision on the celebrated case of the gay sailor, Keith Meinhold,[48] Hatter said that the government had failed to prove a need for its antihomosexual policy. It had not shown that the ban against homosexuals served to achieve such goals as discipline, morale, and order, and he noted that the only available studies indicated that there is no scientific evidence for the government's position on gays and lesbians.[49] Judge Hatter ordered that Meinhold be reinstated in the Navy where he serves today without apparent problems.

Hatter was right. The military has no empirical evidence that homosexuals will disrupt morale. What they do have is opinion surveys of enlisted soldiers saying they *expect* homosexuals to disrupt morale. But the best available evidence on this question has been accumulated since the Meinhold decision, and it indicates that the soldiers are wrong.

The best evidence says that homosexuals will not disrupt morale. The evidence is what happened when the Canadians dropped their ban against homosexuals.

Canada is a country very much like the United States, and Canada's experts predicted, on the basis of survey data obtained from the Canadian soldiers, that dropping the ban would disrupt morale.[50] Then, in October of 1992, the Canadians re-evaluated the evidence and dropped their military ban against homosexuals, and the morale problems they predicted did not materialize.[51]

How is it that so many soldiers can be negative about lifting the ban and still the lifting of the ban fails to cause problems? It happens because the vast majority of soldiers (fully 91 percent of male soldiers) have never been aware of knowing a homosexual, and when they do meet homosexuals, they find them much less offensive than they predict.[52]

The Canadians accepted homosexuals when their ban was lifted, and the data we have indicates that civilian Canadians, in 1987, at least, were only very sightly more liberal about homosexuals serving in the military at that time than were civilians from the United States during the same period.[53]

In addition to Canada, five other countries have lifted their ban against homosexuals since 1972: France, Israel, the Netherlands, Norway, and Australia. None of these countries have had serious problems resulting from the lifting of the ban.[54] Those service members interviewed by the RAND Corporation in countries that have recently lifted the ban "claimed that in their experience there was no significant threat to unit cohesion or organizational performance created by the presence of homosexuals in their militaries, either at home stations or deployed at sea or abroad."[55]

The point is that soldiers can accept homosexuals even though they predict that they cannot. Eighty-eight percent of white soldiers in 1943 felt they could not accept black soldiers, but five years later when blacks were integrated, whites found they were able to accept blacks much more than they expected.[56] The same is true for the acceptance of women. Once they were integrated, they were accepted much more than was expected.[57]

We continue, however, to be warned that lifting the ban against homosexuals will diminish morale. One Army captain, writing anonymously, complained that soldier morale is already compromised by downsizing and indicates that the lifting of the homosexual ban at the same time may prove disastrous. That author said,

> The potential of simultaneously lifting the homosexual ban may push the morale of the armed forces over a precipice. The result–a demoralized military–may prove catastrophic during an emergency deployment.

But, again, this is only fear. The evidence suggests otherwise.

SUMMARY

The military ban makes being homosexual, or sympathizing with homosexuals, such a terrible problem that soldiers can only toss the term around like a hot potato, calling each other faggots and squirming at the thought that they might look like faggots themselves. Even those with no homosexual desire at all are damaged by the fear of looking homosexual to others. It causes them to diminish their expressions of friendship, and to distort their ways of behaving in an effort to convince others that they are not queer.

Psychologically, this is no small price. Human beings need a psychological context in which they can establish a network of people who accept them for who they are and care about them. The American Psychological Association and the American Psychiatric Association agree the ban against homosexuals should be dropped. Such a punitive stance toward homosexuals, and their sympathizers, is psychologically unhealthy for all soldiers.[58]

What we need to do now is look at the ways in which the military treats homosexuals, the damage it causes them personally, and envision new and better ways that will begin to free all of us from the anxiety that the fear of homosexuality causes even among those who experience little or no homosexual desire.

Chapter 8

Stories of Real People Hurt by the Ban

If the ban is wrong because it does not work, or because it is bad for military morale, it is even more wrong because it violates particular individuals who struggle with the secret fact that they find themselves, mysteriously, more attracted to the self-sex than the opposite sex. The military ban that shames and humiliates gay people puts them through an ordeal that hurts them. Since everyone of these people are members of our families the ordeal we cause them is our own ordeal.

The military ban hurts gays because only by doing so can the ban be enforced. It is not easy to catch a homosexual. Doing so requires aggressive investigations and interrogations and sometimes brutal prosecutions. Not only homosexuals are caught in the grips of this trap. Heterosexuals, too, sometimes get tarnished and battered by the enforcement of the military ban against homosexuals.

If the ban is to be enforced, it must be done so aggressively. Even so, the truth is that only a tiny proportion ever do get caught, not more than one in 50 and maybe not more than one in 1,500.[1] Tony and John, for example, from Chapter 5, went through their entire stay in the military without the homosexuality investigators lifting an eyebrow. And they are not alone. Most homosexuals serve their time without being caught. The entire mechanism of the ban exists to prosecute a few.

It is just that homosexuals are hard to catch. After all, most of them look like everyone else and have developed considerable skill in keeping themselves hidden in a homosexual closet.

When a homosexual gets caught it is usually for one of three reasons: the homosexual wanted to get caught, was outwitted, or was accused. The accusation might be a part of a witch-hunt in which the military whips up an intense state of fear so that people will accuse each other, often inaccurately, to reduce their own punishment, or, sometimes, the accusations are just those of a spurned lover or an angry friend.

It is a curious fact that the few token discharges that take place are, proportionally speaking, much more likely to be women. A woman in the military, depending on the particular service and year, is between two and ten times more likely to be booted out for homosexuality than a man is.[2] It is a strange commentary on our earlier observation that heterosexual women are much more comfortable with homosexual women than heterosexual men are with homosexual men. If that is so, why are we so eager to boot out lesbians? If heterosexual women are not that concerned about lesbians, why is our government so concerned with booting out lesbians, especially when the damage we do to the token few is so great?

There are those who will argue that the purpose of the ban is not merely to boot out the token few, but to set an example. This is the deterrence theory of homosexuality. So we will want to ask, do people stop being homosexual if we show them how badly homosexuals can be treated? The data we will look at will tell us "no."

We will begin with a brief overview of how homosexuals do, in fact, get booted out of the military, for there are several different ways this happens and you need these concepts to understand the individual life stories that we will examine.

To see the harm the ban does to people's lives, we need to look at life stories. The irony of these stories is that often closeted homosexuals investigate homosexuals. And the homosexuals that investigators catch are often those who feel most compelled to be honest, who make themselves particularly easy to catch. When they are hard to catch, we only do so by outwitting them with clever and dishonest interrogation techniques, or by pressuring and creating a climate of fear. There are poignant stories here, of people whose only crime was a tentative, anxious, and loving caress, or even less, perhaps, a look, a secret confused desire, and, maybe, even nothing at all. Being prosecuted under the ban put these people through a terrible ordeal, and, in many cases, caused psychological damage to their lives.

As you read these stories, ask yourself if these people are a menace to the heterosexuals around them. Ask if the harm we cause homosexuals substantially decreases homosexuality or if the etiquette of disregard is sufficient for heterosexuals who wish to be spared homosexual involvement.

HOW HOMOSEXUALS GET BOOTED OUT

How do people get booted out of the military for homosexuality? It can happen administratively or through a court-martial.

When it happens administratively, it is as though the person gets fired from the military for doing something that the employer, the military, finds objectionable. There are several kinds of administrative discharges, from honorable to dishonorable, each with different penalties, but even the best, the honorable discharge, results in the accused homosexuals receiving a note in their files. Moreover, on the back of their discharge papers there is a statement in plain English that explains to potential employers that the person was discharged for homosexuality.

A person being booted out administratively may accept the discharge without protest, or may demand a hearing before an administrative board that works much like a court except that hearsay and rumor can be accepted as evidence. Once the discharge is given, it can be appealed with the aid and experience of a private attorney, but it is expensive and almost impossible to get a discharge overturned.

When a person is booted out with a court-martial, on the other hand, the person is convicted of a felony and can go to prison. The advantage of a court-martial over an administrative hearing is that the trial by court-martial does not allow hearsay evidence. However, with a court-martial the penalties are much greater. A person can be penalized for up to five years for a homosexual act, which, according to the court definition includes any kind of genital contact between members of the same sex. The same law makes it illegal, incidentally, for heterosexuals to engage in either oral or anal intercourse.

When a person is court-martialed for homosexuality the charge is often for sodomy, but it can also be for indecent acts, lewd and lascivious conduct, fraternization, or a number of other offenses all of which can be included as separate offenses and added together to increase the time served in prison.

The vast majority of people booted out for homosexuality do not go through a court-martial. In fact, most people discharged do not protest the discharge and are not heard even by an administrative board. Most confess in the process of interrogation, become frightened of what the judicial machinery can do to them, and agree to go quietly. Some are so alarmed by the penalties against homosexuals that they scarcely offer a whimper of resistance. There are even those, as we shall see, who offer themselves for discharge before they have committed homosexual acts.

HOW HOMOSEXUALS GET CAUGHT

Although there are a variety of ways that homosexuals can get discharged, the real question is how they come to the attention of the authorities in order to be prosecuted and discharged. There are three ways: They are outwitted by interrogators and thus confess in spite of themselves, they confess without interrogative pressure, or they can be accused by others.

HOW HOMOSEXUALS GET OUTWITTED

Catching a homosexual requires the art of outwitting someone who feels alone and frightened with intimidation, promises (often false promises), threats and, most of all, skilled questioning. When the interrogation is done successfully the hapless subjects end up implicating themselves and their friends. Most people who investigate and prosecute homosexuals do not like this work.

The following example of an interrogation is a fictional case constructed in conjunction with an agent who conducted such investigations personally for five years.

In reading the example, keep in mind that the task of the interrogator is one of convincing the subject to tell the truth. There is no other agenda. The good interrogator studies the subject to see what techniques will work and is flexible enough to select a technique which will work with the particular subject. Some subjects, for example, need approval, and if they are given approval, (e.g., told that they are not bad for being homosexual, they are just in the wrong place) they will confess. Others are people who will weigh their odds. They need to be convinced that their odds are better if they tell the complete truth (even though this is usually not true). Others, perhaps, might be afraid of parents and friends learning of their homosexuality. These may be led to believe that parents and friends will learn if the investigation continues, but they will not learn if they simply tell the truth and accept an immediate discharge.

There are a variety of ways to convince people to tell the truth, but catching a homosexual by clever interrogation, requires the interrogator to know the needs of the the subject and to satisfy or threaten those needs in exchange for a confession.

Outwitting a Homosexual with Clever Interrogation

A typical interrogation of a homosexual might begin with an investigative agency receiving a phone call. The call comes into a small government office. There might be six metal desks, three of them with young investigators sitting behind them doing paperwork.[3] The phone rings. We'll give these people names and try to create typical characters.

"Agent Thomas," answers a young man who looks more like a bored football player than an agent. His friends call him Charlie. He is 25 years old. He has been in this job a couple of years and feels it does not have enough status. He wishes he could do more exciting police work, have a more prestigious job. An FBI job would be better–better paid, more status.

The voice on the phone is a man's voice. It says, "I think we have something here you guys need to know about."

"What's that?"

"I have this woman sitting here telling me she's a lesbian."

Charlie starts to doodle.

"She looks like she is ready to spill her guts. I think she might name some names. You think you could send someone over to talk to her?"

Charlie glances up at Ken across the way and rolls his eyes. "A lesbian? She told you that?"

Ken groans audibly. Ken is younger than Charlie, perhaps 22.

"That's what she says. Can you get over here?"

"Yeah. We'll get over there in about an hour." There is resignation in his voice.

"Not a sodomy case!" Ken protests. Ken only finished his short ten-week training program three months ago. Both Charlie and Ken see Ken as a kind of apprentice. Ken looks up to Charlie. If Charlie groans about a case, Ken groans. Ken recognizes Charlie hates sodomy cases, but he has, himself, never been on one. He asks Charlie, "Do dykes just come out and tell you that they're dykes?"

"Sometimes," answers Charlie, as he shuffles some papers on his desk. He is feeling, understandably, much more knowledgeable than Ken. Charlie has interrogated about eight of these cases, and developed something of a knack for it. Still the people always amaze him. The truth is they often seem like ordinary human beings and it is hard to imagine that they do the nasty things they do.

The truth is that Charlie does not know much about homosexuality. Although he has a college degree, he has never had a course on homosexuality, never read a book about it, or even an article. What he knows, he learned from his friends talking about homosexuals in the locker room. It is true that when he took this job he had a ten-week training program. They spent a day or so on how to interrogate, and the topic of interrogating a homosexual, specifically, only came up a couple of times. No one discussed what it meant to be homosexual, how a person came to feel that he or she was homosexual, or anything about the statistics on how common homosexual feelings and behavior are.

"Let's go," Charlie tells Ken.

"Now?"

"Now."

Ken groans and reaches for his coat. "Here we go, queer cops to the rescue. Can't we go investigate a homicide?"

Charlie doesn't answer. He does not even laugh. It hits too close to home. Charlie had wanted to be an FBI agent. He's doing this mickey mouse stuff because he did not score the FBI job. "Let's go," he says with a grouch in his voice.

Sitting in the car, Ken says, "What disgusts me is what they do. Do you think about it much when you talk to them? Do you ask them what they do?"

"Sure, I do," Charlie says. "I need to get details so they can't back out of the statement later."

Ken is silent. He sits there reflecting on the magnitude of a homosexual act. What he fails to recognize in this brief moment, as Charlie drives over the urban road, is that the disgust he feels is like the disgust he once felt when he was 11 and learned that his father had to insert his penis in his mother at least twice in order to have created Ken and his brother. At the moment, for Ken, a homosexual is a freak, and he has never met one. He is a little curious. He wonders what they look like.

A few minutes later Ken and Charlie are standing with a heavy, red-faced Navy commander in a big office room filled with typists. The commander speaks, "She's that woman way over there, the one with dirty blond hair. You want me to get her for you?"

"I want an office she has never been in, first," Charlie says, sounding competent. "Something small, empty, if you have it. I want three chairs in it and one desk."

"Is a little writing table okay?"

"Yeah."

"Here's her file."

Charlie and Ken watch the supposed lesbian walk over to the file cabinet, and Charlie says, "I think she walks like a duck, Ken. Remember, if it walks like a duck and quacks like a duck, then it must be a duck."

Ken says out loud, "I think she's an attractive woman. You think she's a dyke?"

"She tells me she's a lesbian," the commander pipes in.

"Hard to believe a good-looking woman like that can be a dyke, huh?" Charlie comments with an air of superiority. "But look at the way she walks. I can tell she's a dyke." He says this, but the truth is he would not have recognized her as a lesbian. He knows this, and he is amazed, too.

Five minutes later Ken and Charlie are in their small, empty office arranging the chairs. Charlie arranges two straight-back chairs facing each other, 18 inches apart. And Ken arranges himself in the back by the desk.

Susan, the confessed lesbian, comes to the door. Charlie looks up at her. She looks 16 and scared to death. She has blue eyes, curly brownish hair, shapely, but a real baby face. "Come in," he tells her and she steps into the room. "Sit here," he says in a casual voice.

"How old are you?" he asks.

"Nineteen," Susan whispers.

And with the routine air of someone who has done this many times before, Charlie loses eye contact while he tells Susan, in a casual, matter-of-fact voice, that she is under investigation for sodomy. As he recites the Miranda he reaches around himself on the floor for his clipboard. He shows her the paper, hands her the pen from his pocket. "Take it," he tells her in a reassuring voice. "Sign here, and date it there. The date," he tells her, "is April 15. Just sign right there." He tells her the date because it will make it easier for her to sign.

She does not hesitate. What she signs is a piece of paper that tells her she has a right to an attorney, a right to remain silent. If she makes incriminating statements they can be used against her. She signs these rights away and hands him the pen.

"Tell me about it," Charlie tells her.

What the young woman tells, while she cries, is a story of a close, nonsexual relationship with another young woman in her barracks, her roommate. It has gone on for several weeks. They felt closer and closer. One day, when Susan had had a bad day, and couldn't get to sleep, she and her friend whispered through the night. Over the next few weeks, Susan felt more and more attached to her roommate, and apparently her roommate did too. Finally, one night, Susan asked this woman to hold her. She could not believe how good it felt.

But the next day, the two overslept and when the housemate threw open their door she found them together. Susan woke with that woman saying, "So you two are a couple of lesbians!" And she heard the door slam. It had happened just that morning, and it left her unnerved.

"I'm glad you came and told us," Charlie says. Charlie's job, now, is to get Susan to confess. He will try to sell her on the importance of telling the truth, of confessing. At this point she has not really said that she has done anything that is homosexual, but Charlie thinks she probably has. He says, "People can't help what they feel, but I admire it when someone tells the truth about it." It is a technique he learned in his training course. He even uses it on homicide cases. "I'm glad you had the self-respect to want to tell the truth. You don't like hypocrisy do you?"

Susan shakes her head no.

Inside, Susan recalls the feelings that she had felt stir in her body the night before. She had felt those feelings once before, when she and her boyfriend had made out last year in the back seat of the car. The feelings were the same. But for the last few months, Susan had found herself strangely attracted to this woman. And here she was lying in bed with her. She had drifted off to sleep and, maybe it was just a dream, felt this woman's warmth against her body, maybe even her hands, but maybe it was just a dream. She cannot bring herself to tell about this experience, cannot believe it really happened. She looks at Charlie. He looks friendly, like he cares. Seeing him caring about her makes her want to cry. But she should not tell them. All the people here know is that she has slept with this woman, and that someone discovered them in bed. She looks down at her hands. Her mind is swimming with confusion.

Charlie speaks again, "It's okay, Susan. There is nothing wrong with being gay. You just love women, and the military doesn't understand that. How long have you known you are gay?" By asking her how long she has been gay, he is telling her that she is gay and that it is okay. These words may comfort her and help her confess.

But the truth is that Susan had only recently begun to wonder if she was gay, and she had never decided for sure. Charlie's confident assertion that she is gay begins to convince her, a little. She had wanted to know. She looks at Charlie with fear and wonder. And he looks back, patiently. He looks like a friend.

"It's okay, Susan," Charlie continues. He remembers his instructors telling him, "Make her feel at ease with it, and she can confess it more easily." "It's okay. Be glad you're not a hypocrite." His challenge now will be to convince her she is a good person for telling exactly what they did. "You know, some people live their whole lives as hypocrites, knowing that they are gay, and never telling. Here you are just 19, and you're willing to admit it. If I were you I would be proud."

Susan looks down, and cries a little. This is so new. She had only considered the possibility that she might be gay for a few days. She had never thought about it before.

"You're too hard on yourself," Charlie continues. "Are you worried what your parents will think?" Charlie is guessing, but this is a common concern.

Susan nods.

"Well they don't have to know. If you do get discharged you can tell them that the military is downsizing. Tell them that your hearing isn't good. We're not going to tell them."

"I also want to stay in the military," she volunteers.

Charlie nods. "Of course," he says. "That's really up to your commanding officer to make that decision. But I believe you will be better off if you do tell us the truth. Your commander will be impressed by your honesty." His statement, however, is not true. Charlie does not believe that her confession will have any positive impact on her life. This is just a trick to promote a confession.

Susan sighs and looks away. Her eyes dart around. She is trying to decide what to do. Then her face floods with emotion and she starts to cry, again.

Charlie's voice is reassuring. "Hey, you're a good person. All you can do is just be honest." It is straight out of the text.

Susan is quiet, whimpering.

"Look," Charlie continues. His voice is reassuring. "Tell me what you did. I understand when two women are together they might kiss, or touch or orally stimulate each other's breasts or genitals. Did you do that or have it done to you?"

Susan cries.

"It's okay, Susan," he tells her. "It would just be better if you told the truth. Just tell me."

"I don't know what really happened," she says. "I was mostly asleep."

"But you know some of what happened, don't you?"

Susan nods.

"Tell me what you know."

"She just held me, like I was in her lap. She put her arms around me. I think she may have touched my stomach, kind of low. But I didn't do anything. I promise. I just laid there."

"I understand, and you were asleep. You just woke up and she was touching you."

"I may have just dreamed it."

"Dreamed what? That she touched your private parts?"

"No! I could feel her leg on my private parts. I think it was her leg!" And Susan starts to sob.

"I understand, and you didn't do anything. Did you?" Charlie is assisting Susan in blaming the other woman. In blaming the other woman, Susan may overlook her confession of surrendering to homosexual touches.

"I didn't do anything! I swear!"

"I know. But you think she had sex on her mind, don't you? That's why you're so upset. Am I right? It's okay." And Charlie smiles and nods acceptingly. "She was seducing you. Isn't that right?"

And Susan nods. "Maybe," she says. Maybe that was it. Susan is whimpering.

Then Charlie pulls out a few more tricks. He asks Susan to show him how low the woman's hand went. And he consoles and reassures, but, somehow, he is never able to get her to say quite enough for him to determine that their interaction could qualify for a sodomy conviction. He is going to have to go for an administrative discharge.

Finally, he sighs. "You know, Susan, I'm going to have to write a report to your commander and tell him what we found out. I'll help you. You can tell him just what you told me, that she touched you, that you did not touch her. Does that sound good?" Charlie wants Susan to focus on blaming the other woman. This will in no way lessen her guilt, but it will make it easier for Susan to confess the homosexuality of the interaction. It will make it easier for Charlie to get a passable confession.

Charlie hands Susan the clipboard and he says, "You write this. 'We did not take our clothes off. Although she touched me with her hands on the lower part of my stomach, I did not touch her in any way . . . ' " And Susan writes. She feels these words exonerate her, but they move her closer to a confession.

And, in the back of the room, Ken is marveling at Charlie's technique. Somehow, it has convinced him that Susan is a homosexual. There are some women, Ken ponders, who prefer women. Mostly, though, Ken is struck by how pretty Susan is. He would have been interested in asking her out on a date. He wonders, secretly, if his own lovemaking would be enough to inspire her to like men.

Then Susan signs this paper. Her confession will not implicate her sufficiently to take her to a court-martial, but it will be enough for her commander to justify an administrative discharge. In a few weeks she will receive her discharge papers, and on the back, it will say, "engaged in homosexual acts," even though, so we might imagine, there was no actual genital contact.

Once again, a military agent has outwitted a "homosexual."

Homosexuals Catching Homosexuals

The details in the fictional account of Charlie interviewing Susan were constructed with the guidance of Linda Gautney, a woman who worked for the NIS[4] herself while trying to put her own homosexuality out of mind.

Linda was just 22 when she went to work as an NIS investigator. Her lesbian inclinations were not conspicuous. Her looks were average, average size, average attractiveness. She wore her dark brown hair at a medium length, but Linda was careful to cast herself with a feminine touch. She wore makeup, contacts, carried a purse, and tried to look feminine. And her average looks were spiced with intelligence and a distinctive Alabama accent. There were plenty of guys interested in dating her.

Linda did not look homosexual, but already, at 22, she had experienced two important romantic relationships with women, and one had lasted nearly two years.

Still, she wanted more than anything to be heterosexual, and she hoped she would eventually fall in love with a man. Her plan was to distance herself from women in hopes that she would meet a man who would inspire the kind of intimate feelings she had had for women. She says, "What I discovered, after many years of angst, was that I had a basic lesbian orientation and that I did not have a choice about my homosexual feelings. I think I could have chosen to marry and have children, even, but I could not have changed my lesbian feelings. And so, although I liked men, and my friends were almost exclusively men, I feel it is unlikely that I would ever have developed the kind of intimate, loving, satisfying relationship with a man that I knew I could have with a woman."

And, so, five years later, still romantically attracted only to women, Linda felt compelled to terminate her job as an investigator for NIS. It is hard to interrogate people for homosexuality when you are struggling with these issues inside yourself.

While Linda worked at NIS, she, like Charlie in our fictional example, knew practically nothing about homosexuality. Even though her degree was with honors, she did not once have a course that explained what homosexuality was, had not read one book, had never discussed the matter with someone who was more informed than she. When she went to work for the NIS, at age 22, she, like Charlie and Ken, went through an intensive ten-week training program on the techniques of investigating crimes, including sodomy, but she was given no in-service training on the nature of homosexuality. The challenge was how to get people to confess, not to understand what they were confessing to.

Not every homosexual who has investigated homosexuals has the courage to disclose this irony. Today, working with a new master's degree in a different field, Linda Gautney has nothing to gain personally from such a disclosure. She is living happily today with her female lover in a quiet and monogamous relationship. Nevertheless, having been a part of the system that prosecutes homosexuals, Linda understands the irony of homosexuals investigating homosexuals and is willing to assist those who try to show what is problematic about the ban.

The Psychological Implications of Interrogation of Homosexuality

The purpose of the interrogation is to achieve a confession. It is a battle of wits and one in which people with lower IQs have a disadvantage,[5] so much so that they can often be led to confess to crimes that they have not even committed.[6] We would expect intelligence to be more important, of course, if the interrogator tried to trick the subject, as Charlie did, with leading and misleading questions.[7] Although we do not know Susan and Charlie's IQs, the fact that Susan was only 19 and Charlie was a 25-year-old college graduate, suggests that he had the edge during this interrogation.

Susan was probably also at a disadvantage emotionally. First, she was young. Young people can be led into confession more easily than older people, and this is especially true if the subject has a tendency, as Susan demonstrated, to feel guilty about things that might not cause so much guilt feelings in others.[8] People who feel guilty in this way may want to confess in the interrogation room just to purify their consciences [9] even if they are not guilty of the actual crime in question.[10] It is as though they lose awareness of the extent to which the interrogator is not really a friend who is motivated to be concerned with the subject's well-being. This kind of confession is more likely, of course, when interrogators use techniques like Charlie's, intended to promote the trust of the subject with reassurance and understanding.[11]

Although Susan confessed, from what we know about her it is psychologically premature for her to accept a homosexual identity. Although she seems to have this inclination inside her, she also has a heterosexual capacity, and it is not clear which is stronger. Rather than have a 25-year-old man who has minimal knowledge about homosexuality convince her that she is gay, we need someone who is more informed to counsel her and assist her in understanding the meaning of her sexual urges. To force her into an identity prematurely is to invite a psychological crisis, and, indeed, to commit a kind of psychological violence against her. Such violence against people is the cost of the ban. It is hard to force people to confess to homosexuality without using tactics capable of causing them psychological harm.

The techniques that Charlie used to press for Susan's confession are different from the ones that would be used with other types of homosexual suspects. People come to an interrogation typically out of their own guilt, but they might come, too, because they are accused by someone. In this case, a sharp interrogator like Charlie, would adapt his techniques. An intuitive reading that the accused knows many other homosexuals, for example, might lead Charlie to say, "We have you. You might as well confess. We have pictures, and the statements of lots and lots of people." And there is nothing in the rule books that would prevent Charlie from saying things like this just because they were not true.

THE EASY CATCH

Given how hard it is to catch homosexuals, it is surprising to learn that there are those who make it easy, who walk into a commander's office and say that they are homosexual. There are a variety of motivations. Sometimes they feel lost and lonely and are eaten up inside with the knowledge that they hide homosexual feelings. They can feel conflicted about their homosexuality and long for acceptance for what they feel they cannot change. Sometimes, on the other hand, when they have found acceptance from parents and friends, they feel a kind of confidence about their homosexuality and disclose it without anticipating how severely homosexuals can be treated.

In the real cases that follow, Karen Stupski is an example of a conflicted homosexual who disclosed her identity as a process of trying to find it. Chris Boadt is an example of a confident homosexual, who had received sufficient acceptance from his peers and parents that he lowered his guard without realizing quite how harshly the military would pounce on him. These are the real names of real people.

The Easy Catch of a Conflicted Homosexual

Karen Stupski is a 27-year-old woman today who is trying to put her life back together. She was discharged from the military for homosexuality even though she had never had a homosexual experience. Her discharge was based entirely on a volunteered confession that her feelings were homosexual.

These homosexual feelings consisted of an awareness that pictures of female bodies were erotic for her, more erotic than pictures of males, and a strong and powerful romantic attachment to Charlotte,[12] who had been a childhood friend. When they were together,

Karen felt inhibited and shy. She never spoke of her feelings, avoiding touching and looking in ways that would make them clear to Charlotte. Still, she imagined that, maybe, Charlotte felt similarly. It was a hope that Karen held onto through the years, through high school, even through college. She confided in her friends in college that she had had lesbian feelings, but she never told Charlotte, and she never had a lesbian experience.

Being from a military family, it was natural for Karen to try for an ROTC scholarship. She got one at Harvard and joined the Navy after graduating with high honors.

Then, suddenly, she was an officer in charge of men. She carried a clipboard and wore the military's version of a baseball cap as she walked around supervising men who were watching the safety practices of the welders, checking for fires. Work was tedious, and she was lonely.

Finally, Karen developed a good friend, not a romantic friend, just a friend. He was driving one day and they were talking when he surprised her by saying, "I'm gay." "I think I am, too," Karen told him and surprised herself. It was a new concept telling people she was gay. She admired the sense of dignity this man displayed. She wanted to feel that comfort with her homosexuality, too.

Hiding her homosexuality felt hypocritical. At night she would see her housemate Penny, a woman who attracted her, and she would think a little of Penny, and even more of Charlotte. Each night she would lie in bed and read lesbian novels, and long to connect romantically with a woman, especially Charlotte.

Then once, when she was on leave back home, Karen found herself in the car with Charlotte driving.[13] Karen looked at Charlotte. Charlotte was a lovely, earthy woman who had long ago captured Karen's heart, and Karen longed to break this silence. Looking down, she braced herself and started to speak.

"There is something I need to say to you," she told Charlotte. And then she said it. "I'm attracted to you." And she explained, with a pretended intellectual detachment, " I have determined this because of how I feel when I'm around you. There is an emotional component as well as a physical component," Karen told her. "My palms sweat. I have an excitement about being with you."

Charlotte stayed calm. Karen's worst fears were stemmed. Charlotte answered with measured words. She said, "Well, Karen, I always valued your friendship, and you've been a close friend, and I am attracted to you as a friend, but for me it's not more than that."

Inside Karen felt a sinking feeling. She had always hoped these feelings were shared by Charlotte. She had secretly believed they were. But at that moment, she felt cold, alone, and like a freak. She was ashamed.

Charlotte continued, with caution and tenderness, "Karen, when I think back about us, I remember noticing that we never touched. I know I'm a physically affectionate person, and I think this distance comes from you. I think you don't want to be touched. Is that true?"

"It's true," Karen responded. "I was afraid that we would touch and I would feel all these feelings, and maybe you wouldn't feel them." And she talked on, describing the way she had hidden her feelings in words that hid them still, hiding the poignancy of her disclosure with dry, unfeeling words.

Charlotte listened, trying to hear the message behind the cold words. "Are you a lesbian?" she asked.

That word stabbed at Karen's heart. "Lesbian," it sounded harsh, but Karen kept her balance. "That's the worst case scenario," she told her. "Probably I'm just bisexual."

As they drove, and talked, in this casual way, sometimes Karen's detached demeanor would slip a little and she would start to cry, just a little.

Charlotte would looked puzzled. She wanted to comfort Karen and did not know how, did not know what she could do, what she could say.

The incident ended later that night after they got to Charlotte's house. Karen said goodbye, and left with both of them feeling embarrassed and awkward. Perhaps, Charlotte had known the desire to touch and hold Karen, too, but that feeling somehow had never become erotic and urgent for her. Yet, still, Charlotte was moved by the urgency that her friend seemed to be feeling.

Back on the base, Karen told her new gay friend about the pain of her disclosure to Charlotte. And as they talked, Karen grew more and more in need of declaring herself a lesbian. She needed to find other women who could love her, other women like herself. That night she lay in her bed listening to music with lesbian lyrics, feeling her loneliness, and the hurt and shame inside her longed to be confessed.

Time passed. A whole year passed, and during that year she continued to fret and worry about what to do about the truth of her lesbian feelings, whom to tell, what to say. And the desire to tell grew increasingly strong.

One day, she told her mother a little about her lesbianism, and she felt comforted and loved.

Then one day, Karen's commander saw her crying. The commander was a short, maternal woman, and she put her arm around Karen's shoulder and told her, "Come into my office and tell me about it."

There in that small office, the commander sat behind her metal desk and said, "Tell me what's wrong."

"I'm a lesbian," Karen told her.

"How do you know?" the commander asked, a little shocked.

And Karen explained how she had had these feelings since she was a child, and how she felt attracted to women, but, she added, "I have never had a homosexual experience."

Karen felt her commander's sadness and concern. "I have to write you up," she told her.

"Yes." Karen had expected it.

With her disclosure, a great sense of relief came over Karen. She called her father, the military man. He was proud of her career, and she spoke with apprehension. "I have told them," she said to him, "that I'm a lesbian."

"You will always be sorry for having done this," he responded.

But she did not feel sorry. That night she and her friends, even her brother, went out to celebrate Karen's new emotional freedom. She had freed herself from the prison of her hypocrisy.

When Karen resigned from the military, she wrote a letter telling of her reasons:

> I identify as lesbian because I am in love with a woman and have desired women sexually. For a long time I did not want to admit this because it contradicted everything I had been taught I should feel. However, I could not deny the truth in my body

> and my spirit, and have come to understand and accept my feelings completely.[14]

Later she withdrew her resignation and let them discharge her. She wanted them to know that she was doing this because it was honest, not because she wanted to leave the military.

The Easy Catch of the Overconfident Homosexual

Sometimes the volunteered homosexual confession comes more out of self-acceptance than self-doubt. In the military, self-confidence in a homosexual needs to be paired with caution or it can lead to some unpleasant surprises. This can happen when homosexuals get enough acceptance by their parents and friends that they let down their guard and expose themselves. Chris Boadt is an example of such a homosexual. He is an articulate, thoughtful young man who, unlike Karen, now holds a job in the civilian world that provides him with a similar level of prestige and pay.

When Chris joined the military at 22 he, like Karen Stupski, had felt homosexual feelings, but he had never had a homosexual experience. After he began experimenting, he told one of his heterosexual friends who accepted this and continued to befriend him. Then, when his mother asked him one day, in a casual voice, "Chris, are you gay?" he answered "yes," and she was accepting. She told Chris that she and his father had thought he was.

Chris' parents were so supportive that they joined a politically active group of parents of homosexuals who argue for accepting homosexuals in public meetings. They tell homosexual youths not to "coddle" their parents by trying to protect them from the truth of their homosexuality.

Gradually, Chris began to feel that it was okay to be gay. At this point he was involved in a long-term, monogamous, committed relationship, and there was little chance that he would be detected by the homosexuality investigators.

But all of this acceptance by everyone gave him false confidence. His problems started one day when Chris' commanders were doing a routine security clearance on him. Chris sat in his commander's office answering standard questions. Then, embedded in all the others, came the question, "Are you a homosexual?"

And Chris said, "Yes," much like he had answered his mother when she asked him.

But with the commander, the response was different. Within minutes the security police were in the office and he was put in handcuffs. He was interrogated all evening and all the next day. When it was finally clear that he had not compromised security, they began to suspect that he was guilty of malingering to get out of going to war, and they threatened to court-martial him and send him to prison for 20 years for malingering. To avoid being court-martialed, Chris had to prove that he was truly gay which he did by finding an old gay magazine in his room, and an old letter. He was given an honorable discharge.

And so Chris Boadt, who had done very well in the military, and was well liked, was, in the end, someone who was easily caught just because he was overconfident.

Psychological Implications of Discharge on the Easy to Catch

Discharging people who tell us the truth about themselves, and publicizing the fact that we do this, tells them, and all who know about it, that homosexuality is something to hide. It encourages everyone who feels homosexual feelings to develop a neurotic adaptation to those feelings, suppressing them, as far as possible, out of consciousness, and disclosing them to no one, not even to a counselor. This, of course, sets them up to live in fear of being accused.

THE ACCUSED HOMOSEXUAL

Since homosexuals can be discharged on the basis of hearsay, it is possible for them to be kicked out of the military on the basis of accusations even when these accusations are untrue. This fact results in three very unfortunate consequences.

First, a few homosexuals get punitive treatments that seem excessive. Second, an atmosphere of fear is constructed. Third, heterosexuals can get kicked out by mistake just by the overzealous prosecution practices.

The real story of Barbara Baum and her lover Laura Hinkley will give us a feel for the level of anxiety that is created by a witch-hunt. Their story, in one way of looking at it, is a touching love story of two young women who found themselves in love for the first time in their lives, and who felt very awkward and confused about the fact that their first love was another woman. Their story is one of how the military complicated their lives during a time of confusion about their sexual identities. They became the anxious victims of one of the nation's biggest homosexual witch-hunts, the witch-hunt of Parris Island in 1989.

Laura and Barbara had committed homosexual acts and were discharged, but heterosexuals, too, can be subjected to misery and psychological damage by the homosexual ban. Moreover, the ordeal that causes this damage is not restricted to those people who actually get discharged.

Although the ban can create a mood of anxiety and misery, homosexuality in the military continues, undeterred.

Lesbians Snared in a Witch-Hunt

They were just two young women sitting on the grass resting from another run. There was a big meet coming up, and they had all the promise of running well. It was just four years before, when she was 18, that Barb's name had been flashed across her hometown paper. she had come in tenth in the state in track. And Laura, a few years older, was a little bit faster, still.

They were two young Marines, and the strange rules of the military forbade these young women from becoming friends because the older one, Laura, 25, blond and lean, with high cheekbones, was a commissioned officer, a captain, and the younger one, Barbara, brunette, small and pretty, quiet and watchful, was merely a corporal. They were only four years apart in age, but Barbara called Laura "ma'am." Friendship between Marines is forbidden between officers and enlisted personnel. It is called fraternization.

But they were not yet violating the rules. It was acceptable for them to run together, and to sit for a while between runs to rest and talk. And so they did, these two young women, one tall, blond captain, and one small, dark, admiring corporal.

As they sat there talking, Barb bragged of the honors she had received in boot camp. Then she found herself telling her attentive listener things she had never told before, sad things like how the neighbor boys in high school had repeatedly raped her limp body while she lay numb and confused in some dark back room. Feeling shame, she would drink and use drugs.

Laura was overwhelmed as she heard these stories. She had never drunk or used drugs, but she remembered her high school teacher catching her alone once and planting a kiss on her mouth–so Laura understood how these things can happen. And, slowly the two women became friends, in violation of the fraternization rules.

First they talked on the grass between runs. Then Barb came over for hot dogs. Then she stayed overnight. One night, going to sleep on the floor, Barb asked Laura to lie with her on the floor, and she did, for inside Laura was growing a need to protect and love this young woman. They did not touch or caress that night, but soon they each knew they were falling in love.

When any person falls in love with another who reciprocates by also falling in love, that person will have a certain magical feeling that makes it very hard to stay apart. And one day, as they were lying there, Laura asked Barbara if she could kiss her. Barb's heart fluttered, and they kissed.

It is true that Barbara had previously had one brief, loveless, sexual affair with another woman on the base. She had let her body be used much as it was by the neighbor boys in high school. But Laura, the proud young captain, had never even considered the possibility of a lesbian romance. She had had romantic affairs with men, and although she had not met the man of her dreams, she had felt the ability in her body to respond to a man. She expected to marry some day.

But here the two of them were in love when even friendship was against the rules. In all that confusion, their caresses were inhibited and anxious, but there were flashes of wonder.

And then, one day, Barbara was told she was being investigated for homosexuality–not for the relationship she was having with Laura, but for the brief loveless affair she had previously had with another woman.

And the wheels of the Marine investigations started turning. Barbara told Laura. They were worried together about their relationship coming under investigation, but Barbara longed for Laura's consolation and advice, and Laura longed to give it. And so they continued to meet while all around them they saw others being investigated for homosexuality. The young captain's eyes were being opened. She had had no idea that lesbianism was common on base.

But Barbara had known. She even knew names. And some of the other women knew of Barb's previous lesbian affair. It was a witch-hunt and all would be questioned for names.

Then one day Barbara was sitting in her lawyer's office reading a statement Barb's previous lover had made, describing what had happened between them. Barb sat there. It is a hard thing to tell the world about the intimacy of sexual experiences, but that is what she had to do. "It's true," she said, "It's basically true."

But because they did not really want Barbara so much as they wanted names, they offered her a bargain if she would name names. Barbara said no, and so they would court-martial her for sodomy.

A court-martial is the military equivalent of a felony trial. The defendant can go to prison. The news media crammed the courtroom. Dressed in her uniform, she stared at the wall at attention while they pronounced her guilty. The handsome blond prosecutor with broad shoulders spoke in his serious voice and asked for 35 years. When the jury returned they sentenced her to one.

Laura watched the sentencing on television as she sat alone with tears in her eyes. Here was Barbara, the small, pretty woman who had loved her, whom Laura had wanted to protect and had dared to kiss. Little Barb. She was put in handcuffs. She would go to prison. There was no one for Laura to tell, no one to talk with.

A month after the trial, risking everything, Laura showed up at the brig. She did not wear her captain's uniform. She went in jeans, in hopes that this would not call attention to herself. They let her wait in the library. Then they brought Barbara in.

Barb had changed. She had lost 20 pounds. Her face was gaunt and strained, distorted even. Then Barb told Laura what she had done. This time when they had pressured her she had given the names of other women who had lesbian experiences. Had she told of Laura? She had resisted telling them that Laura and she had been lovers, but she had told the investigators that she and Laura had just been friends.

It was no small thing that Barbara told that she and Laura were friends. It meant that they could begin investigating Laura for fraternization. Maybe they could also press Laura into a confession. And so this great judicial machinery would now try to crush Laura, too.

"It's okay," Laura told her. "It's okay."

Suddenly, Laura was being investigated. The young blond captain who once ran a marathon for the Marines, who inspected her battalion with pride, who had never loved a woman before, who had never been in love before, who had never even imagined becoming a lesbian, now had to face this shame by herself while her lover sat distraught, abandoned, and helpless in prison.

Laura went to an attorney. She told him the charges.

"I'll tell you what we'll do," he said. "We'll go down and get you a polygraph test. That will intimidate them."

Laura crumbled. "I can't," she said.

"Why not?"

"Because the charges are true."

And so Laura told the lawyer about her circumstances. It was the first time she had told anyone about her love affair with Barb.

Four months later Laura sat before her own hearing board. Her mother and sister held hands in the back of the tension-filled courtroom. Two past boyfriends testified that they had been intimate with her. It argued for her heterosexuality.

Then Laura was allowed to speak for herself. She told about her childhood, how her father had left them, how her mother had raised them with only a bookkeeper's wages. She told of her pride in getting into the Naval Academy and becoming a Marine officer. After about an hour of telling her story, she moved closer to the time of her story with Barbara, and they handed her a sheet of questions.

With the tears rolling down her face, and her head spinning, with her mother and the newspaper reporters listening, she denied the truth. "No," she said, while her lover sat trapped in prison. "No," Laura told them, explaining that she and Barb had only been friends.

Her mother and sister gave a sigh of relief in the back of the courtroom.

A few weeks later, Laura got a call from her attorney. "I don't know how to tell you this," he told her, "but they recommended that if you do not accept a discharge you should be court-martialed for fraternization."

Laura's heart sank and she leaned against the windowsill in shame and tears and told him how she regretted ever having gone to the Naval Academy. And Laura was discharged from the military for fraternization.

A month later Barbara was released from prison and she met Laura in Florida and asked Laura to live with her. Laura longed to live with Barb, but her sister and mother had voiced their objections. Laura's sister called it abnormal.

So Laura decided she would live with Barb, but she would make the relationship "normal" by making it celibate. She told the distraught Barbara. They would live together, forever, she said, but just as friends. They would no longer kiss and lie in each other's arms. So they have lived apart, together, with their broken hearts.

Heterosexuals Snared in the Homosexual Ban

Heterosexuals also appear to get snared in the ban. The Parris Island witch-hunt that captured Barb and Laura began with an angry lesbian who gave the commanders a list of 80 people she accused of being lesbian. About half of these were shown to be heterosexual, but all endured the ordeal of an investigation.[15]

Judith Meade, for example, was a heterosexual whose only violation was accepting comfort after a funeral when she cried on the shoulder of a lesbian. No one even accused her of anything more sexual than that. She was discharged for associating with a lesbian. Some years later, her discharge was overturned, and she is again in the Army although the expense and ordeal of the investigation and discharge were enormous.[16] And there are other examples of heterosexuals snared in witch-hunts, or by wild accusations.[17]

Jack (a pseudonym) was an example of someone who is probably a heterosexual who was snared by a wild accusation. Jack is masculine, even muscular, and he claims to be heterosexual.

His case shows how the prosecution of homosexuality can cause considerable grief whether or not the accused actually engaged in homosexual conduct. The question here is not so much whether Jack is, in fact, heterosexual, but that he could be. Should we make it possible for one soldier to cause all this grief to come to another just by making false accusations?

Jack's accuser was also a sailor. The accuser's story was that one night he was staying as a guest in Jack's mother's house, and Jack, who had been sleeping in another room, got up in the middle of the night, came into the guest's room, and orally copulated him.

Did Jack violate his friend as charged? The friend said yes. Jack said no. What are the possibilities?

One possibility is that Jack did actually copulate his friend, perhaps even sleepwalking into the room to do so. However, in this case, it is curious that his friend did not protest and passively allowed this event to occur. We can conclude, therefore, that there was some degree of consent if the event did occur. One man accepting oral copulation from another man is not likely to be as physically helpless as a woman would be in a similar situation.

But another possibility is that the guest hallucinated the whole thing. We know that the majority of normal people do sometimes awaken in their sleep believing things they have only dreamed to have happened.[18] It is called a hypnopompic hallucination.[19] The guest might have awakened in the night with the dream of being copulated and become convinced that this was the case. Or it could be that the friend made the accusations as a hostile act for reasons that we do not know.

The Navy interrogated Jack and tried to get a confession. When Jack did not confess initially to the NIS, they called in a polygrapher.

Polygraphs, however, are not reliable instruments.[20] They are used, not to collect evidence for legal proceedings, but to assist interrogators whose primary purpose is to exact a confession. And there is evidence that sometimes interrogators are willing to lie to the interrogated in order to elicit that confession.[21] That may have happened in Jack's case.

After the polygraph, Jack was aggressively interrogated by the polygrapher.

"The machine said you lied," he was told.

"No way!" Jack shook his head.

"The machine doesn't lie."

"I didn't lie."

"You're lying right now."

"No."

"Yes, you are. The machine says you lied. You know what you did."

"I did not lie."

In the end, Jack did sign a confession. He says that he signed it merely to get out of the ordeal of the interrogation, and that it was not true. We know that people do sometimes sign confessions that are not true in aggressive interrogations.[22] He signed it, he says, merely to put the matter to rest.

After the confession, Jack did not behave like a guilty person. He told his mother and friends and sought their counsel, and he paid a civilian attorney for assistance.

Perhaps the strangest thing of all is that Jack, after waiting a couple of years, tried to reenlist in the Navy, and the Navy accepted him, even though they had sent him a letter discharging him for homosexuality.

But if scrutiny of this case raises more questions than it answers it is because the Navy was trying to prosecute a person for an action that was surely nothing more than consensual sex when, perhaps, even that was a false charge. Do we feel so strongly that homosexuality must be eradicated that we are willing to risk overprosecuting in this way?

Do Witch-Hunts and Accusations Deter Homosexuality?

Does the practice of aggressively punishing homosexuals discourage homosexuality? Sometimes, at least, it seems to have the opposite effect. Witch-hunts can drive homosexuals underground, causing them to cherish each other's devotion all the more. People who feel persecuted often cling together and the strength of their hurt heals over into mutual bond.

That is what happened in the case of Barbara Baum and Laura Hinkley. Even when Laura felt that visiting Barbara in prison was likely to bring investigations on herself, the knowledge that Barbara had protected her name drove Laura to Barbara, enhancing her devotion and her willingness to risk punishment to protect her.

Also, for the vast majority of homosexuals who are not being prosecuted, the awareness that a few are being prosecuted aggressively, does not appear to be a deterrent. Trying to keep homosexuals from being homosexual does drive some people, such as Karen Stupski, into homosexual conflict and anxiety, but it does not seem to keep them from feeling homosexual desire.

Trying to keep people from feeling homosexual by scaring the wits out of them is about as likely to be successful as trying to keep people anywhere from falling in love just by scaring them with horror stories of divorce. Oh, there will be a few whose romantic vision is weak enough, or whose need for public approval is great enough, that they will suppress their attraction into an inner wound of neurotic confusion and unacknowledged desire, but the healthiest among them will find a way to channel that desire to some homosexual outlet that they can navigate in a culture that tries to outsmart homosexuals.

And so navigating the culture creates a game of mutual intrigue, where the hunted assumes the garb of the heterosexual during the day, and becomes the avowed homosexual in some private space. It is healthier than complete suppression into neurotic loneliness, perhaps, but it is not as healthy, clearly, as the life of those who, like Chris Boadt, find acceptance and love not only from a lover but from the heterosexual world as well.

Tony, you will recall, was married and maintained his homosexual lifestyle by frequent visits to tearooms (hidden rest rooms where homosexuals congregate) and other settings. He is an example of how the homosexual learns to navigate the culture that would lynch him.

Tony was asked if he was aware of the danger of getting caught, if he knew of the witch-hunts. What follows is his response to that question. The version here is abbreviated slightly. Notice that Tony believed that witch-hunts were happening, but that belief did not prevent him from having sexual encounters. In Tony's case, this awareness seems to have made him more cagey, and to choose quick anonymous sex rather than meaningful homosexual relationships. Tony said:

> Witch-hunts, yeah, I was aware of several. . . .
>
> When I was in Illinois, a couple of the women were investigated . . . . One of their friends who claimed that she wasn't a

lesbian, told me that during the investigation the Office of Special Investigations (OSI) agents would quote things that were said between them while they were in the dining hall. Apparently, agents were sitting close enough to them to eavesdrop on their conversations. The women said that they were being followed and harassed every step of the way. They didn't know who to trust. They ended up hating everyone.

A friend of mine in Japan was also investigated. He used to go to gay bars in Okinawa, and believed that OSI agents went to the bars and took pictures of American men who were there. Then they would find out who they were and start investigations. He was one of those men, and four of his friends got caught, too. But they denied that they were gay, said that they were just having a good time in the wrong place, and drinks were cheap. Again, because there was no admission of being gay, and no proof or witnesses, the investigation dragged on and on without conclusion. The . . . agents just kept bringing in more people to question, hoping that they could get more clues to prosecute these men. Eventually, the investigation stopped, but everyone knew about it and that there was no proof, so these guys had to lay low for the remainder of their tours of duty. They were afraid to move; it was really sad how penned up and isolated these guys were. It was also rumored that some of the gay men and women in Okinawa would get married to each other to collect more money for spouse support, and hide their identities from the authorities. I never met anybody who did that, though.

A couple of my friends in Hawaii were also investigated. One of them was scared into sharing names, places, and dates on two others, and that testimony was enough to throw them all out. I felt really bad about that, because two people had their lives disrupted because someone else couldn't keep his mouth shut. I guess that the line of questioning was so intense that it looked like the movies, lights in the eyes, good cop/bad cop, etc.

Although many heterosexuals may have some homosexual desire, it is fantasy to imagine that one could suppress a strong homosexual orientation with a witch-hunt. One might drive it underground where it festers into a wound. One might distort it into an intrigue to outsmart the hunters, but if these cases make anything clear, they tell us that homosexual desire, and perhaps any romantic desire, does not fade in a context of shame. It merely hurts.

THE HOMOSEXUAL WHO OUTWITS THE INTERROGATOR

And, finally, there are the cases of homosexuals who outwit the system only to find themselves psychologically damaged by it anyway.

In Chapter 5, we studied the case of Edward, a 76-year-old man, who today is an inactive, but closeted homosexual. The account in Chapter 5 took his life to the point that he told his wife of his homosexuality and they got a divorce.

What happened next was that Edward, at around 40, was called back into service and he did so well that he began to dream of becoming a general.

Then one day, as he was drinking with a friend in the officers' bar, he observed from a second floor window a homosexual acquaintance, Thompson, traipsing across an empty field laughing and joking with five outlandishly foppish companions.

"For God's sake, look at that mob!" Edward told his heterosexual companion.

"Look at that!" laughed the companion.

Before long this foppish Thompson was standing at Edward's table. "Come join us tonight," Thompson invited. They were going to a film. Secretly Edward recognized the film as homoerotic and he wanted to go. And later, over at the bar, Edward told Thompson to meet him at his apartment.

As Edward left, he climbed into his parked Volkswagen alone, waved to his drinking companion up at the window, and drove off. But on the way he began to worry. Would his drinking companion know?

When he arrived at his apartment, Thompson and his companions were waiting. The apartment was small. There was a bedroom with two single beds, and a living room with a few easy chairs.

Stepping inside, Edward said to Thompson, "I want to talk to you. Come into the bedroom."

Only Edward and Thompson know, of course, exactly what happened in that room, but it took only 15 or so minutes. Edwards says he chastised Thompson. "You're very foolish," Edward says he told him.

Although Edward left for the movie, he got cold feet. Half way there, he made excuses and went back home.

Nothing happened for a few months. Then, one day, a call came into Edward's office. The voice on the phone said, "This is General Fredericks; could you come over for a minute please?"

Crossing the hallway into the General's spacious office, Edward heard the General say, "I'm damn sorry Colonel, and I don't know what the hell this is all about, but I want you to report for an interrogation. Go to building 36."

Edward drove his Volkswagen over to the interrogation building. This had never happened to him before.

It was a small, cheap building, cold in the winter, equipment lying around, metal tables, few people. In a moment, a tall interrogator with rumpled clothes came to meet him. Edward was led into a small office.

The interrogation office contained three metal folding chairs and three separate, small writing tables. The tall rumpled man sat down in one of the chairs, Edward in another, and a shorter heavyset man stood. The first day was cordial and easy.

On the second day, the tall rumpled man began speaking aggressively. He sat accusing Edward of being homosexual while the stockier man paced the room slowly offering sympathetic remarks which the rumpled man disregarded. Edward had heard of this good guy, bad guy technique. It was supposed to make people want to confess.

But in the beginning, it did not work. For example, Edward was shown some phony notes. "A man who visits your house regularly gave us these," the rumpled man said. "They tell us when the two of you have sex." But Edward knew this was not true. They tried other tricks, but Edward was not flustered.

Then they hit on something. They talked of the day that Edward had met his foppish companions at the officers' club. Not only did they know these companions had met Edward at his apartment, but they knew, as well, that Edward had asked Thompson to come, for a few moments, into his bedroom.

Edward was flustered. How could this be?

"What were you doing while you were in your bedroom with Thompson?" the rumpled interrogator pressed.

"I was giving him hell for coming around with this bunch," Edward answered.

"Did you think Thompson was gay?"

"Sometimes I wondered."

"Why didn't you do something about it?"

And so the interrogation went on and on all day.

That night, Edward paced the floor in his apartment. The next day, the rumpled man told Edward he had paced in his apartment. And the accusations, and excuses, began again.

Edward longed to surrender to this accuser, just to say, "Oh, it's true! I am a homosexual!" But he steeled himself. Only a homosexual would be so soft. He would not do it. And the day went on and on.

On the fourth day, Edward began to formulate a plan. He would fake a heart attack. It was a scary thing to do, but he needed a plan.

And on the fifth day, Edward stood up, grabbed his chest, and cried out that he couldn't breathe. "This is terrible!" he gasped as the interrogators rushed him into a car.

"We just want to get at the truth. We don't want to kill you," he heard them say as they raced him to the hospital.

Edward was gasping, but there was no pain in his chest.

What is strange about what happened next is that the doctors covered for him. Did they know of his situation? Was there a group of doctors who were sympathetic to the plight of homosexuals? Edward would never know.

And so the interrogation was over, but one wonders whether such heavy-handed interrogation contributed to Edward's psychological scars as he sits today, with his buddies, a closeted, celibate homosexual at age 76.

SUMMARY

Perhaps the biggest problem with the ban against homosexuals is not that it works so poorly to catch homosexuals, and not that it damages military morale by making men afraid of heterosexual friendship, but that it is so psychologically harmful to a token group of people who get caught in its snare with so little respect for their humanity.

But if the military is to get rid of even a few homosexuals, it has no choice. It is hard to catch homosexuals. One must be cagey and one must be tough, and even then, only those who are most vulnerable, most confused, most conflicted, or most overconfident, are likely to be snared in the net.

And those few, when we catch them and shame them, do not stop homosexuals from being homosexual. How could it be otherwise? Have human beings ever stopped loving and lusting when we tried to shame them?

Chapter 9

How It Would Work in Our Post Cold War Military

Now that America is the world's only superpower, we are using our military forces increasingly: for nonbelligerent missions, to provide disaster relief, to quiet civil disturbances, and, more than ever, to give humanitarian aid. If our military is to be successful in these nontraditional missions, we will need to quiet the masculine imagery in our minds that has been left over from generations of brutal warfare. Psychologically, lifting our ban on gays should help us shift to the new, more tolerant era. Gays, of course, can be as tough and masculine as straights if we need that, but the prejudice that disdains gays (or women, for that matter) is a prejudice that can blind our military leaders, and the soldiers they command, to the strategic usefulness, on occasion, of a gentler touch.

In the spring of 1993, the first American soldiers landed on the quiet, predawn beaches of Somalia. We Americans watched from the safety of our living rooms as the drama unfolded on our television screens. There they were, our soldiers, halfway around the world, slithering on the sand with their weapons strapped to their bodies. They had come to save the starving Somalia children. Many thousands of children had already died, and our soldiers had come to save those who were still at risk.

But it was an odd mission. We had not long thought of our soldiers as saving people's lives. The American military is a fighting machine–the greatest fighting machine the world has ever known–and saving lives involves a little different imagery. But still, here it was, the American military, doing something positive for the hapless people in Somalia.

Then, the next day, in the dawn light, we saw a vision of the graceful Somalis standing on the hill flashing grateful white-toothed smiles and waving enthusiastically at our young soldiers. Through the week, we watched these soldiers as they wove their way through the dirt streets in this foreign land. Gradually their cautious expressions began to soften, and they joked and smiled with the Somali youngsters. These people were glad to see us, and we were glad to help.

Of course, there were those who resented our coming. The children were starving because the clan leaders were fighting over the scarce food. The hungry looters in the bushes could hardly be grateful that we were assisting the other side. But, nevertheless, we were here to help the starving, and surely a modern American soldier, strapped with weapons, would be able to get the food past the barefoot looters who hid in the bushes.

But it was not all that easy. At this writing, 35 Peacekeeper's lives have been sacrificed in Somalia, and 170 Americans have been wounded. The operation has cost us 981 million dollars.[1]

And, unfortunately, we have alienated the people we came to help. Perhaps, it is because we killed many of the Somali people in the process of getting food to the starving. We do not know exactly how many we killed and wounded, but certainly many more Somalis died than did Americans. And so the people who welcomed us from the hillside when we came to their country were angrily dragging the dead body of an American soldier through their streets the next year.

This mission in Somalia, with all its promise and rough spots, is symbolic of our awkward transition into new kinds of military engagements. Now that the cold war is over, America has the luxury of turning its gigantic military establishment into a new kind of institution, one that not only wages wars of destruction and defends American soil and interests against real enemies, but an institution which aids and assists people around the world. That is what America intends to do. And, in the spirit of this new vision, Somalia was a fledgling effort to adapt our war-trained soldiers to the delicate task of saving starving children.

There was much that was right about what we did in Somalia. If our skill was limited, it was limited because our military is burdened with the traditions of conventional war. The soldiers who carried food to Somali children were soldiers trained in our cold war training institutes. If we are to succeed in humanitarian missions such as Somalia, we cannot send a military that thinks with the traditional logic of warfare, in terms of dominating and conquering enemies. For the American military can be deadly, and it is not humanitarian to kill people or to destroy their lands.

It is not even humanitarian to make them conform narrowly to our values. Humanitarian goals require, above all, a respect for difference. And if we are to implement our newfound generosity with the aid of our military, the military culture needs to evolve into one that honors human difference, even fights for the right of people to be different.

How much difference should we respect? A lot. There will always be those who are too different for our culture to tolerate, those who believe in harming or taking from others. But it is the cultural foundation of the American society that we respect differences, even deep religious and value differences, especially when those who are different respect our differences as well.

If we have tolerated a military that imposes rules on people's private and discreet sex lives, it is because we were so threatened by mushroom clouds that we dared not tamper with the system that had protected us. Today's military will battle enemies again, but it is not the same. There is an enormous difference between living in a world with a nuclear arms race between two deadly superpowers, and living in this post cold war world society. We will not abandon our military, of course, but neither will we need to hide behind its skirts.

Acceptance of homosexuals in the military, and acceptance of women, should be a part of the American military's transition to a culture more tolerant of diversity. This is part of what is good about America. Wherever possible, we tolerate and accept diversity, not only diversity of "benign skin color" but religious and values diversity, and the behavior consistent with those diverse values. We only ask that our own difference be accepted as well.

THE PROS AND CONS OF A SHIFT IN MILITARY PHILOSOPHY

There is much to be gained if the military does adapt to its new role. There are many starving and wounded people in the world, and the American military is uniquely equipped to move enormous quantities of foods, supplies, and materials when needed by humanitarian missions.

Moreover, we will be doing our economy a favor if we find new tasks for our military.[2] Back in the 1980s when there were much bigger dangers to threaten us, we expanded our military to be fully 10 percent of our national employment.[3] Drastically cutting its budget now means massive job losses[4] that can inflict structural damage upon our national economy. The humanitarian missions that the world seems to need can create a more favorable economic environment.[5]

But this shift of focus to humanitarian interventions will require us to rethink the philosophy of our military culture.[6] Until very recently, international policy did not allow other countries to engage in humanitarian interventions. International policy during the cold war protected the sovereignty of the state over the individual rights of its citizens.[7] That cold war policy told us, "In international law the state is clearly sovereign and has the ultimate legal right to say what should be done within its jurisdiction."[8] This even gave states the right to kill its citizens or allow them to starve. We could not intervene.

But things have changed, and it is now possible to engage in humanitarian missions. Since the passing of the cold war,[9] both the United Nations and NATO have reinterpreted international law to allow humanitarian interventions,[10] and America has been increasingly involved in nontraditional military missions ever since.[11] "All the branches of the American armed services are pondering how extensively America should be involved in humanitarian interventions which do not involve permission of the host governments."[12]

American readiness to engage in humanitarian peacekeeping missions stretches across party lines. President Bush sent U.S. troops to Somalia with Clinton's blessing. And we will continue to engage in such humanitarian missions for it seems to us that "U.N. peacekeeping holds the promise to resolve many of this era's conflicts."[13]

But again, these new missions require new skills and a different philosophy. Even conservative military theorist Charlie Moskos has told us the success of most of these operations has depended on "administrative and logistical skills, not to mention health-care and social-work skills, . . . [much more] than tactical insight, marksmanship, or courage under fire."[14]

The question now is whether our traditional military values that were intended to make us victorious over a hostile enemy can evolve sufficiently for us to be successful in this new kind of mission.

CAN THE MILITARY CHANGE?

Can the military change enough to take advantage of the opportunity of humanitarian intervention without making a mockery of our international policy? The evidence we have examined in this book suggests that it can change, and that this change will be fostered by official tolerance of self-identified homosexuals. The military is likely to change because it needs to change.

In the past, the military has changed when it needed to change. When we needed more soldiers, it integrated the military and accepted blacks, and then later, when we needed more soldiers again, it accepted women.[15]

The kind of change we need now is not just in the number of soldiers, but in the mindset of the military. We need a military that is more respectful of diversity, more respectful of different value systems, even a military less inclined to interpret all missions in terms of force. And we need a military less afraid of abandoning its tradition when that tradition no longer serves our national purpose.

What is at stake in accepting homosexuals in the military is not loss of cohesion and morale. As we have seen in every case in which homosexuals have been accepted, they have personally managed their identities in a way that does not cause disruption, mostly by disclosing their identities cautiously and discreetly. When people meet self-identified homosexuals, they discover that they are less personally objectionable than they had imagined them to be. It is possible for heterosexuals to have friendships with homosexuals, to be their companions, without sexual involvement or even sexual innuendos. There is every reason, therefore, to presume that we could lift the ban against homosexuals without disruption to cohesion and morale, and no reason to maintain the ban but prejudice.

What is at stake is the false belief that a person's sexual orientation is a malignant and critically important fact about that person, that "Sexual orientation is . . . the most profound of human behavioral characteristics."[16] What is critically important about human beings, at least in this modern age, is not their sexual orientation but their ability to respect and honor each other's differences.

HOMOSEXUALS IN THE NEW MILITARY

Our military leaders have opposed lifting the ban on the grounds that homosexuals will invade the privacy of heterosexuals and that they will disrupt military morale, but a review of the most relevant data tells us otherwise.

When gay soldiers have been reinstated, their colleagues have not rebelled. Just as Keith Meinhold and Justin Elzie were reinstated without causing their colleagues to rebel, so we can expect other troops to adapt to homosexuals among them in the vast majority of cases.

Moreover, the evidence tells us that most homosexuals will not disclose their identities casually to heterosexuals,[17] and so the military will not change very dramatically as a result of dropping the ban. Homosexuals will be there, as before, and, as before, they will be discreet about who they are. They are likely to be particularly discreet with people whom they judge to be uncomfortable with homosexuality. Lifting the ban will protect homosexuals from court-martial, from arbitrary discharges, and from some level of harassment, but it will not protect them from personal prejudices. They will have to manage their identities as they do now in civilian life to protect themselves, as best they can, from that.

When gay people do tell others that they are homosexual, they are likely to do so with dignity and tact, in a way that engenders the respect of heterosexuals, not their contempt.[18] In fact, many heterosexuals will find that they are surprisingly comfortable being friendly with homosexuals, that gay people are much more like straight people than they had expected, that it is possible to enjoy the companionship of homosexuals, to feel care and concern for homosexuals, and to trust them–and that it is possible to do these things without becoming homosexual as a consequence.

Nevertheless, some cultural changes will eventually begin to happen in the military. These changes will be particularly constructive for homosexuals, who will become much less vulnerable to unfair and arbitrary treatment that can do much to destroy their lives. It will help them to find meaningful and honest relationships rather than merely engage in flurries of fleeting secret sexual encounters.

And it will promote changes that will be generally positive for heterosexuals, as well. Presently, it is possible for heterosexuals to be mistakenly discharged for homosexuality. That would no longer be possible. People would no longer bring grief on themselves for letting it be known that they have friends who are homosexual. Moreover, it would no longer be possible for women, or men, to be pressured to perform heterosexually just to prove that they are not gay. Gradually, perhaps, being called a faggot or a lesbian will have less sting and, since heterosexuals can be called these things as well as homosexuals, this, too, should be positive for heterosexuals.[19]

As to concern about being embarrassed around homosexuals in situations of toileting or undress, heterosexuals are likely to learn here, too, that their fears are much worse than the reality. Just as we all learn, to our surprise, that modesty is typically protected by a widely practiced etiquette of disregard, so heterosexuals will learn that homosexuals are quite willing and able to practice this etiquette in their presence. Homosexuals are not likely to leer at heterosexuals anywhere, but they are much less likely to do so in the military than in civilian life, for soldiers are much more accountable for their discourteous behavior than are civilians.[20]

Most heterosexuals know little about homosexuality, and what they know is based on fiction. When they meet people who call themselves homosexual, the myths they have accepted will start to fade. When people learn more about homosexuality, they will learn that Colin Powell was wrong when he implied that homosexuality was a malignant behavioral characteristic that is likely to cause straight people to feel their privacy is invaded and generally disrupt military morale.

WHAT CAN BE DONE TO FACILITATE THE CHANGE

There are, however, things that both straights and gays can do to facilitate a successful transition to a military that does not discriminate against gays.

Straights can learn about gay people so that they do not think about them stereotypically. Although our myths about gays may make them seem to be birds of a feather, they vary as widely as one can imagine. They can be as wise as Socrates in ancient Greece, or the genius philosopher Ludwig Wittgenstein in modern times. And they can be foolish and make mistakes, just as straight people can. They can be charming, or unpleasant, masculine or feminine, beautiful or ugly. They can also be friends and fight for the right of straight people to be straight. Although a few might behave in ways that straights will find offensive, they are no more likely to do so than straights. Remember, as we have seen, the evidence is that men who rape and assault other men are likely to be heterosexual, raping and assaulting in an effort to dominate and control.

There are things that gays, too, can do to facilitate this transition to an era that no longer needs to ban gays from the military. First, gays can disclose that they are gay with thoughtfulness as to what this means to the listener, recognizing that it is natural in our society for people to be a little apprehensive about what it means to be gay. Gays need to make their disclosure in a setting that assures the listener that the disclosure is not a sexual or romantic invitation.

If the disclosure is not confused with a sexual invitation, then it will become a source of pride and dignity. For example, the discreet behavior in showers that seems to a closeted gay like a lie that hides the private homosexual truth, now becomes a dignified form of etiquette that gays use with people believed to be straight. It is part of a show of mutual respect. It is not enforceable as an etiquette, and it does not imply that the gay person is blind in these settings. Instead, it is merely a graceful veneer that is used to make everyone as comfortable as possible.

SUMMARY AND CONCLUSION

American men today are struggling to free themselves from the straitjacket of our psychologically repressive society, for ours is a civilization that tames men's passions and blunts the spirit of adventure, leaves them sitting numb and passive behind their desks, or methodically screwing yet one more bolt on just another engine.

Ours is a culture that leaves many men struggling with the sense of meaninglessness in their lives.

And for American men, the military has always been a handy way out of this civilized straitjacket. For what is wilder than strapping a weapon across one's chest and sailing out across the seas to right the wrongs of the world? If combat brings terror, and it surely does, the energy of terror combined with belief in the value of the mission, at least, has made many soldiers feel alive.

There was a charm in our grandfather's military–especially the old John Wayne military–when everyone knew who the enemy was. It was an institution that guided each confused son through the mysteries of manhood, left him with stories that he would never tell, a V.A. loan on the family house, and maybe a medal or two to show his own sons. It was like Boy Scouts only much, much better, because the victories were important for everyone and the bullets were real.

Is it any wonder that a man who has gone through this military passage into manhood might be reluctant to allow this grand old institution to evolve and change? Yet all but the most sentimental know that this grandfather's military cannot be faked. Whatever was good about the old military institution was possible only because its battles were real, that the victories made the world a better world.

What is real today is different from what was real then. The bushmen in Somalia may shoot real bullets, but they are not real enemies. Their power, their training, does not qualify them to be real enemies of the American military.

The soldiers who fight them as enemies are fighting their grandfather's battles. They have not understood that they come to these shores as friends, as liberators, friends even of the people who shoot at them. Killing these people is no more honorable than shooting the annoying little boy who steals into the backyard and takes apples from the apple tree.

Perhaps, another world is dawning. President Bush spoke of the "New World Order." It is the post cold war society. There are new rules here. We Americans have never known a world like this. We have all been raised in a world full of angry enemies. We are a people who learned, as children, to hide under our desks to protect ourselves from the biggest, most fearsome weapons our minds could fathom, bombs so destructive that they could destroy the very earth we walked on many times over. We are the generation who grew up with the terrible vision of a mushroom cloud over our heads.

Who would have ever thought we would have mourned the passing of that world? But we do. It was a simple world of good and evil, and a world without such common rules confuses us, we who have grown up under the fear of the mushroom cloud.

The new world is still hidden behind the fog of our tomorrow, but it is possible to discern some of its shape: It will be a world vastly complicated by the fact that we have no formidable enemy, and until we understand what it is like not to have such an enemy, we will feel frustrated, over and over, by the fact that our many battles never seem to end the way battles should, by a simple victory or defeat.

But what is most important about this new world order is that we will have the ability, more than we could ever have imagined, to make choices to enhance what is so good about our culture. And, now, freed from the urgency of a threatening enemy, we can redesign the institution that protects our lives by making it more consistent with our national values.

If no dominant enemy will truly threaten our lives, then we have the choice more than ever to make our military a more democratic force, to make it more consistent with the values that form the foundation of the world's only remaining superpower. To choose otherwise is to try to anchor ourselves in a world that exists no longer, like middle-aged folk wearing hippie T-shirts and bell-bottom pants.

And a military that accepts homosexuals will be a good military. There may need to be a period of adjustment, a period in which those who have never known a homosexual learn that they are not freaks, learn they are human beings who struggle, like the rest of us, in their relationships to find happiness.

It is no longer right for us to blind ourselves to the truth about human nature, the unspeakable truth that many people are attracted to and fall in love with their own sex. If this is the way humans are, then we can manage our lives with the awareness of that fact. Pretending there is no homosexual feeling has not made it disappear. It has merely made us hypocrites. Our soldiers do not need to be protected from these simple truths. Letting this truth be known is not likely to make them homosexuals. If it is hard to stamp out homosexuality, then it will be equally hard to stamp out heterosexual desire.

But it will help to create a world in which those with hidden homosexual feelings can tell someone about it. It will help many people find a life of dignity and acceptance, and many of these people will identify, eventually, as heterosexual.

For our policy of pretending there are no homosexuals is a festering wound in our culture. Millions of people ache from this problem, many whom you know and care about. Telling the world that they are good enough to be in your military, that you will let them give their lives for their country, that you will trust them to be honorable with your sons and daughters, that you will love and respect them if they are your sons and daughters, will begin to heal the ugly wound of our hypocrisy.

Notes

CHAPTER 1

1. Shilts gives evidence that the military actually eases up on its antihomosexual rules when it needs people to fight. Shilts, R. What's fair in love and war. *Newsweek,* 1993, 121(5).

2. Kramer explains President Clinton's policies on gays in the military. Kramer, M. Don't settle for hypocrisy. *Time*, 1993, 142(4), 41.

3. Benecke, M. M. & Dodge, K. S. Lesbian baiting as sexual harassment: Women in the military. In Warren Blumenfeld (Ed.), *Homophobia: How We All Pay the Price*. Boston: Beacon Press, 1992; Benecke, M. M. & Dodge, K. S. Military women in nontraditional job fields: Casualties of the Armed Forces' war on homosexuals. *Harvard Women's Law Journal*, 1990, 13, 215-250.

4. *We hold these truths to be self-evident, that all men are created equal, that they are endowed by their Creator with certain unalienable Rights, that among these are Life, Liberty, and the pursuit of Happiness.–That to secure these Rights, Governments are instituted among Men, deriving their just Powers from the Consent of the Governed.–That whenever any Form of Government becomes destructive of these Ends, it is the Right of the People to alter or to abolish it, and to institute new Government, laying its Foundation on such Principles, and organizing its Powers in such form, as to them shall seem most likely to effect their Safety and Happiness.*

5. Towell, P. Military dismissals. *Congressional Quarterly Weekly Report*, February 6, 1993, 51(6), 274.

6. Personal communication with Allan Bérubé, 12/04/93. Bérubé, A. *Coming Out under Fire: The History of Gay Men and Women in World War Two*. New York: The Free Press, 1990.

7. Bayer, R. *Homosexuality and American Psychiatry: The Politics of Diagnosis*. New York: Basic Books, 1981.

8. See: Office of the Secretary of Defense Working Group Memorandum, 8 June 1993, "Recommended DoD Homosexual Policy Outline."

9. A version of this expressed by the judge in the case of *Steffan v. Dick Cheney,* 1991. In his opinion, Judge Gasch said:

> In the Military Establishment and for those who attend the Naval Academy, the policy of separating men and women while sleeping, bathing and "using the bathroom" seeks to maintain the privacy of officers and the enlisted when in certain states of undress. The embarrassment of being naked between the sexes is prevalent because sometimes the other is con-

> sidered to be a sexual object. The quite rational assumption in the Navy is that with no one present who has a homosexual orientation, men and women alike can undress, sleep, bathe, and use the bathroom without fear or embarrassment that they are being viewed as sexual objects. (*Steffan v. Cheney,* Civil action No. 88-3669-Og, U.S. District Court, District of Columbia, Dec. 09, 1991, pp. 27-28.)

A similar statement of the privacy argument was made by Charles Moskos, a professor at Northwestern University, chairman of the Inter-University Seminar on Armed Forces and Society and author of the recent book *The Military–More Than Just a Job?* Moskos said:

> Sex between [military] service members does undermine order, discipline and morale. So does invasion of sexual privacy. That is why the military separates the living quarters of men and women. Even in field conditions, the privacy of men and women is maintained to the maximum degree possible. Nowhere in our society are the sexes forced to endure situations of undress in front of each other. Should we have "empirical research" on the effects on military efficiency of mixed male/female bathing? Most women–and many men–dislike being stripped of all privacy before the opposite sex. Similarly, most heterosexual men and women dislike being exposed to homosexuals of their own sex. If feelings of privacy for women are respected regarding privacy from men, then we must respect those of straights with regard to gays. (The quotation is excerpted from a newspaper commentary by Moskos. [cf., Moskos, C. Why banning homosexuals still makes sense. *Navy Times*, March 30, 1992].)

Also, see a similar argument presented by Colin Powell on page 49 of Chapter 2.

It should be noted that before making the privacy argument for banning homosexuals, Moskos dismissed the persuasiveness of the AIDS argument on the grounds that "HIV testing in the military makes the health argument untenable. Further, what if a cure or prevention for AIDS were to be discovered tomorrow? Is the way then clear for homosexuals in the military?" And he dismissed the argument that homosexuals were susceptible to blackmail saying, "If one's sexual proclivities do not have to be concealed, they can hardly be the basis for extortion."

10. National Defense Research Institute. *Sexual Orientation and U.S. Military Personnel Policy: Options and Assessment.* Prepared for the Office of the Secretary of Defense, MR-323-OSD, RAND, 1993.

11. Towell, P. Military dismissals. *Congressional Quarterly Weekly Report,* February 6, 1993, 51(6), 274.

12. Navy secretary quits in 1991 convention sex-abuse furor. *Facts on File* July 2, 1992, 52(2693), 484; Naval operations: Sexual harassment. (Sexual harassment case resulting from Tailhook convention.) *Economist*, July 4, 1992,

324(7766), A29; Report details abuses at 1991 naval aviators' convention. (Tailhook scandal) (includes related article), *Facts on File,* April 29, 1993, 53(2735), 305.

13. Seifert, R. Constructions of masculinity–The military as a discursive power. *Argument*, 1992 34(6), 859-872; Donald, R. R. Masculinity and machismo in Hollywood's war films. In Steve Craig (Ed.), *Men, Masculinity, and the Media,* Newbury Park: Sage Publications, 1992.

14. For a very partial listing consider: Edwards, G. R. A critique of creationist homophobia. In Richard Hasbany (Ed.), *Homosexuality and Religion*. Binghamton, NY: The Haworth Press, 1989, 95-118; Heron, A. (Ed.) *Towards a Quaker View of Sex*. London: Friends Home Service Committee, 1963; McNeil, J. *The Church and the Homosexual*. Kansas City, MO: Sheed, Andrews, and McMeel, 1976; Gramick, J. Rome speaks, the Church responds. In Jeannine Gramick & Pat Furey (Eds.), *The Vatican and Homosexuality*. New York: Crossroad, 1988, 93-104; Ashley, B. M. Compassion and sexual orientation. In Gramick & Pat Furey (Eds.), *The Vatican and Homosexuality*. New York: Crossroad, 1988, 105-111; Cooper, A. No longer invisible: Gay and lesbian Jews build a movement. In R. Hasbany (Ed.), *Homosexuality and Religion*. Binghamton, NY: Harrington Park Press, 1989; Nugent, R. & Gramick, J. Homosexuality: Protestant, Catholic and Jewish issues: A fishbone tale. In R. Hasbany (Ed.), *Homosexuality and Religion*. Binghamton, NY: Harrington Park Press, 1989; Boswell, J. *Christianity, Social Tolerance, and Homosexuality*. Chicago: University of Chicago Press, 1980; Jones, H. K. *Toward a Christian Understanding of the Homosexual*. New York: Associated Press, 1966; Scanzoni, L. *Is the Homosexual My Neighbor? Another Christian View*. San Francisco: Harper & Row, 1978.

15. Chandler, R. *The Times* poll: Americans like Pope but challenge doctrine. *Los Angeles Times*, 23 August 1987, p. 20. Cited in Gramick, J. Rome speaks, the Church responds. In Jeannine Gramick & Pat Furey (Eds.), *The Vatican and Homosexuality*. New York: Crossroad, 1988.

16. This conclusion is based on the author's conversation with several key people who monitor personnel policy for the Canadian military. It is based in part on a conversation on 06/18/93 with Ron Dickenson, Acting Director of Personnel–Policy 2 at the National Defense Headquarters in Ottawa, Canada. Dickenson indicated that no one has asked to resign from the military because of homosexuals, or submitted a grievance saying they do not want to be in the service because of the removal of the ban against homosexuals, or in any other way that can be detected, caused a disruption in the smooth running of the military. This information was also confirmed by George Logan, the official whom Ron Dickenson replaced in June of 1993, and on August 17, 1993, it was confirmed by Frank Pinch, PhD, who is the recently retired Director General, Personnel Policy Division, who indicated he was still in contact with those members of the Canadian forces who would know if there was any disruption due to the new policy which dropped the ban against homosexuals in the Canadian military. As of August 17, 1993, therefore, the lifting of the ban against homosexuals in the Cana-

dian military had lasted approximately ten months without a disruptive incident. Also see: Fisher, L. Armed and gay. *Maclean's,* May 24, 1993, 106(21), 14-16.

17. The military report on homosexuals given to Secretary Aspin, July 1993, suggested that the legal policy of foreign countries accepting homosexuals is made workable because in these countries "few servicemembers openly declare their homosexuality due to fears of baiting, bashing, and negative effects to their careers." Office of the Secretary of Defense Working group memorandum, 8 June 1993, "Recommended DoD Homosexual Policy Outline."

18. Akin, Scott R. & Gallagher, John. Class struggle. *Advocate*, March 9, 1993 (2 pages).

19. Henry III, William. A mindset under siege. *Time*, November 30, 1992, 40-42.

20. See for example: President Clinton spends too much time on gay rights say a majority of Americans in a *U.S. News & World Report* Poll. *U.S. News & World Report Press Release.* Saturday, June 26, 1993; Herek, G. M. Beyond "homophobia": A social psychological perspective on attitudes toward lesbians and gay men. *Journal of Homosexuality*, 1984, 10, 1-21; Herek, G. M. Stigma, prejudice and violence against lesbians and gay men. In J. C. Gonsiorek & J. D. Weinrich (Eds.), *Homosexuality: Research Implications for Public Policy.* Newbury Park, CA: Sage, 1991, 60-80; Schneider, W. & Lewis, I. A. The straight story on homosexuality and gay rights. *Public Opinion*, February/March, 1984, 7, 16-20, 59-60; Saad, L. & McAneny, L. Americans deeply split over ban on gays in military. *The Gallup Poll Monthly*, February, 1993, 6-11.

21 Dunkle, J. H. & Francis, P. L. The role of facial masculinity/femininity in the attribution of homosexuality. *Sex Roles*, 1990, 23(3-4), 157-167; Addison, W. E. Beardedness as a factor in perceived masculinity. *Perceptual & Motor Skills*, June 1989, 68(3, Pt. 1), 921-922.

22. Dunkle, J. H. & Francis, P. L. The role of facial masculinity/femininity in the attribution of homosexuality. *Sex Roles*, 1990, 23(3-4), 157-167.

CHAPTER 2

1. Military sociologist Charles Moskos argues, for example, "Nowhere in our society are the sexes forced to endure situations of undress in front of each other. . . . If feelings of privacy for women are respected regarding privacy from men, then we must respect those of straights with regard to gays" and Judge Gasch argues "The embarrassment of being naked between the sexes is prevalent because sometimes the other is considered to be a sexual object. The quite rational assumption in the Navy is that with no one present who has a homosexual orientation, men and women alike can undress, sleep, bathe, and use the bathroom without fear or embarrassment that they are being viewed as sexual objects." Moskos, C. Why banning homosexuals still makes sense. *Navy Times*, March 30, 1992; *Steffan v. Cheney,* Civil action No. 88-3669-Og, U.S. District Court, District of Columbia, Dec. 09, 1991, pp. 27-28.

2. See Stephens, W. N. *A Cross-Cultural Study of Modesty and Obscenity and Pornography*. Vol. 3., Washington, DC: U.S. Printing Office, 1971; Antoun, R. T. On the modesty of women in Arab Muslim Villages: A study of the accommodation of traditions. *American Anthropologist*, 1968, 70(4), 671-697; Crawley. E. Nudity and dress. In M. E. Roach & J. B. Eicher (Eds.), *Dress, Adornment, and the Social Order.* New York: John Wiley & Sons, 1965, 46-49; Felding, W. J. *Strange Customs of Courtship and Marriage*. New York: Garden City Publishing, 1942.

3. Goldman and Goldman studied 838 children between the ages of five and 15 from Australia, Canada, Sweden, the United Kingdom, and the United States. They found the North American subjects the most prudish and the Australians the least. Nevertheless, by 13 years old, most children (53 percent) answered that children in warm countries should wear clothes. Smith, Moore, Armonk, Weinberg, Whiting, and Child, and Sears et al. have all independently found Americans to be more prudish than most others of European backgrounds. Goldman, R. J. & Goldman, J. D. Children's perceptions of clothes and nakedness: A cross-national study. *Genetic Psychology Monographs*, 1981, 104(2)9, 163-185; Smith, H. A modest test of cross-cultural differences in sexual modesty, embarrassment and self-disclosure. *Qualitative Sociology*, 1980, 3(3), 223-241; Moore, Barrington. *Privacy, Studies in Social and Cultural History.* Armonk, NY: M. E. Sharpe, Inc., 1984; Weinberg, M. Sexual modesty, social meanings, and the nudist camp. *Social Problems*, 1964, 12, 311-318; Whiting, John W. M. & Child, I. L. *Child Training and Personality: A Cross-Cultural Study.* New Haven: Yale University Press, 1953. pp. 48, 73; Sears, R., Maccoby, E., & Levin, H. *Patterns of Child Rearing*. Evanston, IL: Row, Peterson, 1957.

4. Malchow, C. W. *The Sexual Life*. St. Louis: C.V. Mosby Co., 1923, pp. 60-61; See also Walters, R. G. *Primers for Prudery: Sexual Advice to Victorian America*, Englewood Cliffs, NJ: Prentice-Hall, 1974; Rugoff, M. *Prudery and Passion: Sexuality in Victorian America.* New York: G. P. Putnam's Sons, 1971.

5. Muir, F. *An Irreverent and Almost Complete Social History of the Bathroom.* New York: Stein & Day, 1983.

6. Perin, N. *Dr. Bowdler's Legacy. A History of Expurgated Books in England & America.* New York: Atheneum, 1969.

7. Wilcox, D. *Ethical Marriage*, pp. 56-57 Cited in Haller, J. S. & Haller, R. M., *The Physician and Sexuality in Victorian America.* Urbana: University of Illinois Press, 1974.

8. Coben, S. *Rebellion against Victorianism: The Impetus for Cultural Change in 1920s America.* New York: Oxford University Press, 1991; Ditzion, S. *Marriage, Morals, and Sex in America.* New York: W. W. Norton, 1969.

9. For a popular and interesting account of the rise and fall of Victorian prudishness see Coleman, Emily & Edwards, B. *Body Liberation. Freeing Your Body for Greater Self-Acceptance, Health, and Sexual Satisfaction*. Los Angeles: J. P. Tarcher, 1977; For a legal reference see Shils, E. B. Privacy: Its constitution and vicissitudes. *Law and Contemporary Problems*, 1966, 31, 281-306.

10. The quote is from Stone, but many other authors have commented on the pre-Victorian liberalism. It appears, even, that the Victorians were reacting against the increased liberalism of their parents, whose childhoods were touched by the still active radical spirit of the American and French revolutions. Stone, L. *The Family, Sex and Marriage in England, 1500-1800: The Abridged Edition*, New York: Harper Torchbooks, 1979, p. 394; D'Emilio and Freedman also talk of the pre-Victorian liberalism regarding sexual matters. D'Emilio, J. & Freedman, E. B. *Intimate Matters: A History of Sexuality in America.* New York: Harper & Row, 1988, p. 41-42; Rugoff, M. *Prudery and Passion.* New York: G. P. Putnam's Sons, 1971, p. 39-40.

11. A recent survey of Americans' comfort with nudity that was reported in the *Economist* showed that the public and government are increasingly comfortable with nudity in America. Topfree, bottomfree. *Economist,* 1992, August 15, 324(7772), A19.

12. It was Buss's work that suggested the importance of ridicule and teasing in the indoctrination of modesty embarrassment. Buss, A. H. *Self-Consciousness and Social Anxiety,* San Francisco: W. H. Freeman, 1980.

13. Parke, R. D. & Sawin, D. B. Children's privacy in the home: Developmental, ecological and child-rearing determinants. *Environment and Behavior,* 1979, 11(1), 87-104.

14. The synopsis of the childhood development of modesty is based on Parke's study, (op. cit.) and also the following studies: Rosenfeld, A., Siegel-Gorelick, B., Haavik, D., Duryea, M., Wenegrat, A., Martin, J., & Bailey, R. Parental perceptions of children's modesty: A cross-sectional survey of ages two to ten years. *Psychiatry,* 1984, 47, 351-365; Buss, A. H., Iscoe I., & Buss, E. H., The development of embarrassment. *The Journal of Psychology,* 1979, 103, 227-230; Maccoby, E. & Jacklin, C. *The Psychology of Sex Differences.* Stanford, California: Stanford University Press, 1974. The development of modesty appears to happen at a similar age in Britain. See: Newson, J. & Newson, E. *Four Years Old in an Urban Community,* London: Allen & Unwin, 1968; For an example of an article guiding parents in the art of modesty instructions, see: Segal, Julius & Segal, Zelda. "Standards on Nudity," *Parents Magazine,* May, 1990, 65(5), 211. (Guidelines for children) (five and six year olds).

15. Yeazell explains how the culture of feminine bodily modesty was enhanced by the novels of the Victorian period. These novels depicted the modest woman as particularly desirable. Yeazell, R. B. *Fictions of Modesty: Women and Courtship in the English Novel.* Chicago: University of Chicago Press, 1991.

16. Ellis, H. *Studies in the Psychology of Sex.* (especially "The Evolution of Modesty") New York: Random House, 1942 (first published in 1905).

17. In addition to describing the comfort traditional Japanese felt toward nudity with the opposite sex, Down explains that nudity in Japan often has a different meaning than it does for Westerners. In Japan it is often sentimental and evokes feelings about family and motherhood. Down, J. F. Nudity in Japanese visual media: A cross-cultural observation. *Archives of Sexual Behavior,* 1990, 19(6), 583-594.

18. Asayama, S. Sexual behavior in Japanese students: Comparisons for 1974, 1960, and 1952. *Archives of Sexual Behavior,* 1976, 5(5), 371-390.

19. For a colorful description of the development of etiquette in the court society of Louis XIV, see Elias, N. *The Court Society*, Edmund Jephcott (trans.). New York: Pantheon Books, 1983.

20. Hill's nineteenth century etiquette manual described how the word etiquette originated in the court of Louis XIV. Little invitations called *etiquettes* were printed with rules of conduct on the back. The only people invited to the court were aristocrats, but before long, the rules on the "etiquettes" were conformed to by commonfolk as well. Hill wrote, "After America emerged from the violent turmoil of the Revolution and later survived the upheaval of the Civil War, the people of the young nation settled down to the business of living normal lives, educating themselves and improving their lot in life. Refinement and good living became of primary importance, not just to the rich, but to every American. Books of instruction for all social situations were devoured by the ambitious population." The introduction of modesty as a sign of aristocracy might also have been fostered by the poverty of the day. Lower class families often lived in the same room and slept in the same bed. Baynes discusses this situation in Scotland in the early part of the twentieth century. *Hills Manual: Never Give a Lady a Restive Horse–a 19th Century Handbook of Etiquette–Selections reprinted without change from the pages of Professor Thomas E. Hill's Justly Famous Volumes on 19th Century Rules of Etiquette*. New York: The World Publishing Co., 1969. Trevor-Roper tells us that the new etiquette in the court of Louis XIV replaced a coarseness of manners that had existed before that time. Trevor-Roper, H. R. *The Age of Louis XIV and Other Selected Writings*. New York: Washington Square Press, 1963, especially pp. 124-125; Baynes, J. *Morale: A Study of Men and Courage*. New York: Frederick Praeger, 1967; Coleman, Emily & Edwards, B. *Body Liberation. Freeing Your Body for Greater Self-Acceptance, Health, and Sexual Satisfaction*. Los Angeles: J. P. Tarcher, 1977.

21. The Victorian authors Haines & Yaggy tell us, "The union of gentleness of manners with firmness of mind are noticeable in the true gentleman." And Victorian author Weaver says, ". . . The gentleman and lady are not natural products, but human beings trained to the courtesies and amenities of good society. They are common human beings educated into the fine forms and spirit of high and noble intercourse." Haines, T. L. & Yaggy, L. W. *The Royal Path of Life: Aims and Aids to Success and Happiness*. Chicago: Western Publishing House, 1882, 357-362; Weaver, G. S. *The Heart of the World or Home and Its Wide Work*, 18th edition. Chicago: Elder Publishing Co., 1882, p. 288.

22. See, for example, Armstrong, who said, "Now it has appeared to me that the popular idea of education is altogether too narrow and limited, and thus an art like 'manners' receives too little attention in comparison with its importance. The cultivation of good behavior, proper conduct under all circumstances, style, politeness, noble action and bearing–in a word, manners–is the greatest part of education, and is in fact the end to be aimed at." Armstrong, R. O. *Education and Manners. Self-Culture,* 1898, Vol. 8, 241-242.

23. Laslett, B. The family as a public and private institution: An historical perspective. *Journal of Marriage and the Family*, 1973, 35, 480-492.

24. Muir, F. *An Irreverent and Almost Complete Social History of the Bathroom*. New York: Stein & Day, 1983.

25. Victorian physician William J. Robinson tells his readers that nothing more damning can happen to a young woman than to get pregnant before she is married, and he blames her parents for her great misfortune. What is so striking is the Victorian confidence that such misfortune could not happen to his own daughter. One imagines how horrified he would have been if it had. Robinson said,

> Suppose you are the parents of a girl to whom a misfortune has happened. I admit it is a misfortune, a catastrophe. Probably the greatest catastrophe that, under our present social system, can happen to an unmarried young woman. What are you going to do? Are you going to disgrace her–incidentally disgracing yourselves–are you going to kick her out of the house, condemning her to a suicide's grave, or to a life that is often worse than death? Or are you going to stand by her in her dark hours, to shield her, to surround her with a wall of protection against a cruel and wantonly inquisitive world, and thus earn her eternal gratitude, and put her on the path of self-improvement and useful social work? Which shall it be? But before you decide, kindly bear in mind that your girl is not entirely to blame; that some of the blame lies with you. If she had been properly brought up, this would not have happened. I know such a thing could never happen in my household. (273-274)

Robinson, W. J. *Woman: Her Sex and Love Life*. New York: J. J. Little and Ives, Co., 1917, 273-274.

26. Harris reports the statistics on the Victorian birthrate. The Victorian era brought a drastic decline in the number of children a woman had. Before this era, the average woman bore 7.04 children. In 1900 the average woman had 3.56 children. Lewin tells us that this drop in birthrate happened without mechanical or chemical contraceptives, that is by abstinence. Harris, B. *Beyond Her Sphere: Women and the Professions in American History*. Westport, CT: Greenwood Press, 1978, p. 54, cited in Lewin, M. The Victorians: The psychologists and psychic birth control. In M. Lewin (Ed.), *In the Shadow of the Past: Psychology Portrays the Sexes*. New York: Columbia University Press, 1974.

27. The influential Victorian sexologist, Krafft-Ebing, wrote, "Women . . . if physically and mentally normal, and properly educated, have but little sensual desire." (p. 14). Krafft-Ebing, R. von. *Psychopathia Sexualis: A Medico-Forensic Study*. New York: Pioneer Publications, Inc., 1939.

28. Both Weaver (1882) and Haines & Yaggy (1882), for example have made this point. Weaver said, "Woman's worth to man comes partly from her strong home instincts. She anchors him and holds him from roving, keeps him at one place and one thing, civilizes him and applies his great powers to civilizing uses. He, left to himself, is a barbarian; she inclines to civilization, loves her home, locality and country, and so holds him to her strong impulses and devotes him to an order of life that founds society and promotes civilization. This quality in woman shows that man is not complete without woman. 'It is not good for him to

be alone.' He is not at his best when alone. She utilizes, completes and puts him in such orderly ways as best to use his power and promote his higher interests. Man need not hesitate to acknowledge his indebtedness to woman in the higher and better things of his life, because the facts in the case are becoming clear to all thoughtful minds" (p. 37). Haines explains that good women assume this power to control their men, and complains that lesser women frequently are unable to assert this power. He does not complain that men do not have the power to control themselves. Haines says, "Young women ought to hold steady moral sway over their male associates, so strong as to prevent them from becoming such lawless rowdies. Why do they not? Because they do not possess sufficient force of character. They have not sufficient resolution and energy of purpose. Their virtue is not vigorous. Their moral wills not resolute." Haines, T. L. & Yaggy, L. W., *The Royal Path of Life: Aims and Aids to Success and Happiness.* Chicago: Western Publishing House, 1882. Weaver, G. S. *The Heart of the World or Home and Its Wide Work*, 18th edition. Chicago: Elder Publishing Co., 1882.

29. Marcus, S. *The Other Victorians: A Study of Sexuality and Pornography in Mid-Nineteenth-Century England.* New York: Basic Books, 1966, p. 2.

30. Marcus, S. *The Other Victorians: A Study of Sexuality and Pornography in Mid-Nineteenth-Century England.* New York: Basic Books, 1966, 282-283.

31. Although Sigmund Freud, Havelock Ellis, and other rebels against sexual repression at the end of the Victorian period helped society overcome the damaging psychological consequences of sexual repression for women, the Victorian belief that only men are sexual was complicated by the unnoticed fact that women could not attest to their sexuality, or show it in any way, without enormous loss of status. The evidence is that as late as the 1970s, women still suppressed their sexuality in the service of creating a mood of asexual propriety, and that this sexual distortion continues to distort and damage the relationship between men and women. Klassen, A. D., Williams, C. J., & Levitt, E. E. *Sex and Morality in the United States: An Empirical Enquiry under the Auspices of the Kinsey Institute.* Middletown, CT: Wesleyan University Press, 1989.

32. Weinberg, G. Becoming a nudist. *Psychiatry*, 1966, February, 15-24.

33. Markee, N. L, Carey, I. L., & Pedersen, E. L. Body cathexis and clothed body cathexis: Is there a difference? *Perceptual & Motor Skills*, 1990, 70(3, Pt2) 1239-1244.

34. Solomon, G. F. & Solomon, J. C. Shyness and sex, *Medical Aspects of Human Sexuality*, 1971, 5(5), 10-19. Bryan, W. J. The effective use of nudity in treating sexual problems. *Journal of the American Institute of Hypnosis*, 1972, 13(2), 71-73, 76-78.

35. The excerpt is taken from the ABC News *Nightline* transcript for Show #2867 (p. 1), which was on the air 05/19/92. According to the transcript, Powell actually made this statement 02/05/92.

36. Other examples of officials using the modesty folklore to argue for the ban against homosexuals are included in Chapter 1, footnote 9.

CHAPTER 3

1. Maginnis works in the Army's Office of the Inspector General, Washington, DC. He has a master's degree from the Naval Postgraduate School. Maginnis, R. L. A case against lifting the ban on homosexuals. *Army*, January 1993, 43(1) 37-40.

2. The quotation is from Chuck Schoen of Clear Lake, California who is head of a local gay-veterans chapter. Mentioned in Henry III, William. A mindset under siege. *Time*, November 30, 1992, 40-42.

3. "The physician's demeanor is highly stylized. . . . He demonstrates that he is the detatched professional. . . . Since intimacy can be introduced into instrumental physical contact by a 'loving' demeanor (lingering, caressing motions and contact beyond what the task requires), a doctor must take special pains to insure that his demeanor remains a brisk, no-nonsense show of efficiency." Emerson, J. P. Behavior in private places: Sustaining definitions of reality in gynecological examinations. *Recent Sociology*, 1970, 2, 74-97; also see Domar, A. D. Psychological aspects of the pelvic exam: Individual needs and physician involvement. *Women & Health*, 1985-1986, 10(4), 75-90; Henslin, J. & Briggs, M. Dramaturgical desexualization: The sociology of the vaginal examination. In J. Henslin (Ed.), *Studies in the Sociology of Sex*. New York: Appleton-Century Crofts, 1971, 243-277; Lief, Harold & Fox, Renee. Training for detatched concern. In H. I. Lief, V. F. Lief, & N. R. Lief. (Eds.), *The Psychological Basis of Medical Practice*. New York: Hoeber Medical Division, Harper & Row, 1963; Lawler, Jocalyn. A social construction of the body: Nurses' experiences. Unpublished Doctoral Dissertation, 1990, University of New South Wales, Australia, DAI 5110.

4. The following is taken from a letter to a journal by a physician in the year 1820:

> I give you the following imperfect relation of a case which occurred a short time since, in the circle of my practice that you may publish it, or make remarks upon it as you shall deem expedient.
>
> Near the middle of February, I was called to visit Miss __________, aged 17, found her apparently in the first stage of a common catarrhal fever, and made use of the usual remedies; but her recovery was slow, and I soon began to suspect some morbid affection of the system that had hitherto escaped my notice. The symptoms however were considerably moderated in their violence, and at length assumed the form of a mild remittent. With the intention of exciting a more healthy action of the liver, I gave her submurriated mercury in alternate doses. In the mean time I had learnt from her mother that she had never menstruated; that for a long time previous to her last attack, she was at such times subject in a greater or less degree to the usual distress attendant on painful menstruation. Her countenance was of the chlorotic kind. Bark and other tonics were given her to a considerable extent, without any evident effect. In three or four weeks from the time I first saw her she was attacked much as at first, but complained of more distress. The stomach, and indeed all the viscera

seemed to suffer alternately, but the contents of the pelvis suffered most. At this late period, I learnt that she had a tumified abdomen, that it was most prominant at first on one side, but was now equally diffused. I at first suspected an ascites, but on discovering no evident fluctuation, concluded it might be a dropsy of the ovaria. There were many symptoms however, that I could with difficulty account for on that supposition, and the idea of an imperforate vagina suggested itself. I explained myself to the mother, and urged the necessity of an examination. The patient was unwilling, and the mother would not urge it. I called for counsel. They admitted it might be so, but thought it more probably dropsy of the liver, or uterus, etc. Of course nothing was done. She gradually wasted away, the subject of the most intense suffering, which I thought now I could well account for. I left her about the middle of April, for the purpose of performing a journey and was absent four weeks. During my absence I consulted Drs.________, gentlemen of deserved eminence in the profession. They both pronouced it to be an imperforate vagina, and censured me for having too easily given up an examination. I resolved if my patient lived til I returned, though it might be to late to save her, to do the utmost in my power. She died a day or two before I returned, and had suffered excruciating distress to the last. An intelligent woman who assisted in dressing her for the grave, informed me that she discovered a tumor protruding from the vagina, of an uncommon appearance, which from her description, I have no doubt, was the vagina itself, imperforate and distended with the menstrual fluid. I taked unqualified blame to myself for having, while I was aware of her condition, not withstanding the opposition of the patient and friends neglected to take measures for her relief.

May 31, 1820 *We have printed the above as communicated by the writer, without alternations. It furnishes a most important lesson to physicians. The names are suppressed for obvious reasons. Ed.

Anonymous. A case of imperforate vagina which terminated fatally. *The New-England Journal of Medicine and Surgery,* 1820, January, 9(1), 243-244.

5. Casler, L. Nudist camps. *Medical Aspects of Human Sexuality,* 1971, 5(5), 92-98.

6. Craig Smith, Dennis. *The Naked Child: The Long-Range Effects of Family and Social Nudity.* Palo Alto, CA: R & E Research Associates, Inc., 1981, p. 75.

7. Hartman, W. E. & Fithian, M. A. *Treatment of Sexual Dysfunction.* Long Beach, CA: Center for Marital and Sexual Studies, 1972.

8. Story compared 100 nudists with a matched sample of 100 non-nudists and found that compared to non-nudists fewer social nudists had had nontraditional sexual experiences, and that, nevertheless, nudists were more likely than non-nudists to feel guilty about sex. Story, M.D. A comparison of social nudists and non-nudists on experience with various sexual outlets. *Journal of Sex Research,* 1987, 23(2), 197-211.

9. The comfort of art students and the administrators' sense of propriety is protected by putting nudity in the context of classroom routine and having the model relate to the students only in this role. Jesser, C. & Donovan, L. Nudity in the art training process: An essay with reference to a pilot study. *Sociological Quarterly*, 1969, 10, 355-371; Also see: Manzella, David B. Nude in the classroom. *American Journal of Art Therapy*, 1973, 12(3), 165-182.

10. Paruresis is the inhibition of the ability to urinate in a public place. Mild degrees merely delay the flow of urine. Severe paruresis makes urination impossible. Rees and Leach have demonstrated that there are three kinds of paruresis, each resulting from embarrassment about a different aspect of the toileting: visual, auditory, and olfactory. Women are more concerned with auditory aspects and men more concerned with visual. About 70 percent of men suffer from some degree of paruresis and about 45 percent of women. Rees, Bill & Leach, Debbie. The social inhibition of micturition (paruresis): Sex similarities and differences. *Journal of American College Health Association*, 1975, 23, 203-205; Gerald Koocher questioned the ethics of studying lavatory behavior. Koocher, G. Bathroom behavior and human dignity. *Journal of Personality and Social Psychology*, 1977, 35(2), 120-121.

11. Middlemist et al. reported a study of 60 lavatory users in a three-urinal lavatory. A researcher stood immediately adjacent to the subject, one urinal removed or was absent. The closer the researcher stood to the subject, the longer the delay of the onset of urination. Reid and Novak found in another study that if at all possible, men chose urinals that had a urinal separating them from anyone else using the rest room at the same time. Middlemist, R. D., Matter, C. F., & Knowles, E. Personal space invasions in the lavatory: Suggestive evidence for arousal. *Journal of Personality and Social Psychology*, 1976, 33(5), 541-546; Reid, E. & Novak, P. Personal space: An unobtrusive measures study. *Bulletin of the Psychonomic Society*, 1975, 5(3), 265-266.

12. In one study, college coeds were put in a situation where several people used the bathroom at the same time (some used the toilet while others took a bath). Girls who experienced this at home were less self-conscious, but they all adapted. Vivona, Charles & Gomillion, Merilee. Situation morality of bathroom nudity. *Journal of Sex Research*, May 1972, 8(2), 128-135.

13. These distinctions are similar to those made by a number of authors. See: Sherif, C. W., Sherif, M., & Nebergall, R. E. *Attitude and Attitude Change: The Social Judgment Involvement Approach*. Philadelphia,: W. B. Saunders Co., 1965; Keisler, C. A., Collins, B. E., & Miller, N. *Attitude Change: A Critical Analysis of Theoretical Approaches*: New York: John Wiley & Sons, 1969; Goffman, E. Attitudes and rationalizations regarding body exposure. In M. E. Roach and J. Eiocher (Eds.), *Dress, Adornment, and the Social Order*. New York: John Wiley, 1965, 50-52.

14. During Victorian times women were sometimes praised for being stoical and resisting going to a gynecologist in order to preserve their modesty. Rugoff, M. *Prudery and Passion: Sexuality in Victorian America*. New York: G. P. Putnam's Sons, 1971, p. 107.

15. See Sherif, C. W., Sherif, M. & Nebergall, R. E. *Attitude and Attitude Change: The Social Judgment Involvement Approach*. Philadelphia: W. B. Saunders Co., 1965.

16. Shawver, L. & Kurdys, D. Shall we employ women guards in male prisons? *The Journal of Psychiatry and Law*, 1987, 15(2), 154-159.

17. About 20 to 40 percent of both sexes experience the problem to a slightly troublesome degree (Williams & Degenhardt, 1954; Reid & Novak, 1975), however the vast majority of people seem to experience it in at least a slight degree and it is made worse by the amount of exposure a person feels subject to, and by the proximity of other people in the lavatory (Middlemist, Matter, & Knowles, 1976). People manage mild versions of the problem by avoiding toileting until most people have left the rest room, or, more simply, routinely choosing a urinal far from other people (Reid & Novak, 1975). Williams, G. W. & Degenhardt, E. T. Paruresis: A survey of a disorder of micturition. *The Journal of General Psychology*, 1954, 51, 19-29; Reid, E. & Novak, P. Personal space: An unobtrusive measures study. *Bulletin of the Psychonomic Society*, 1975, 5(3), 265-266; Middlemist, R. D., Matter, C. F., & Knowles, E. Personal space invasions in the lavatory: Suggestive evidence for arousal. *Journal of Personality and Social Psychology*, 1976, 33(5), 541-546.

18. Wahl, C. W. & Golden, J. Psychogenic urinary retention. Report of six cases. *Psychosomatic Medicine*, 1963, 25(6), 543-555.

19. Williams, G. E. & Johnson, A. M. Recurrent urinary retention due to emotional factors: A case report. *Psychosomatic Medicine*, 1956, 18(1), 77-80; Chapman, A. H. Psychogenic urinary retention in women: A report of a case. *Psychosomatic Medicine*, 1959, 21(2), 119-122.

20. Elliot, R. A case of inhibition of micturition: Unsystematic desensitization. *The Psychological Record*, 1967, 17, 525-530; Lamontagne, Y. & Marks, I. M. Psychogenic urinary retention: Treatment by prolonged exposure. *Behavior Therapy*: 1973, 4, 581-585; Anderson, L. T. Desensitization in vivo for men unable to urinate in a public facility. *Journal of Behavior Therapy and Experimental Psychiatry*, 1977, 8,105-106; Orwin, A. Treatment of a situational phobia: A case for running. *British Journal of Psychiatry*, 1974, 125, 95-98; Zgourides, G. D. Paruresis: Overview and implications for treatment. *Psychological Reports*, 1987, 60(3, pt. 2), 1171-1176.

21. Vivona and Gomillion studied women getting used to a bathroom in a college dorm which did not provide modesty doors for the tub. They describe a process in which the women became more and more confident that they could protect each other's modesty sentiments by conforming to an etiquette of disregard. Vivona, C. & Gomillion, M. Situation morality of bathroom nudity. *Journal of Sex Research*, 1972, 3(2,) 123-135.

22. While most women experience anxiety due to bodily modesty when they are first exposed to a gynecological exam, almost all who experience it adapt and become more comfortable with it. (Haar, Halitsky, & Stricker, 1977; Millstein, Adler, & Irwin, 1984). Interestingly, there is a tendency for women to be less embarrassed with women examiners (Haar, Halitsky, & Stricker, 1975; Seymore et

al., 1986; Alexander & McCullough, 1981) especially those who have experienced women examiners (Seymore et al., 1986). Haar, E., Halitsky, V., & Stricker, G. Patients' attitudes toward gynecologic examination and to gynecologists. *Medical Care*, 1977, 15(9), 787-795; Haar, E., Halitsky, V., & Stricker, G. Factors related to the preference for a female gynecologist. *Medical Care*, 1975, 13(9), 782-790; Millstein, S. G., Adler, N. E., & Irwin, C. E. Sources of anxiety about pelvic examinations among adolescent females. *Journal of Adolescent Health Care*, 1984, 5(2), 106-111; Seymore, C., DuRant, R. H., Jay, M. S., Freeman, D., Gomez, L., Sharp, C., & Linder, C. W. Influence of the position during the examination and the sex of the examiner on patient anxiety during pelvic examination. *Journal of Pediatrics*, 108(2), 312-317, February 1986; Alexander, K., & McCullough, J. Women's preference for gynecological examiners: Sex versus role. *Women and Health,* 1981, 6, 123.

And while most people feel a modesty anxiety when they first enter a nudist beach situation, they too adapt quickly. Casler, L. Nudist camps. *Medical Aspects of Human Sexuality*, 1971, May, 92-98; Weinberg, M. Sexual modesty, social meanings, and the nudist camp. *Social Problems*, 1964, 12, 311-318; Firestone, I., Lictman, C. M., & Evans, J. R. Privacy and solidarity: Effects of nursing home accommodation on environmental perception and sociability preferences, *International Journal of Aging and Human Development*, 1980, 11(3), 229-241; Jesser, C. & Donovan, L. Nudity in the art training process: An essay with reference to a pilot study. *Sociological Quarterly*, 1969, 10, 355-371.

23. Unwanted sexual arousal is harder for people with certain neurotic personality configurations. See, for example, Warwick et al. However, most people are capable of diminishing their sexual arousal if they choose to do so. The management of sexual arousal is enhanced, however, if there are acceptable outlets. Warwick, Hilary M., & Salkovskis, Paul M. Unwanted erections in obsessive-compulsive disorder. *British Journal of Psychiatry*, 1990, December, 157, 919-921.

24. Berger and his colleagues made short tapes of interviews with homosexual and heterosexual males and females (24 in total, six in each group) and found that a sample of 143 heterosexual and homosexual men and women could not identify homosexual subjects at a level beyond chance. However, particular individuals could, and those most able to do so were female homosexuals. Berger, G., Hank, L., Rauzi, T., & Simkins, L. Detection of sexual orientation by heterosexuals and homosexuals. *Journal of Homosexuality*, 1987, 13(4), 83-100. Hencken, J. D. Conceptualizations of homosexual behavior which preclude homosexual self-labeling. Special Issue: Bisexual and Homosexual Identities: Critical Clinical Issues. *Journal of Homosexuality,* 1984, 9(4) 53-63.

25. Henkin, J. The sociology of the secret: Techniques for the neutralization of stigma among male homosexuals. Unpublished Doctoral Dissertation, 1984, City University of New York, DAI 4501; Nemeyer, L. Coming out: Identity congruence and the attainment of adult female sexuality. Unpublished Doctoral Dissertation, 1980, Boston University School of Education, DAI 4105; Cornelius, D. L. An applicaton of rules-based theory of interpersonal communication: The rules of taboo communication within a "gay community." Unpublished Doctoral Disserta-

tion, 1980, Florida State University, DAI 4103; deMonteflores, C. & Schultz, S. J. Coming out: Similarities and differences for lesbians and gay men. *Journal of Social Issues*, 1978, 34(3), 59-72; Wells, J. W. & Kline, W. B. Self-disclosure of homosexual orientation. *Journal of Social Psychology*, 1987, 127(2), 191-197.

26. Town, J. P. & Harvey, J. H. Self-disclosure, attribution and social interaction. *Social Psychology Quarterly*, 1981, 44(4), 291-300.

27. Sepekoff asked both heterosexual males to imagine a situation ("I am soaping my genitals while showering with other males and I get an erection I can't hide"), and asked subjects to indicate their degree of discomfort. Both homosexual and heterosexual males were highly uncomfortable in such a situation and there was no difference detectable in the degree of their discomfort. Sepekoff, B. The development of an instrument to measure homophobia among heterosexual males. Unpublished Doctoral Dissertation, 1985, New York University, DAI 4701.

28. Sinclair and Ross compared the quantity of homosexual socialization and sexually transmitted diseases in two Australian states, one prior to decriminalization of homosexuality and one eight years after decriminalization. There was no evidence that decriminalization increased sexual solicitation or sexually transmitted diseases. Bell has discussed the way in which these laws deny constitutional rights to homosexual males. Sinclair, K. & Ross, M. W. Consequences of decriminalization of homosexuality: A study of two Australian states. *Journal of Homosexuality*, 1985, 12(1), 119-127; Bell, J. J. Public manifestation of personal morality: Limitations on the use of solicitation statutes to control homosexual cruising. *Journal of Homosexuality*, 1979-1980, 5(1), 97-114.

29. The service that this recruit was in has not been accurately clarified. It was a story told to the author by a recruit who left the military because of feeling uncomfortable with hiding the fact that he was gay.

CHAPTER 4

1. Yet 52 percent of Americans oppose teaching children about what it means to be gay in sex education in public schools. *U.S. News and World Report Press Release*, Saturday, June 26, 1993.

2. Homosexual graffiti is more common on male bathroom walls than heterosexual graffiti, and it is at least as common as heterosexual graffiti on female bathroom walls. Flora, K. S. Privies, privacy and political process: Some thoughts on bathroom graffiti and group identity. In H. Kellerman (Ed.), *Group Cohesion: Theoretical and Clinical Perspectives*. New York: Grune & Stratton, 1981.

3. There are many more myths than the five that are listed here. These five myths, however, are probably learned the earliest and form the core of what we think of as homosexual.

4. Lochhead, Carolyn. Raucous house hearing on military's gay ban. *San Francisco Chronicle*, May 6, 1993, A1, A19.

5. One study indicates that one American adult in three knows somebody who is homosexual. Other research (see note 43) indicates the figure is more like

half. Herek, G. M., Capitanio, J. P., & Glunt, E. K. *Intergroup contact predicts heterosexuals' attitudes toward gay men.* Paper presented at the meeting of the American Psychological Society, San Diego, CA, 1992.

6. Several studies show that most homosexuals and lesbians are traditionally masculine and feminine much as are heterosexuals. McDonald, G. J. & Moore, R. J. Sex-role self-concepts of homosexual men and their attitudes toward women and male homosexuality. *Journal of Homosexuality,* 1978. 4(1), 3-14; Jones, R. W. & De Cecco, J. P. The femininity and masculinity of partners of heterosexual and homosexual relationships. *Journal of Homosexuality,* 1982, 8(2), 37-44; Storms, M. O. Theories of sexual orientation. *Journal of Personality and Social Psychology,* 1980, 38(5), 763-792.

7. Berger and his colleagues found that although some people thought they could detect homosexuals, most could not. Berger, G., Hank, L., & Rauzi, T. & Simkins, L. Detection of sexual orientation by heterosexuals and homosexuals. *Journal of Homosexuality,* 1987, 13(4), 83-100.

8. Harry, J. & DeVall, W. *The Social Organization of Gay Males.* New York: Praeger; 1978. Peplau, L. A. What homosexuals want in relationships. *Psychology Today,* March 1981, 28-38.

9. Bell, A. P. & Weinberg, M. S. *Homosexualities: A Study of Diversity among Men and Women.* New York: Simon & Schuster, 1978, p. 325; Blumstein, P. & Schwartz, P. *American Couples: Money, Work, Sex.* New York: William Morrow, 1983; Harry, J. *Gay Couples,* 1984. New York: Praeger; McWhirter, D. P. & Mattison, A. M. *The Male Couple: How Relationships Develop.* Englewood Cliffs, NJ: Prentice-Hall, Inc., 1984; Saghir, M. T. & Robins, E. *Male and Female Homosexuality: A Comprehensive Investigation.* Baltimore: Williams & Wilkins, 1973. See research reviews as well: Harry, J. Gay male and lesbian family relationships. In E. Macklin (Ed.), *Contemporary Families and Alternative Life-styles: Handbook on Research and Theory.* Beverly Hills, CA: Sage, 1983; Larson, P. C. Gay male relationships. In W. Paul & J. D. Weinrich (Eds.), *Homosexuality as a Social Issue.* Beverly Hills, CA: Sage, 1982; Peplau, L. A. & Gordon, S. L. The intimate relationships of lesbians and gay men. In E. R. Allgeier & N. B. McCormick (Eds.). *Gender Roles and Sexual Behavior.* Palo Alto, CA: Mayfield, 1982.

10. Steffensmeier, D. & Steffensmeier, R. Sex differences in reactions to homosexuals: Research continuities and further developments. *The Journal of Sex Research,* 1974, 10, 52-67; Milham, J., San Miguel, C. C., & Kellogg, R. A. Factor analytic conceptualization of attitudes toward male and female homosexuals. *Journal of Homosexuality,* 1976, 2, 3-10.

11. Nineteenth-century sexologist, Havelock Ellis tells us that Westphal was the first to study homosexuality (i.e., sexual inversion), publishing his first works in 1870, but, he explains, the most important medical theorist on this topic was probably Richard von Krafft-Ebing. Krafft-Ebing considered homosexuality to be a perversion. If we reflect on the concept of a perversion, it seems to be a precursor to the concept of mental illness. It implies a distortion of what is natural, but the resulting problem is understood more on the model of an unfortunate defor-

mity than on the model of an ongoing disease process. If one considers Krafft-Ebing's theory of perversion to be a medical model, however, the medical model of homosexuality stretches back to the Victorian period. The history of the medical model of homosexuality has been deduced here from the account of Havelock Ellis. Ellis, H. Sexual Inversion. *Studies in the Psychology of Sex, Vol. I.* New York: Random House, 1905, p. 65. Westphal's work is listed only as published in the *Archiv für Psychiatrie,* 1870; Krafft-Ebing, R. von. *Aberrations of Sexual Life: A Medico-Legal Study for Doctors and Lawyers.* Arther Viv Burbury (trans.), Springfield, IL: Thomas, c. 1959.

12. Freud's judgment about homosexuality is, perhaps, most revealed in a letter he wrote to an American mother in 1935:

> Homosexuality is assuredly no advantage, but it is nothing to be ashamed of, no vice, no degradation, it cannot be classified as an illness; we consider it to be a variation of the sexual function produced by a certain arrest of sexual development. Many highly respectable individuals of ancient and modern times have been homosexuals, several of the greatest men among them. (Plato, Michelangelo, Leonardo da Vinci, etc.) It is a great injustice to persecute homosexuality as a crime and cruelty too . . .
> . . . If (your son) is unhappy, neurotic, torn by conflicts, inhbited in his social life, analysis may bring him harmony, peace of mind, full efficiency, whether he remains a homosexual or gets changed.

Taken from: Historical notes: A letter from Freud. *American Journal of Psychiatry,* 1951, 786.

13. Rado, S. *Psychoanalysis of Behavior II.* New York: Grune & Stratton, 1962.

14. Bieber and his colleagues based their research on 106 homosexual and 100 heterosexual patients whose data was contributed to the project by 77 psychiatrists. These psychiatrists completed a questionnaire about the patients covering information about family. Bieber, I., Dain, H., Dince, P. R., Drellich, M. G., Grand, H. G., Gundlach, T. H. Kremer, M. W., Rifkin, A. H., Wilbur, C., & Bieber, T. B. *Homosexuality: A Psychoanalytic Study of Male Homosexuals.* New York: Basic Books, 1962.

15. The recent studies, at least in English-speaking countries, challenge the Bieber theory of homosexual aetiology. Bigner, J. J. & Jacobsen, R. B. Parenting behaviors of homosexual and heterosexual fathers. *Journal of Homosexuality,* 1989, 18(1-2), 173-186; Ross, M. W. & Arrindell, W. A. Perceived parental rearing patterns of homosexual and heterosexual men. *Journal of Sex Research,* 1988, 24, 275-281; Robertson, G. Parent-child relationships and homosexuality. *British Journal of Psychiatry,* 1972, 121, (564), 525-528.

16. Kinsey and his colleagues led people to see homosexuality as common within the human community. Ford and Beach did the same for the animal kingdom. Kinsey, A., Kinsey, A. C., Pomeroy, W. B., & Martin, C. E., *Sexual Behavior in the Human Male.* Philadelphia: Saunders, 1948; Ford, C. S. & Beach, F. A. *Patterns of Sexual Behavior.* New York: Harper and Brothers, 1951.

17. For example, a study by Evelyn Hooker indicated that homosexuals did not appear to be more mentally ill than heterosexuals on psychological tests. Hooker, M. A. The adjustment of the male overt homosexual. *Journal of Projective Techniques*, 1957, 21, 17-31; also see: Gonsiorek, J. C. Results of psychological testing on homosexual populations. *American Behavioral Scientist*, 1982, 25, 385-396; Gonsiorek, J. C. The empirical basis for the demise of the illness model of homosexuality. In J. Gonsiorek & J. Weinrich (Eds.), *Homosexuality: Research Implications for Public Policy*, Newbury Park, CA: Sage, 1991, 115-136; Hart, M., Roback, H., Tittler, B., Weitz, L., Walston B., & McKee, E. Psychological adjustment of nonpatient homosexuals: Critical review of the research literature. *Journal of Clinical Psychiatry*, 1981, 39, 604-608; Reiss, B. F. Psychological tests in homosexuality. In J. Marmor (Ed.), *Homosexual Behavior: A Modern Reappraisal*, New York: Basic Books, 1965, 296-311.

18. The influence of the gay community on the shift of psychiatric opinion toward a less medical model of homosexuality has been well chronicled by Bayer. Bayer, R. *Homosexuality and American Psychiatry: The Politics of Diagnosis*. New York: Basic Books, 1981.

19. Bayer has provided us with a very readable description of the politics involved in this change. Bayer, R. *Homosexuality and American Psychiatry: The Politics of Diagnosis*. New York: Basic Books, 1981.

20. By 1990, only 3 percent of psychiatrists saw homosexuality as a mental illness. However, 9 percent of general practitioners (e.g., MDs) saw homosexuality as a mental illness. Bhugra, D. Doctors' attitudes to male homosexuality: A survey. *Sexual & Marital Therapy*, 1990, 5(2), 167-174.

21. Miles says, "A major part of the problem of the difficulty of being a homosexual man is the widespread perception of the entire group as predatory, sexually voracious, promiscuous and faithless" (p. 155). The RAND report included data showing that 38 percent of male Army soldiers, and 29 percent of women soldiers, either agreed, or agreed strongly, that openly gay and lesbian soldiers will try to seduce straight soldiers. Miles, Rosland. *Love, Sex, Death and the Making of the Male*. New York: Summit Books, 1991; National Defense Research Institute, *Sexual Orientation and the U.S. Military Personnel Policy: Options and Assessment*. Prepared for the Office of the Secretary of Defense, MR-323-OSD, RAND, 1993, p. 461.

22. Allgeier, A. R. & Allgeier, E. R. *Sexual Interactions* (2nd ed.). Lexington, MA: Heath, 1988.

23. Wooden, W. S. & Parker, J. *Men Behind Bars: Sexual Exploitation in Prison*. New York: Plenum Press, 1982, p. 145.

24. Research reported by Akers et al., shows that these custodial prisons have larger proportions of homosexual activity than prisons which do not segregate staff and prisoners to this extent. This study reported data on seven prisons which were rated according to how custodial they were. Those that were very different from custodial prisons were the treatment prisons which were rich with staff that had continued interaction with the inmates. Akers and his colleagues found that there was a significant correlation between the degree to which the institution

was custodial and the prevalence of homosexual activity. Akers, R. L., Hayner, N. S., & Gruninger, W. Homosexual and drug behavior in different types of prisons. In E. Segarin, & D. E. MacNamara, *Corrections: Problems of Punishment and Rehabilitation*. New York: Praeger, 1972, 70-79.

25. The way in which dominant male prisoners can control a prison through rape and threats of rape when the prison staff is lax has been well documented. Davis, Alan. Sexual assaults in the Philadelphia prison system. In David Petersen & Charles Thomas (Eds.), *Corrections: Problems and Prospects*. Englewood Cliffs, NJ: Prentice Hall, 1975; Wooden, W. S. & Parker, J. *Men Behind Bars*. New York: Plenum, 1982; Aldridge, R. G. Sexuality and incarceration. *Corrective and Social Psychiatry and Journal of Behavior Technology, Methods and Therapy*, 1983, 29(3), 74-77; Nacci, P. L. & Kane, T. R. Sex and sexual aggression in Federal prisons: Inmate involvement and employee impact. *Federal Probation*, 1984, 48(1), 46-53; Rothenberg, David. Sexual behavior in an abnormal setting. *Corrective and Social Psychiatry and Journal of Behavior Technology, Methods and Therapy*, 1983, 29(3), 78-81; Scacco, A. M. *Rape in Prison*. Springfield, IL: C. C. Thomas, 1975.

26. For many years, a number of authors (e.g., Gagnon, Kirkham) have stated their impression that the prison "jocks," as they are often called, who rape and threaten others, are, in fact, themselves heterosexual and use rape merely as a control device. Segarin, however, followed five prison "jocks" who were prone to rape and dominate in prison, and evaluated their sexual adjustment on parole. He found that on parole they tended to be heterosexual, and heterosexually violent. Kirkham, G. L. Homosexuality in prison. In J. M. Henslin (Ed.), *Studies in the Sociology of Sex*. New York: Appleton-Century Crofts, 1971; Gagnon, J. H. & Simon, W. The social meaning of prison homosexuality. In Robert Carter & Daniel Glaser (Eds.), *Correctional Institutions*. Philadelphia: Lippincott, 1972, p. 225; Segarin, E. Prison homosexuality and its effects on post-prison sexual behavior. *Psychiatry*, 1976, 245-257; also see: Wooden, W. S. & Parker, J. *Men Behind Bars: Sexual Exploitation in Prison*. New York: Plenum Press, 1982; Scacco, A. M. *Male Rape: A Casebook of Sexual Aggressions*. New York: AMS Press, 1982; Bowker, L. H. *Prison Victimization*. New York: Elsevier, 1980; Marquart, J.W. Prison guards and the use of physical coercion as a mechanism of prisoner control. *Criminology*, 1986, 24(2), 347-367.

27. Relevant to understanding the difference between prison homosexuality and civilian homosexuality is the finding that 59 percent of delinquent homosexuals, in one sample, preferred a feminine male partner, whereas only 29 percent of nondelinquents preferred this masculine role. Gebhard, P. & Johnson, A. *The Kinsey Data*. Philadelphia: W. B. Saunders, 1979.

28. We do not know, of course, if prison rape is occurring until the scandal breaks out.

29. Rape is criminal. The evidence is that homosexuals are less criminal than heterosexuals and that bisexuals are more criminal than heterosexuals. Lesbians are more criminal than heterosexual females, but less criminal than heterosexual males.

Ellis, L., Hoffman, H., Burke, D. M. Sex, sexual orientation and criminal and violent behavior. *Personality & Individual Differences.* 1990, 11(12), 1207-1212.

30. Bell, A. P. & Weinberg, M. S. *Homosexualities: A Study of Diversity among Men and Women.* New York: Simon & Schuster, 1978; Laner, M. R. Permanent partner priorities: Gay and straight. In J. P. De Cecco (Ed.). *Gay Relationships.* Binghamton, NY: Harrington Park Press, 1987.

31. Gomulka, E. T. Position Paper on the DoD Policy on Homosexuality. July 20, 1992.

32. Beane, J. Choiceful sex, intimacy and relationships for gay and bisexual men. In Franklin Abbot (Ed.), *Men & Intimacy: Personal Accounts Exploring the Dilemmas of Modern Male Sexuality.* Freedom, CA: The Crossing Press, 1990.

33. De Cecco, J. P. Obligation versus aspiration. In J. P. De Cecco (Ed.), *Gay Relationships.* Binghamton, NY: Harrington Park Press, 1987, p. 3.

34. See: Peplau, L. A. Research on homosexual couples: An overview. In J. P. De Cecco (Ed.), *Gay Relationships.* Binghamton, NY: Harrington Park Press, 1987.

35. "In a sample of men who had AIDS, only 2% of homosexually, 7% of bisexually and 27% of heterosexually identified men, respectively, reported engaging in oral or anal sex with anonymous male partners during the one-year period (studied)." Doll, L. S., Petersen, L.R., White, C. R., Johnson, E. S., Ward, J. W., & the Blood Donor Study Group. Homosexually and nonhomosexually identified men who have sex with men: A behavioral comparison. *The Journal of Sex Research,* 1992, 29(1), 1-14.

36. This version of Jess Jessop's story is taken from a more detailed account reported in Humphrey, M. A. *My Country, My Right to Serve.* New York: Harper Collins, 1988, 139-143.

37. Taken off of the military forum on Compuserve, October 2, 1993.

38. But exactly what the people polled believe is hidden by subtle differences in the different surveys. For example, in a *Los Angeles Times* survey in 1985, there were two questions that seem, on superficial analysis, quite similar, yet produced very different statistics in terms of how many people accepted homosexuality. Compare the wording of the two questions:

1. What about sexual relations between adults of the same sex? Do you think it is always wrong, or almost always wrong, or wrong only sometimes, or not at all wrong?
2. What is your attitude toward homosexuality? Do you personally approve of homosexual relations between consenting adults . . . or do you think it's all right for other people, but not for yourself . . . or do you oppose it for everyone?

Both of these questions are different ways of asking, "What do you feel about homosexuality?" But the first question got a lot more condemning response from people than the second. In answering the first question people said, in general, that homosexuality was almost always wrong and in answering the second question they said that they were halfway between approving of it in general and approving of it just for other people but not for themselves.

Nevertheless, the proportion of Americans that are negative about homosexuals hovers around 50 percent. More specifically, in a study by Turner and his colleagues 53 percent said that homosexuality was an unacceptable lifestyle, and, similarly, *U.S. News & World Report* indicated that 50 percent disapproved of extending current civil rights laws to cover gays and lesbians.

Los Angeles Times, poll no. 126 and 101 reported in: Price, V., & Hsu, M. L. Public opinion about AIDS policies: The role of misinformation and attitudes toward homosexuals. *Public Opinion Quarterly,* 1992, 56, 29-52. Turner, B. & Support Staff. Gays under fire. *Newsweek,* September 14, 1992, 35-40. Aguero, J. E. & Bloch, L. President Clinton spends too much time on gay rights say a majority of Americans in a *U.S. News & World Report* Poll. *U.S. News & World Report Press Release.* Saturday, June 26, 1993.

39. Saad, L. & McAneny, L. Americans deeply split over ban on gays in military. *The Gallup Poll Monthly,* February 1993, pp. 6-12.

40. About 45 percent approve of homosexuals in these questions, and about 5 percent tell us they are not sure.

41. Levitt and Klassan (1974) found that nearly 70 percent believed that male homosexuals act like women, and 56 percent believed that all homosexuals fear the opposite gender. *U.S. News & World Report* says that 46 percent believe that gays and lesbians choose to be gay. Levitt, E. & Klassen, A. Public attitudes toward homosexuality: Part of the 1970 national survey by the Institute for Sex Research. *Journal of Homosexuality,* 1974, 1(1), 29-43. Aguero, J. E. & Bloch, L. President Clinton spends too much time on gay rights say a majority of Americans in a *U.S. News & World Report* Poll. *U.S. News & World Report Press Release.* Saturday, June 26, 1993.

42. A *U.S. News & World Report* study found that people who believe homosexuals are born gay are more likely to believe we should protect gays' civil rights than people who believe they choose to be gay. Aguero and Bloch found that the subjects who had the most negative attitude were those who had negative affect toward them and believed that homosexuality was a learned, as opposed to an inborn, problem. These authors also found that men are more negative toward homosexuals than women. Aguero, J. E., Bloch, L. President Clinton spends too much time on gay rights say a majority of Americans in a *U.S. News & World Report* Poll. *U.S. News & World Report Press Release.* Saturday, June 26, 1993.

43. According to a *U.S. News & World Report,* 46 percent say that they don't know either, and another 2 percent say that they are unsure, which means, given rounding errors that about 54 percent of people do know a gay. *Newsweek* published a survey nine months earlier that seems supportive although the questions make a direct comparison impossible. According to *Newsweek* 43 percent of people have a friend or acquaintance who is gay. Twenty percent work with someone whom they know is gay and 9 percent have a gay person in their family. If one presumes that there is some overlap so that some people who have gay friends also work with gays, and so forth, then it is reasonable to suppose that

around half of people, or a few more, know a gay. Aguero, J. E. & Bloch, L. President Clinton spends too much time on gay rights say a majority of Americans in a *U.S. News & World Report* Poll. *U.S. News & World Report Press Release*. Saturday, June 26, 1993. Turner, B. and support staff. Gays under fire. *Newsweek*, September 14, 1992, 35-40.

44. A February 1993 Gallup Poll found that whereas 50 percent of Americans disapproved of lifting the ban, only 31 percent of those who had known a homosexual disapproved of lifting the ban. This study found that 27 percent of Americans (combining males and females) had known a homosexual. *U.S. News & World Report* did a similar poll and found much the same thing, as have Herek (1991, 1984); and Schneider and Lewis (1984). Aguero, J. E. & Bloch, L. President Clinton spends too much time on gay rights say a majority of Americans in a *U.S. News & World Report* Poll. *U.S. News & World Report Press Release*. Saturday, June 26, 1993; Herek, G. M. Beyond "homophobia": A social psychological perspective on attitudes toward lesbians and gay men. *Journal of Homosexuality*, 1984, 10, 1-21; Herek, G. M. Stigma, prejudice and violence against lesbians and gay men. In J. C. Gonsiorek & J. D. Weinrich (Eds.), *Homosexuality: Research Implications for Public Policy*. Newbury Park, CA: Sage, 1991, 60-80; Schneider, W. & Lewis, I. A. The straight story on homosexuality and gay rights. *Public Opinion*, February/March, 1984, 7, 16-20, 59-60; Saad, L. & McAneny, L. Americans deeply split over ban on gays in military. *The Gallup Poll Monthly*, February, 1993, 6-11.

45. Furnham, A. & Taylor, L. Lay theories of homosexuality: Etiology, behaviors and "cures." *British Journal of Social Psychology*, 1990, 29(2), 135-147; Ficarrotto, T. J. Racism, sexism, and erotophobia: Attitudes of heterosexuals towards homosexuals. *Journal of Homosexuality*, 1990, 19(1), 111-116; Whitley, B. E., Jr. The relationship of heterosexuals' attributions for the causes of homosexuality to attitudes toward lesbians and gay men. *Personality and Social Psychology Bulletin*, 16(2), June 1990, 369-377; Herek, G. M. Homosexuals' attitudes toward lesbians and gay men: Correlates and gender differences. *Journal of Sex Research*, 25, 451-477; Gentry, C. S. Social distance regarding male and female homosexuals. *Journal of Social Psychology*, 1987, 127, 199-208; Herek, G. M. Beyond "homophobia": A social psychological perspective on attitudes toward lesbians and gay men. *Journal of Homosexuality*, 1984, 10, 1-21.

46. Apparently no study has challenged the general finding that men are more tolerant of lesbianism than of male homosexuality. Similarly, studies generally show that men are less tolerant of homosexuals in general than women are. However it is not clear (the data goes both ways) whether women are more or less tolerant of lesbians than they are of homosexual men.

Two studies (Turnbull & Brown, 1977; Belkin, 1982) present data saying that women are equally tolerant of lesbians and male homosexuals, but Gurwitz and Marcus (1978), and Gross et al., (1980) present data saying women are more tolerant of male homosexuals, and D'Augelli and Rose (1990) present data saying women are more tolerant of lesbians. Milham et al. (1976) suggest women are less tolerant of lesbians but less negative toward them, nevertheless, than men are of male homosexuals. So, although it is clear that men are more tolerant of lesbians, this kind of differential intolerance is not as apparent in women's attitudes. Turnbull, D. & Brown, M. Attitudes toward homosexuality and male and female reactions to homosexual and heterosexual slides. *Canadian Journal of Behavioral Science*, 1977, 9(1), 68-80; Belkin, B. M. Homophobia in women. Unpublished Doctoral Dissertation, 1982, Adelphi University, Gurwitz, S. & Marcus, M. Effects of anticipated interaction, sex and homosexual stereotypes on first impressions. *Journal of Applied Social Psychology*, 1978, 8(1), 47-56; Gross, A. E., Green, S. K., Storek, J. T., & Vanyr, J. M. Disclosure of sexual orientation and impressions of male and female homosexuals. *Personality and Social Psychology Bulletin*, 1980, 6(2), 307-314; D'Augelli, A. & Rose, M. L. Homophobia in a university community: Attitudes and experiences of heterosexual freshmen. *Journal of College Student Development*, 1990, 31(6), 484-491; Milham, J., San Miguel, C. C., & Kellogg, R. A. Factor analytic conceptualization of attitudes toward male and female homosexuals. *Journal of Homosexuality*, 1976, 2(1), 3-10; Men's apparent general intolerance towards all homosexuality (female as well as male) as reported in many studies (Price, 1982; Nyberg & Alston, 1977; Thompson & Fishburn, 1977; Minnegerode, 1976; Larsen, Reed, & Hoffman, 1980; Glassner & Owen, 1976; Newman, 1985; Herek, 1988; Wells, 1989; Steffensmeier & Steffensmeier, 1974; Weis & Dain, 1979; Weinberg, 1972) appears to have been a consequence of the fact that most men (73 percent) use the term "homosexual" to refer exclusively to male homosexuals (whereas only 37 percent of women refer only to men with this term), (cf. Black & Stevenson, 1985). Furthermore, those few men who do use the word "homosexual" to refer to both female and male homosexuals are very signficantly more tolerant than those who use it to refer only to males (Black & Stevenson, 1985). This means that when men are asked how they feel about "homosexuals" they often tell us how they feel about male homosexuals and many men feel more negatively about male homosexuals than about lesbians (Turnbull & Brown, 1977; Gurwitz & Marcus, 1978; Gross et al.; and D'Augelli & Rose, 1990; Milham, San Miguel, & Kellogg, 1976; Price, J. H. High school students' attitudes toward homosexuality. *The Journal of School Health*, 1982, 52(8), 469-473; Nyberg, K. L. & Alston, J. P. Homosexual labeling by university youths. *Adolescence*, 1977, 12(48), 541-556; Thompson, G. H. & Fishburn, W. R. Attitudes toward homosexuality among graduate counseling students. *Counselor Education and Supervision*, 1977, December, 121-130; Minnegerode, F. A. Attitudes toward homosexuality: Feminist attitudes and sexual conservatism. *Sex Roles*, 1976, 2, 347-352; Larson, P. C. Gay male relationships. In W. Paul & J. D. Weinrich (Eds.) *Homosexuality as a Social Issue*. Beverly Hills, CA: Sage, 1982; Glassner, B. & Owen, C. Variation in attitudes toward homosexuality. *Cornell Journal of Social Relations*, 11, 161-176; Newman, B. S. Development of heterosexual attitudes toward lesbians. Unpublished Doctoral Dissertation, 1985, University of Pittsburgh; Herek, G. M. Heterosexuals' attitudes toward lesbians and gay men: Correlates and gender differences. *Journal of Sex Research*, 1988, 25(4), 451-477; Wells, J. W. Teaching about gay and lesbian sexual and affectional orientation using explicit films to reduce homophobia. *Journal of Humanistic Education and Development*, 1989, 28(1), 18-34; Steffensmeier, D. & Steffensmeier, R. Sex differences in reactions to homosexuals: Research continuities and further developments. *The Journal of Sex Research*, 1974, 10, 52-67; Weis, C. B. & Dain, R. N. Ego development and sex attitudes in heterosexual and homosexual men and women. *Archives of Sexual Behavior*, 1979, 8(4), 341-355; Weinberg, G. *Society and the Healthy Homosexual*. New York: St. Martin's Press, 1972.

47. Sigelman, C. K., Howell, J. L., Cornell, D. P., Cutright, J. D., & Dewey, J. C. Courtesy stigma: The social implications of associating with a gay person. *The Journal of Social Psychology*, 1991, 131(1), 45-56.

48. Data has been reported showing that homophobia is highly correlated with the desire to maintain proper social roles for men and women. Britton, D. M. Homophobia and homosexuality: An analysis of boundary maintenance. *The Sociological Quarterly*, 31(3), 423-439.

49. Men who are more negative about homosexuality also appear to be men who feel more need to avoid any behavior that hints of femininity in themselves. Chitwood, K. L. The relation of attitudes toward the male role, attitudes toward homosexuality, and sex-typed characteristics to traditionality of occupational choice among college men. Unpublished Doctoral Dissertation, 1980, New York University, DAI 4207; Dunbar, J., Brown, M., & Amoroso, D. Some correlates of attitudes toward homosexuality. *Journal of Social Psychology*, 1973, 89, 271-279; Thompson, E. H., Grisanti, C. & Pleck, J. H. Attitudes toward the male role and their correlates, *Sex Roles*, 1985, 13(7-8), 413-427; McRoy, D. T. Gay and heterosexual men's friendships: The relationships between homophobia, antifemininity and intimacy (friendships). Unpublished Doctoral Dissertation, 1990, California School of Professional Psychology–Los Angeles, DAI 5112; Morin, S. F. & Garfinkle, E. M. Male Homophobia. *Journal of Social Issues*, 1978, 34, 29-47.

50. Sigelman and her colleagues found that intolerance of gays had a profound affect on people's inclination to see nonsex role stereotype behavior as evidence of a person being gay. Heterosexuals who were homophobic were much more likely to see nonmasculine behavior as evidence that a man was gay or had significant homosexual tendencies ($F(1,108) = 17.06$, $p. < .0001$) The tendency to see nonstereotyped images as evidence of homosexuality was not affected by homophobia. Sigelman, C. K., Howell, J. L., Cornell, D. P., Cutright, J. D., & Dewey, J. C. Courtesy stigma: The social implications of associating with a gay person. *The Journal of Social Psychology*, 1991, 131(1), 45-56. Dunbar, too, found that men who were homophobic were more likely to think more feminine men were homosexual. Dunbar, J., Brown, M., & Amoroso, D. Some correlates of attitudes toward homosexuality. *Journal of Social Psychology*, 1973, 89, 271-279.

51. The majority of men who are homophobic are not angry with homosexuals unless they cannot avoid them, or avoid seeing evidence of their homosexuality. The fact that some homophobic people react angrily, or politically, in order to avoid, and to continue to avoid, the object which makes them anxious, however, should not be surprising. It is not diagnostic of a phobia, certainly, but a clinician

would not be surprised, for example, if a woman agoraphobic were to react angrily if her family were to threaten to force her to be social. Furthermore, people who are prejudiced do not need to be angry toward the objects of their prejudice. Pre-Civil War southerners were not always angry, for example, at their slaves. They simply disdained them.

Leibman described such a phobic reaction. He was with a young man who suddenly realized the clerk they were dealing with in a store was gay. The young man rushed outside, and when Leibman joined him the young man emoted, "Ugh, I hate faggots. God how I hate them. God, if one of them touched me, I'd break his nose. I'd just bash his face in." And men like this sometimes do bash in the faces of the homosexuals they hate. Liebman, Marvin. *Coming Out Conservative*. San Francisco: Chronicle Books, 1992, p. 246.

52. Sokolov, E. *Perception and the Conditioned Reflex*. New York: Macmillan, 1963.

53. Shields, S. A. & Harriman, R. E. Fear of male homosexuality: Cardiac responses of low and high homonegative males. In John P. De Cecco (Ed.), *Bashers, Baiters & Bigots: Homophobia in American Society*. Binghamton, NY: Harrington Park Press, 1985, 53-68.

54. Russell, P. & Gray, C. D. Prejudice against a progay man in an everyday situation: A scenario study. *Journal of Applied Social Psychology*, 1992, 22(21), 1676-1687.

55. Price, J. H. High school students' attitudes toward homosexuality. *The Journal of School Health*, 1982, 52(8), 469-473; Nyberg, K. L. & Alston, J. P. Homosexual labeling by university youths. *Adolescence*, 1977, 12(48), 541-556; Thompson, G. H. & Fishburn, W. R. Attitudes toward homosexuality among graduate counseling students. *Counselor Education and Supervision*, 1977, December, 121-130; Minnegerode, F. A. Attitudes toward homosexuality: Feminist attitudes and sexual conservatism. *Sex Roles*, 1976, 2, 347-352; Larsen, P., Reed, M., & Hoffman, S. Attitudes of heterosexuals toward homosexuals: A Likert-type scale and construct validity. *The Journal of Sex Research*, 1980, 16, 245-257; Glassner, B. & Owen, C. Variation in attitudes toward homosexuality. *Cornell Journal of Social Relations*, 1976, 11, 161-176; Newman, B. S. Development of heterosexual attitudes toward lesbians. Unpublished Doctoral Dissertation, 1985, University of Pittsburgh, DAI 4705; Herek, G. M. Heterosexuals' attitudes toward lesbians and gay men: Correlates and gender differences. *Journal of Sex Research*, 1988, 25(4), 451-477. Wells, J. W. Teaching about gay and lesbian sexual and affectional orientation using explicit films to reduce homophobia. *Journal of Humanistic Education and Development*, 1989, 28(1), 18-34; Steffensmeier, D. & Steffensmeier, R. Sex differences in reactions to homosexuals: Research continuities and further developments. *The Journal of Sex Research*, 1974, 10, 52-67; Weis, C. B. & Dain, R. N. Ego development and sex attitudes in heterosexual and homosexual men and women. *Archives of Sexual Behavior*, 1979, 8(4), 341-355; Weinberg, G. *Society and the Healthy Homosexual*. New York: St. Martin's Press, 1972.

56. Women are allowed to have more intimate nonsexual friends (McRoy, 1990), to touch and gaze intimately (Ellsworth & Ross, 1975), and to disclose intimately with women without violating their sex role. And the increased amount of physical intimacy involved in lesbian lovemaking simply seems, to the male mind, at least, less a violation of traditional femininity than the violation of masculinity that occurs when men are sexually intimate with each other (Paul, 1984; McRoy, D. T. Gay and heterosexual men's friendships: The relationships between homophobia, antifemininity and intimacy (friendships). Unpublished Doctoral Dissertation, 1990, California School of Professional Psychology, Los Angeles, DAI 5112; Ellsworth, P. & Ross, L. Intimacy in response to direct gaze, *Journal of Experimental Social Psychology*, 1975, 11, 592-613; Paul, J. P. The bisexual identity: An idea without social recognition. In John P. De Cecco & M. G. Shively (Eds.), *Origins of Sexuality And Homosexuality*, Binghamton, NY: Harrington Park Press, 1984.

57. The relative importance of males conforming to male gender roles compared to females conforming to female gender roles starts early. Little boys are likely to be more censured when they violate masculinity guidelines than are little girls when they behave in a more masculine way (Fling & Manosevitz, 1972; Hartley, 1959; Lansky, 1967), and the same appears to be true for college students (Seyfried and Hendrick, 1973). And, when they are grown, research shows that women's sex role guidelines are seen as more vague and trivial than are men's. (Hayes & Leonard, 1983) Also, finally, because homosexuality violates traditional sex roles, it is not surprising that men seem more afraid of the homosexual role whether or not they have homosexual impulses (Morin & Garfinkle, 1978; Fling, S., & Manosevitz, M. Sex typing in nursery school children's play interest. *Developmental Psychology*, 1972, 7, 146-152; Hartley, R. E. Sex role pressures and the socialization of the male child. *Psychological Reports*, 1959, 5, 457-468; Lansky, L. M. The family structure also affects the model: Sex-role attitudes in parents of preschool children. *Merrill-Palmer Quarterly*, 1967, 13, 139-150; Seyfried, B. A., & Henderick, C. When do opposites attract? When they are opposite in sex and sex-role attitudes. *Journal of Personality and Social Psychology*, 1973, 25, 15-20; Hayes, S. C. & Leonard, S. R. Sex-related motor behavior: Effects on social impression and social cooperation. *Archives of Sexual Behavior*, 1983, 12, 415-426; Morin, S. F. & Garfinkle, E. M. Male homophobia. *Journal of Social Issues*, 1978, 34, 29-47.

58. In fact, both men and women are more likely to know a lesbian than a gay male. One study showed, for example, that whereas about 64 percent of women know a lesbian, only about 14 percent of men know a gay man (Whitley, 1990). Interestingly, a 1970 data sample (reported in 1989) showed that at that time more people knew of a male homosexual (38 percent) than knew of a lesbian (24 percent). The data suggests, therefore, that lesbians are more open about their lesbianism than they were 20 years ago and that gay men are more circumspect, perhaps due to the stigma promoted by AIDS. Whitley, B. E., Jr. The relationship of heterosexuals' attributions for the causes of homosexuality to attitudes toward

lesbians and gay men. *Personality and Social Psychology Bulletin*, 1990, 16(2), 369-377; Klassen, A. D., Williams, C. J., & Levitt, E. E. *Sex and Morality in the United States: An Empirical Inquiry under the Auspices of the Kinsey Institute*. Middletown, CT: Wesleyan University Press, 1989.

59. This conclusion is based on a survey reported in a *U.S. News & World Report* press release which also indicates that women who do not work outside the home appear less likely to know a gay person than men are. Since anyone who knows a gay person is likely to approve of gays more than someone who does not, the difference between male and female approval of gays may be even more striking than it is at first glance. Aguero, J. E. & Bloch, L. President Clinton spends too much time on gay rights say a majority of Americans in a *U.S. News & World Report* Poll. *U.S. News & World Report Press Release*. Saturday, June 26, 1993.

60. Faderman, L. *Surpassing the Love of Men: Romantic Friendship and Love beween Women from the Renaissance to the Present.* New York: William Morrow, 1981; Jeffreys, S. *The Spinster and Her Enemies: Feminism and Sexuality, 1880-1930.* London: Pandora, 1985.

61. Wood-Allen, Mary, M.D. *What a Young Woman Ought to Know.* Philadelphia: The Vir Publishing Co., 1905, 177-178.

62. Klassen, A. D., Williams, C. J., & Levitt., E. E. *Sex and Morality in the United States: An Empirical Inquiry under the Auspices of the Kinsey Institute.* Middletown, CT: Wesleyan University Press, 1989.

63. See footnote 47 in Chapter 4.

CHAPTER 5

1. The stories told here are abbreviated summaries of very extensive verbal or written interview material during 1993. Each subject has reviewed the material and agreed that it reflected the facts in his case. They were told by men who knew the author was writing a book on homosexuals in the military, but they were not acquainted with the author's theories. One of the subjects, Edward, was the relative of an ex-patient. He was interviewed for a total of about eight hours, in part in the presence of another person. Acquaintances with the other four were made over a computer online system. Telephone calls were made. In some cases pictures were sent. The interview here consisted of the author sending the subject questions which they answered at their leisure. These stories are a compilation of what they said. Their stories were told in a series of between eight and 20 lengthy responses to a set of questions.

2. This process can be broken up in a number of different ways, and has been, but most people who consider themselves homosexual and have a homosexual lifestyle have followed this sequence of experiences. For similar attempts to analyze the formation of a healthy homosexual identity see Cass, 1984; Troiden, 1988; and the collected essays contained in De Cecco and Shively (1984); Cass, Vivienne C. Homosexual identity formation: Testing a theoretical model. *Journal*

of Sex Research, May 1984, 20(2):143-167; Troiden, Richard R. Homosexual identity development. *Journal of Adolescent Health Care*, March 1988, 9(2):105-113; De Cecco, J. P. & Shively, M. G. (Eds.), *Origins of Sexuality and Homosexuality.* Binghamton, NY: Harrington Park Press, 1984.

3. The fact that lesbianism is viewed with less opprobrium today than male homosexuality was documented in the previous chapter. The research reviewed there showed that both men and women view lesbianism less negatively than men view male homosexuality.

4. Richardson and Hart, 1981, and Rust, 1993 have emphasized the way some people's identity can be fluid. The concept of bisexuality sometimes helps prevent a person going through the stage of shame. It allows the satisfaction of fluid desires without the inevitable formation of a homosexual identity. Richardson, D. & Hart, J. The development and maintenance of a homosexual identity. In John Hart & Diane Richardson (Eds.), *The Theory and Practice of Homosexuality.* London: Routledge & Kegan Paul, 1981; Rust, P. C. "Coming out" in the age of social constructionism. *Gender & Society*, 1993, 7(1), 50-77; See also: Blumstein, P. W. & Schwartz, P. Lesbianism and bisexuality. In Erich Goode (Ed.), *Sexual Deviance and Sexual Deviants.* New York: Morrow, 1974, 278-295; Blumstein, P. W. & Schwartz, P. Bisexuality in men. *Urban Life*, 1976, 5, 339-358; Blumstein, P. W. & Schwartz, P. Bisexuality: Some psychological issues." *Journal of Social Issues*, Vol. 5(2) 33, 30-45.

5. Data reported on nonhomophobic societies show a similar level of reported homosexuality as the United States. Whitam, F. L. & Mathy, R. M. *Male Homosexuality in Four Societies: Brazil, Guatemala, the Philippines, and the United States.* New York: Praeger, 1986.

6. For example, one man who considers himself exclusively gay today says:

> In fourth grade a little girl arrived named Deborah . . . I developed the biggest little-boy crush on her. And she liked me back!! It was emotional.

Then Deborah moved away. When she moved back in the sixth grade, the romance continued. The story continues:

> I was sitting on a log back in the swamp next to Debbie when my body woke up. We had played kissy-kissy before and were the big romance of the school, but this kiss was different and I knew exactly how though no one had told me to expect feelings like this. It was very powerful. School ended and she and her family moved again.

Then, just about the same time, this future gay man discovered a boy named Timmy. They touched each other in the locker room when they changed for swimming.

> It was slippery and wet. If it was fun it was only because it was part of the whole swimming experience. It was also where I saw Joe. I couldn't figure out why but I was attracted to him and his body in a new and very

> strong way. It was the way I was attracted to Debbie when we sat on the log in the forbidden swamp. I thought he was beautiful. . . . To me it was no big deal. It seemed as natural to think how nice Timmy looked as it was to kiss Debbie.

7. A gay soldier says:

> My family never talked about it . . . I just always assumed that I would be attracted to women, get married and raise a family like my father and mother, and like their parents, and their parents' parents.

8. Hetrick, E. & Martin, A. Developmental issues and their resolution for gay and lesbian adolescents. Special Issue: Psychotherapy with homosexual men and women: Integrated identity approaches for clinical practice. *Journal of Homosexuality*, 1987, 14 (1-2), 25-43.

9. Another gay man also referred to the dictionary. He says,

> I knew in 7th grade and I knew I had better not bring it up. But I was very hungry for information. There was no one to ask. . . . And I certainly was not going to be seen talking with those unfortunates who had not managed to escape the label. They were so weird, so strange, they were untouchable. But mostly they were what I did not want to be. I would rather have death. But I wore out every "H" section and index in twelve libraries. I remember the first time I found an "H" section torn out, as I would many times. My head raced a little as I realized another guy, maybe just like me, stood there doing the same thing.

10. Cathy Reback worked with 28 women in the initial stages of changing from a heterosexual to a lesbian sexual identity. She found that sexual activity was the least salient variable she studied in causing women to choose a lesbian identity. Often women who became lesbian were not sexually active as lesbians but claimed a lesbian identity because of emotional attachment with another woman rather than sexual involvement. Reback, C. J. The Social Construction of Sexualities: A Study of Redefining Identity (Lesbian Identity Formation, Symbolic Interactionism, Women's Studies). University of California, Santa Cruz, 1986, DAI 47(06), SECA 2321. Also see: Lewis, L. The coming-out process for lesbians: Integrating a stable identity. *Social Work*, 1984, 29(5), 464-469.

Women who think of themselves as lesbians in the 1980s and 1990s might well have thought of themselve as heterosexuals in earlier years.

11. In a study by Berger and his colleagues, it was found that some women were able to identify homosexuals better than chance, but the group of men and women as a whole were not able to detect homosexuals better than chance. Berger, G., Hank, L., Rauzi, T. & Simkins, L. Detection of sexual orientation by heterosexuals and homosexuals. *Journal of Homosexuality*, 1987, 13(4), 83-100. Data from the Kinsey Institute indicates that among homosexuals in prison with extensive homosexual experience, only 22.6 percent are obvious for their homosexuality. Gebhard, P. H., Gagnon, J. H., Pomeroy, W. B., & Christenson, C. V. *Sex Offenders: An Analysis of Types*. New York: Harper & Row, 1965, (p. 652).

12. Weinberg and Williams surveyed 2,497 homosexuals in three countries and found that commitment to a deviant identity is positively related to stability of self-concept and self-esteem and negatively related to measures of psychological maladjustment. They found about 70 percent of homosexuals who mostly pass as heterosexuals anticipate a great deal of discrimination if they were to disclose their homosexuality.

They also found that the most important factor in the social and psychological development of the homosexual was social involvement with other homosexuals. Male homosexuals who are more socially involved with other homosexuals find it easier to deal with the heterosexual world. Also, those who are more socially involved with other homosexuals tend to have fewer psychological problems. Hammersmith, S. K. & Weinberg, M. S. Homosexual identity: Commitment, adjustment, and significant others. *Sociometry,* March 1973, 36(1), 56-79.

They also found that 32 percent of U.S. homosexuals who are highly known anticipate discrimination and 20 percent worry about exposure of homosexuality. On the other hand, 69 percent of those only slightly known anticipate a great deal of discrimination and 56 percent worry about exposure (p. 195).

Homosexuals are about evenly divided between those who feel they are quite known about and those who feel they are little known. (see p. 184 and 195). Weinberg, M. S. & Williams, C. J. *Male Homosexuals*. New York: Oxford University Press, 1974.

13. Eichberg, R. *Coming Out: An Act of Love*. New York: Dutton, 1990, p. 13.

14. Dank, B. Why homosexuals marry women. *Medical Aspects of Human Sexuality*, 1972, 15-23.

15. Ross, M. W. *The Married Homosexual Man: A Psychological Study*. Boston: Routledge and Kegan Paul, 1983, 73.

16. The available research suggests that when homosexual men marry successfully, it is often the companionship and the love for their children that keeps the marriage together. The inability to share intimately with their wives is often a reason for the breakup. The sexual aspect of a heterosexual marriage is largely unsatisfactory for homosexual men, but not the reason for the breakup. Ross, M. W. *The Married Homosexual Man: A Psychological Study*. Boston: Routledge and Kegan Paul, 1983, 53.

17. Ross, M. W. *The Married Homosexual Man: A Psychological Study*. Boston: Routledge and Kegan Paul, 1983, 122.

18. Recall that Tony was married. This pattern of promiscuous sex may be particularly likely for married homosexuals. At any rate, Humphreys found that 54 percent of men who frequented tearooms like Tony were currently married. Humphreys, L. *Tearoom Trade*. Chicago: Aldine, 1970.

19. Good and Troiden explain how promiscuous sex is likely to be associated with emotional superficiality. Goode, E. & Troiden, R. R. Correlates and accompaniments of promiscuous sex among male homosexuals. *Psychiatry*, 1980, 43(1), 51-59.

20. This pattern of disclosure in the development of meaningful friendships is well researched. Waring, E. M. & Chilune, G. J. Marital intimacy and self-disclo-

closure. *Journal of Clinical Psychology,* 1983, 39, 183-190; Miller, G. R. & Steinberg, M. *Between People: A New Analysis of Interpersonal Communication.* Palo Alto, CA: Science Research Assoc., 1975; Morton, T. L. Intimacy and reciprocity of exchange: A comparison of spouses and strangers. *Journal of Personal and Social Psychology,* 1978, 36, 72-81; Ehrlich, H. J. & Graeven, D. B. Reciprocal self-disclosure in a dyad. *Journal of Experimental Social Psychology,* 1971, 7, 389-400; Cozby, P. C. Self-disclosure, a literature review. *Psychological Bulletin* 1973, 79, 73-91; Goffman, Erving. *The Presentation of Self.* Garden City, NY: Doubleday, 1959, p. 188-189; Altman, I. & Taylor, D. A. *Social Penetration: The Development of Interpersonal Relationships.* New York: Holt, 1973; Altman, I. Privacy regulation: Culturally universal or culturally specific? *Journal of Social Issues,* 1977, 33(3), 66-84; Altman, I. *The Environment and Social Behavior.* Monterey, CA: Brooks-Cole. 1975; Altman, I. Privacy: A conceptual analysis. *Environment and Behavior,* 1976, 8, 7-29; Altman, I. & Chemers, M. M. *Culture and Environment.* Monterey, CA: Brooks-Cole, 1980; Altman, I., Vinsel, Anne & Brinn, Barbara B. Dialectical conceptions in social psychology: An application to social penetration and privacy regulation. *Advances in Experimental Social Psychology* 1981, 14, 107-159; Jourard, S. M. *Self-Disclosure: An Experimental Analysis of the Transparent Self.* New York: Wiley, 1971; Jourard, Sidney M. Some psychological aspects of privacy. *Law and Contemporary Problems,* 1966, 31(2), 307-318; Chilune, G. J. Self-disclosure and its relationship to marital intimacy. *Journal of Counseling and Clinical Psychology,* 1984, Vol. 40(1), 216-219.

21. Clark, D. *Loving Someone Gay.* New York: Signet, 1977; Martin, A. D. Learning to hide: The socialization of the gay adolescent. *Adolescent Psychiatry,* 1982, 10, 52-65.

22. The quote is from Ruth Weatherford, a lesbian psychologist in San Francisco, personal interview, November 16, 1993.

23. Sedgwick says, "Even at an individual level, there are remarkably few of even the most openly gay people who are not deliberately in the closet with someone personally or economically or institutionally important to them. . . . Even an out gay person deals daily with interlocutors about whom she doesn't know whether they know or not; it is equally difficult to guess for any given interlocutor whether, if they did know, the knowledge would seem very important. . . and there can be few gay people, however, courageous and forthright by habit, however fortunate in the support of their immediate communities, in whose lives the closet is not still a shaping presence." Sedgwick, Eve Kosofsky. *Epistemology of the Closet.* Berkeley: University of California Press, 1990, (pp. 68-69).

24. "A national poll conducted for the *San Francisco Examiner* found that 54% of the respondents had revealed their sexual orientation to their coworkers." Hatfield, L. D. Gay life is getting better. *San Francisco Examiner,* A15, June 30 1989. Cited in Anderson, C. W. & Smith, R. Stigma and honor: Gay, lesbian, and bisexual people in the U.S. military. In L. Diamant (Ed.), *Homosexual Issues in the Workplace.* Washington, DC: Taylor & Francis, 1993.

25. David Cornelius found that the first questions homosexuals asked themselves in deciding whether to disclose their homosexuality was whether the lis-

tener could be "trusted" to deal with the information in a nonjudgmental way. Cornelius, David Lee. An application of a rules-based theory of interpersonal communication: The rules of taboo communication within a "gay community." Unpublished Doctoral Dissertation, 1980, Florida State University, DAI 4103.

26. Wells and Kline found their subjects were careful in choosing the heterosexuals to whom they disclosed their homosexuality. When they chose to do so it was to feel honest in the relationship, to develop the relationship in a more meaningful (intimate) way, to educate the heterosexual people about gays, and for their own sense of honor and integrity. Wells, J. W. & Kline, W. B. Self-disclosure of homosexual orientation. *Journal of Social Psychology*, 1987, 127(2), 191-197.

27. Several studies have found that the decisions for homosexuals to disclose in particular cases were more determined by the homosexual's judgment about whether that person could accept their homosexuality than whether the homosexual accepted his or her own homosexuality. Franke, R. & Leary, M. R. Disclosure of sexual orientation by lesbians and gay men: A comparison of private and public processes. *Journal of Social and Clinical Psychology*, 1991, 10(3), 262-269; Cain, R. Relational contexts and information management among gay men. *Families in Society*, 1991, 72(6), 344-352.

28. Schneider, B. E. Coming out at work: Bridging the private/public gap. *Work and Occupations*, 1986, 13(4), 463-487.

29. For example, Peter Fisher urges disclosure. He says:

> Every time a homosexual denies the validity of his feelings or restrains himself from expressing them, he does a small hurt to himself. He turns his energies inward and suppresses his own vitality. The effect may be scarcely noticeable: joy may be a little less keen, happiness slightly subdued, he may simply feel a little run-down, a little less tall. Over the years, these tiny denials have a cumulative effect. (p. 249)

A similar argument is made by Rob Eichberg:

> In this book I am calling on all of us to be willing to come out further. I am calling on us to express ourselves more fully and be more willing to say who we are and what we value. If you are homosexual and "pass" as heterosexual, I am asking that you disclose your homosexuality and realize that by hiding your sexual orientation you have contributed to the prevailing stereotypes of what it is to be gay and can make a major contribution to changing those stereotypes. If you are heterosexual and know someone who is gay, I am asking that you come out as well. You too have supported oppression by not stating that you have a son, daughter, mother, father, cousin, friend, or acquaintance who you care about who is gay. (p. 17)

Fisher, Peter. *The Gay Mystique: The Myth and Reality of Male Homosexuality*. New York: Stein and Day, 1972; also see Minton, Henry L. & McDonald, Gary J. Homosexual identity formation as a developmental process. In John P. De Cecco and Michael G. Shively (Eds.), *Bisexual & Homosexual Identities, Criti-*

cal Theoretical Issues: Origins of Sexuality and Homosexuality, Binghamton, NY: Harrington Park Press, 1984, 102; Rob Eichberg is cofounder of a gay rights political action committee in Los Angeles–The Municipal Elections Committee of Los Angeles (MECLA), p. 3; Eichberg, R. *Coming Out: An Act of Love.* New York: Dutton, 1990.

30. Dank, B. M. Coming out in the gay world. *Psychiatry,* 1971, 34, 180-195; Weinberg, M. S. & Williams, C. J. *Male Homosexuals.* New York: Oxford University Press, 1974.

31. The rise of this ethic can be traced to the Stonewall Riot of 1969. See: Herdt, G. & Boxer, A. Introduction: Culture, history and life course of gay men. In G. Herdt (Ed.). *Gay Culture in America.* Boston: Beacon, 1992, 1-28.

32. This point is related to a point made by De Cecco and Shively who argue that there should be a conceptual shift from thinking of homosexuality in terms of an identity, which inevitably carries with it the mythology of a biological identity, and replace it with an analysis of the homosexual relationship. De Cecco, J. P. & Shively, M. From sexual identity to sexual relationships: A contextual shift. In J. P. De Cecco & M. G. Shively (Eds.), *Origins of Sexuality and Homosexuality.* Binghamton, NY: Harrington Park Press, 1984.

33. Once men accept their homosexuality, they are less inclined to engage in the tearoom promiscuity that Tony did, and that many Americans find objectionable. Klassen et al. found that Americans object less to homosexuals in loving and committed relationships than to homosexual promiscuity. Humphreys found that 54 percent of the men who use a tearoom (a public rest room for making sexual contact) are married. Rogers and Turner report that men who have homosexual contact in the United States are *much* less likely to be married than the general population. Thus, it seems that if we allow men to accept their homosexuality and avoid marrying for purposes of disguise, we may reduce their tendency to use tearooms, and increase their acceptance by Americans by engaging in homosexual behavior in more loving relationships. Klassen, A. D., Williams, C. J., & Levitt, E. E. *Sex and Morality in the United States: An Empirical Inquiry under the Auspices of the Kinsey Institute.* Middletown, CT: Wesleyan University Press, 1989; Humphreys, L. *Tearoom Trade.* Chicago: Aldine. 1970; Rogers, S. M. & Turner, C. F. Male-male sexual contact in the U.S.A.: Findings from five sample surveys, 1970-1990. *The Journal of Sex Research,* 1991, 28(4), 491-519.

34. The DoD report concludes that homosexuals in foreign militaries do not typically disclose because they are afraid of "baiting, bashing and negative effects to their careers." However, the fact that they do not disclose is much more easily researched than are the reasons that they do not disclose. The military's hypothesis is that it is fear of physical and career consequences that prevents disclosure. The data reviewed in this chapter suggest that the homosexual hides his (or her) identity because of anticipated negative reactions that are much more subtle than the DoD suggests. Otjen, J. P., DaVitte, W. B., Miller, G. L., Redd, J. S., & Loy, J. M. (The Office of the Secretary of Defense Working Group), *Memorandum for the Secretary of Defense (Recommended DoD Homosexual Policy),* June 8, 1993, p. 14.

CHAPTER 6

1. The results of the Guttmacher study are reported in an article by Billy et al. The methodology is further described in a report by Tanfer. Billy, J. O. G., Tanfer, K., Grady, W. R., & Klepinger, D. The sexual behavior of men in the United States. *Family Planning Perspectives*, 1993, 25(2), 52-60; Tanfer, K. National survey of men: Design and execution. *Family Planning Perspectives*, 1993, 25(2), 83-86.

2. One article stated that conservative leader, Phyllis Schlafly, whose son was confirmed last year as being gay, said "It shows politicians they don't need to be worried about 1% of the population." And, similarly, gay activists were presumably concerned with ACT UP cofounder Larry Kramer saying, "They don't worry about 1%. This will give Bill Clinton a chance to welch on promises." Panton, P. & Toufexis, A. The shrinking ten percent. *Time*, April 26, 1993, 141, 17(April 26, 1993), 27.

3. Donovan reviewed the different definitions of homosexuality used by a wide variety of researchers and found a "fundamental inconsistency" in the way they defined them. Donovan, J. M. Homosexual, gay, and lesbian: Defining the words and sampling the populations. *Journal of Homosexuality*, 1992, 24(1/2), 27-47.

4. They would have been called "bisexual."

5. Why did the Guttmacher study get the attention and respect it did if it had such an odd definition of homosexuality? The reason was that the Guttmacher study was intended to measure AIDS-related activity. It was funded to do that, not to measure homosexual activity in our ordinary sense of the term.

Kori Tanfer, coauthor of the 1 percent study, made the following remarks to the author on January 5, 1993.

> The purpose of our research was not to estimate the true proportion of the gays in the population. There are other research techniques that would be more appropriate for that. We were trying to estimate levels of activity that put people at risk for AIDS and STDs, and so we had a very narrow definition of gay activity, more narrow than one would use if the purpose of the research was to measure the true proportion of gays in the population. We did not include, for example, homosexual hand holding, kissing, caressing, or even mutual masturbation. We did not count people as gay just because they had gay fantasies or homosexual desire. Because we were only interested in behaviors that put people at risk for AIDS and STDs, a person had to engage in either oral or anal intercourse in order to be considered homosexual in our study.

What is here being called the Guttmacher 1 percent study is: Billy, J. O. G., Tanfer, K., Grady, W. R., & Klepinger, D. The sexual behavior of men in the United States. *Family Planning Perspectives*, 1993, 25(2), 52-60; Tanfer, K. National survey of men: Design and execution. *Family Planning Perspectives*, 1993, 25(2), 83-86.

6. "Even if no sexual activity had occurred, a growing body of policy supported the view that a homosexual personality could readily be identified, and that such persons were to be barred from military service at induction or separated from the service upon discovery." National Defense Research Institute, *Sexual Orientation and U.S. Military Personnel Policy: Options and Assessment.* Prepared for the Office of the Secretary of Defense, MR-323-OSD, RAND 1993, p. 5-6.

7. Socarides was one of the authors who helped to popularize the notion of "latent homosexuality." To explain the term, he says:

> There is much confusion in the use of the term, latent homosexuality. Correctly it means the presence in an individual of the underlying psychic structure of true homosexuality without sexual orgastic activity with a person of the same sex. (p. 98)
> The latent homosexual may or may not have any conscious knowledge of his preference for individuals of the same sex for orgastic fulfillment. There may be a high degree of elaboration of unconscious homosexual fantasies and homosexual dream material. He may live his entire life span without realizing his homosexual propensities, functioning marginally on a heterosexual level, sometimes being married and having children. (p. 99)
> It is misleading and incorrect to assume that because an individual, due to regression, has dreams of wishing to be admired, loved and taken care of by older, authoritative and protective men he is suffering from homosexuality in its latent form. This is simply an infantile adaptation of extreme dependency and has no connection with the complex of psychodynamic factors which are responsible for true homosexuality, manifest or latent. (p. 100)

Socarides, C. W. *The Overt Homosexual.* New York: Grune & Stratton, 1968.

8. The concept of a "true homosexual" has been used even in the recent literature to make a distinction between true homosexuals and those who merely behave like homosexuals. Gutstadt has made a similar point about heterosexuals, arguing that in addition to true heterosexuals, there are pseudo heterosexuals who merely act like heterosexuals. Soloff, P. H. Pseudohomosexual psychosis in basic military training. *Archives of Sexual Behavior,* 1978, 7(5), 503-510; Gadpaille, W. J. Homosexuality in adolescent males. *Journal of the American Academy of Psychoanalysis*, 1975, 3(4), 361-371; Druss, R. G. Cases of suspected homosexuality seen at an army mental hygiene consultation service. *Psychiatric Quarterly,* 1967, 41(1), 62-70; Gutstadt, J. P. Male pseudoheterosexuality and minimal sexual dysfunction. *Journal of Sex and Marital Therapy,* 1976, 2(4), 297-302. See Shawver (1977) for a general discussion of the way scientific labels get created and how they mislead the unwary. (Shawver, L., Reserach variables in psychology and the logic of their creation. *Psychiatry,* 1977, 40(1), 1-16.

9. Karen Machover is the researcher who introduced and popularized this test. She and many others found that most males (boys and men) do in fact draw male figures first and most females draw females. Their conclusion that the drawing of the opposite sex first indicated an identity with the opposite sex has

been challenged by the great majority of the recent literature. And the study (Janzen et al.) that does show some statistical relationship between homosexuality and the gender of the first drawing shows a minimal relationship so that it would not be possible to use this test to reliably identify homosexuals. See Kahill, S. Human figure drawing in adults: An update of the empirical evidence 1967-1982. *Canadian Psychology*, 1984, 25(4), 269-292; Farylo, B., & Paludi, M. A. Research with the Draw-A-Person Test: Conceptual and methodological issues. *Journal of Psychology*, 1985, 119(6), 575-580; Roback, H. B., Langevin, R., & Zajac, Y. Sex of free choice figure drawings by homosexual and heterosexual subjects. *Journal of Personality Assessment*, 1974, 38(2), 154-155; Janzen, W. B. & Coe, W. C. Clinical and sign prediction: The Draw-A-Person and female homosexuality. *Journal of Clinical Psychology*, 1975, 31(4), 757-765.

10. Salzman, L. "Latent" homosexuality. In Judd Marmor (Ed.), *Sexual Inversion: The Multiple Roots of Homosexuality*. New York: Basic Books, Inc., 1965.

11. In a study by Berger and his colleagues, it was found that some women were able to identify homosexuals better than chance, but the group of men and women as a whole were not able to detect homosexuals better than chance. Berger, G., Hank, L., Rauzi, T. & Simkins, L. Detection of sexual orientation by heterosexuals and homosexuals. *Journal of Homosexuality*, 1987, 13(4), 83-100.

12. Specifically this study found that in a sample of men who had sex with other men, 23 percent had a primary female partner and 20 percent had children. Twenty-one percent had not disclosed their homosexual behavior to family, friends, or colleagues. Doll, L. S., Petersen, L.R., White, C. R., Johnson, E. S., Ward, J. W., & the Blood Donor Study Group. Homosexually and nonhomosexually identified men who have sex with men: A behavioral comparison. *The Journal of Sex Research*, 1992, 29(1), 1-14.

13. Cornelius, David Lee. An application of a rules-based theory of interpersonal communication: The rules of taboo communication within a "gay community." Unpublished Doctoral Dissertation, 1980, Florida State University, DAI 4103.

14. William Earl's study suggests that about 15 percent of men who have homosexual sexual activity are married or engaged to a woman and that only a very small fraction of these women are aware of their partner's homosexual activity. Earl, W. L. Married men and same-sex activity: A field study on HIV risk among men who do not identify as gay or bisexual. *Journal of Sex & Marital Therapy*, 1990, 16(4), 251-257.

15. Coleman, E. The married lesbian. *Marriage and Family Review*, 1989, 14, 3-4, 119-126.

16. The following studies show no difference in the masculinity and femininity of homosexuals when compared to heterosexuals. McDonald, G. J. & Moore, R. J. Sex-role self-concepts of homosexual men and their attitudes toward women and male homosexuality. *Journal of Homosexuality*, 1978, 4(1), 3-14; Jones, R. W. & De Cecco, J. P. The femininity and masculinity of partners of heterosexual and homosexual relationships. *Journal of Homosexuality*, 1982, 8(2), 37-44; Storms, M. O. Theories of sexual orientation. *Journal of Personality and Social Psychology*, 1980, 38(5), 763-792; also see: Connell, R. W. Very straight

gay: Masculinity, homosexual experience, and the dynamics of gender. *American Sociological Review*, 1992, 57(6), 735-751.

17. Nunngesser, L. G. *Homosexual Acts, Actors, and Identities*. New York: Praeger, 1983, p. 41.

18. Green, R. *The Sissy Boy Syndrome, and the Development of Homosexuality*. New Haven: Yale University Press, 1987. Green gives examples of very feminine boys who became heterosexual adults although he found that boys who were more feminine as children were more likely to be homosexual as adults.

19. In the older literature, homosexuals are often described as suffering from an impaired masculine self-image (Bieber et al., 1962), a "flight from masculinity" (Kardiner, 1963, p. 27), a "primary feminine identification" (Freud, 1905/53, p. 226), or a "secret longing to play the female's less demanding role" (Ruitenbeek, 1963, p. 120). Bieber, I., Dain, H., Dince, P., Drellich, M., Grand, H., Gundlach, T., Kremer, M., Rifkin, A., Wilber, C., & Bieber, T. *Homosexuality: A Psychoanalytic Study of Male Homosexuals*. New York: Basic Books, 1962; Kardiner, A. The flight from masculinity. In H. M. Ruitenbeck (Ed.), *The Problem of Homosexuality in Modern Society*. New York: E. P. Dutton, 1963; Freud, S. Three essays on the theory of sexuality (Originally published in 1905). In J. Strachey (Ed.), *The Standard Edition of the Complete Psychological Works of Sigmund Freud*. New York: Macmillan, 1953; Ruitenbeek, H. M. (Ed.). *The Problem of Homosexuality in Modern Society*. New York: E. P. Dutton, 1963.

20. Several studies have found their lesbian subjects to be about as feminine and masculine as heterosexual women. Jones, R. W. & De Cecco, J. P. The femininity and masculinity of partners of heterosexual and homosexual relationships. *Journal of Homosexuality*, 1982, 8(2), 37-44; Stokes, K., Kilmann, P. R., & Wanlass, R. L. Sexual orientation and sex role conformity. *Archives of Sexual Behavior*, 1983, 12(5), 427-433; Storms, M. O. Theories of sexual orientation. *Journal of Personality and Social Psychology*, 1980, 38(5), 763-792. Several other researchers have found their lesbian subjects to be about as feminine as heterosexual women but somewhat more masculine. Ponse, B. Lesbians and their worlds. In J. Marmor (Ed.), *Homosexual Behavior: A Modern Appraisal*. New York: Basic Books, 1980, 157-175; Finlay, B. & Scheltema, K. E. The relation of gender and sexual orientation to measures of masculinity, femininity and androgyny: A further analysis. *Journal of Homosexuality*, 1991, 21(3), 71-85; Oberstone, A. K. & Sukonek, H. Psychological adjustment and lifestyle of single lesbians and single heterosexual women. *Psychology of Women Quarterly*, 1976, 1(2), 172-188; Oldham, S., Farnill, D., & Ball, I. Sex-role identity of female homosexuals. *Journal of Homosexuality*, 1982, 8(1), 41-46; LaTorre, R. A., & Wendenburg, Kristina. Psychological characteristics of bisexual, heterosexual, and homosexual women. *Journal of Homosexuality*, 1983, 9(1), 87-97.

21. Lever et al. analyzed a sample of 6,982 men who reported having sexual experience with both males and females. Two-thirds thought of themselves as heterosexual. Similar proportions were reported in a smaller study. Doll studied 209 HIV-positive men who reported having sex with other men and found that only one-third identified themselves as homosexual with the rest only slightly more likely to identify themselves as bisexual than heterosexual. Lever, J., Ka-

nouse, D. E., Rogers, W. H., Carson, S., & Hertz, R. Behavior patterns and sexual identity of bisexual males. *The Journal of Sex Research*, 1992, 29(2), 141-167; Doll, L. S., Petersen, L.R., White, C. R., Johnson, E. S., Ward, J. W., & the Blood Donor Study Group. Homosexually and nonhomosexually identified men who have sex with men: A behavioral comparison. *The Journal of Sex Research*, 1992, 29(1), 1-14.

22. For a more complete analysis of how one can explain homosexual interest in oneself, and homosexual behavior, without applying the label "homosexual" to oneself, see Hencken, J.D. Conceptualizations of homosexual behavior which preclude homosexual self-labeling. In John De Cecco (Ed.), *Gay Personality and Sexual Labeling*. Binghamton, NY: The Haworth Press, 1985.

23. Carrier, J. M. & Magna, J. R. Mexican and Mexican-American male sexual behavior and spread of AIDS in California. *The Journal of Sex Research*, 1991, 28, 425-441.

24. Zarit, J. Intimate look of the Iranian male. In Arno Schmitt & Jehoda Sofer (Eds.), *Sexuality and Eroticism Among Males in Moslem Societies*. Binghamton, NY: The Haworth Press, 1992, 55-60.

25. Khan, B. Not-so-gay life in Karachi: A view of a Pakistani living in Toronto. In Arno Schmitt & Jehoda Sofer (Eds.), *Sexuality and Eroticism Among Males in Moslem Societies*. Binghamton, NY: The Haworth Press, Inc. 1992, 93-104.

26. Necef, M. U. Turkey on the brink of modernity: A guide for Scandinavian gays. In Arno Schmitt & Jehoda Sofer (Eds.), *Sexuality and Eroticism Among Males in Moslem Societies*. Binghamton, NY: The Haworth Press, Inc. 1992, 71-75.

27. Doll, L. S., Petersen, L. R., White, C. R., Johnson, E. S., Ward, J. W., & the Blood Donor Study Group. Homosexually and nonhomosexually identified men who have sex with men: A behavioral comparison. *The Journal of Sex Research*, 1992, 29(1), 1-14.

28. Lever, J., Kanouse, D. E., Rogers, W. H., Carson, S., & Hertz, R. Behavior patterns and sexual identity of bisexual males. *The Journal of Sex Research*, 1992, 29(2), 141-167.

29. Blumstein, P. & Schwartz, P. Bisexuality in men. *Urban Life*, 1976, 5, 339-358.

30. Bell, A. P., & Weinberg, M. S. *Homosexualities: A Study of Diversity among Men and Women*. New York: Simon & Schuster, 1978.

31. For example, Lonnie Barbach, one of the most notable authors on the topic of sex therapy says, "Lesbian fantasies are not uncommon among women, and they make sense. Women are attractive and erotic beings. An aroused woman is sexually exciting." Barbach, L. G. *For Yourself: The Fulfillment of Female Sexuality*. Garden City, NY: Doubleday, 1975, p. 79.

32. This data was reported by Bell and Weinberg on an apparently representative sample. According to one study, for example, only 25 percent of male homosexuals and only 38 percent of lesbians were exclusively homosexual. Bell, A. P.

& Weinberg, M. S., *Homosexualities: A Study of Diversity among Men and Women.* New York: Simon and Schuster, 1978.

33. Several authors report that it is common for lesbians to worry about the extent to which they fantasize about men. Masters and Johnson reported that heterosexual fantasies were the third most common fantasies of women who reported themselves as lesbian. Roth, S. Psychotherapy with lesbian couples: Individual issues, female socialization, and the social context. *Journal of Marital and Family Therapy*, 1985, 11(3), 273-286. Chapman and Brannock found that 85 percent of lesbian-identified women had had sexual contact with men. Saghir and Robins (1973) and Hedblom (1973) also suggest that the majority of lesbians have had heterosexual experience. Chapman, B. E. & Brannock, J. C. Proposed model of lesbian identity development: An empirical examination. *Journal of Homosexuality*, 1987, 14, 69-80; Saghir, M. T. & Robins, E. *Male and Female Homosexuality: A Comprehensive Investigation*. Baltimore: Williams and Wilkins, 1973; Hedblom, J. H. Dimensions of lesbian sexual experience. *Archives of Sexual Behavior*, 1973, 2, 329-341; Masters, W. & Johnson, V. *Homosexuality in Perspective.* Boston: Little, Brown, 1979.

34. Rust reported that only one-third of her sample of 427 subjects said that they were exclusively attracted to women although only one out of six were participating simultaneously in both lesbian and heterosexual relationships. Bell and Weinberg found that half of the lesbian women in their sample were exclusively attracted to women. Rust, P. C. The politics of sexual identity: Sexual attraction and behavior among lesbian and bisexual women. *Social Problems*, 1992, 39(4), 366-386; Bell, A. P. & Weinberg, M. S. *Homosexualities: A Study Of Diversity among Men And Women*. New York: Simon & Shuster, 1978.

35. Chapman et al. found that of women who identified themselves as lesbians approximately 85 percent had heterosexual experience. Chapman, B. E. & Brannock, J. C. Proposed model of lesbian identity development: An empirical examination." *Journal of Homosexuality*, 1987, 14, 69-80.

36. Saghir and Robins, 1973, found similar proportions. They found that about 75 percent of homosexual males have engaged in heterosexual kissing and necking and 50 percent have had heterosexual intercourse with a rate similar to that of heterosexual males, and 50 percent had had a relationship with a woman lasting more than a year and including sexual relations. Saghir, M. T. & Robins, E. *Male and Female Homosexuality: A Comprehensive Investigation*. Baltimore: Williams & Wilkins, 1973.

37. Rogers, S. M. & Turner, C. F. Male-male sexual contact in the U.S.A.: Findings from five sample surveys, 1970-1990. *The Journal of Sex Research*, 1991, 28(4), 491-519. Most of the research on the heterosexual identity of men who engage in homosexual behavior has been conducted in an effort to understand how the HIV virus spreads outside of the homosexual community. See also Peterson, J. & Marin, G. Issues in the prevention of AIDS among Black and Hispanic men. *American Psychologist*, 1988, 43, 871-877; Fay, R. E., Turner, C. F., Klassen, A. D., & Gagnon, J. H. Prevalence and patterns of same-gender contact among men. *Science*, 1989, 243, 338-348.

38. Rothblum, E. D. & Brehony, K. A. The Boston marriage today: Romantic but asexual relationships among lesbians. In Charles Silverstein (Ed.), *Gays, Lesbians and Their Therapists: Studies in Psychotherapy.* New York: W. W. Norton, 1991; Loulan, J. Research on the sex practices of 1,566 lesbians and the clinical applications. *Women and Therapy,* 1988, 7, 221-234.

39. One study reported on over 1,500 lesbians and found that the majority (78 percent) had been celibate at some point, with 35 percent celibate from one to five years and 8 percent celebate for over six years. Loulan, J. Preliminary report on survey of lesbian sex practices. Unpublished manuscript. Cited in Falco, K. L. *Psychotherapy with Lesbian Clients.* New York: Brunner/Mazel, 1991, p. 144; Nichols, M. The treatment of inhibited sexual desire (ISD) in lesbian couples. *Women and Therapy,* 1982, 1(4), 49-66.

40. Leif, H. I. Evaluation of inhibited sexual desire: Relationship aspects. In H. S. Kaplan (Ed.), *Comprehensive Evaluation of Disorders of Sexual Desire.* Washington, DC: American Psychiatric Press, 1985; LoPiccollo, L. Low sexual desire. In S. R. Lieblum, & L. A. Pervin (Eds.), *Principles and Practice of Sex Therapy.* New York. Guilford, 1980; Schover, L. & LoPiccollo, J. Effectiveness of treatment for dysfunction of sexual desire. *Journal of Sex and Marital Therapy,* 1982, 8:179-197; Hawton, K., Catalan, J., Martin, P., & Fagg, J. Prognostic factors in sex therapy. *Behavior Research and Therapy,* 1986, 24, 377-385.

41. Some studies (i.e., Coleman et al. and Masters & Johnson) suggest that lesbians are more sexually responsive than heterosexual women and more sexually responsive in general. Masters and Johnson speculate that lesbian women have sex that is more suited to women, less penetration, less concentration on orgasm. Coleman, E., Hoon, P., & Hoon, E. Arousability and sexual satisfaction in lesbian and heterosexual women. *Journal of Sex Research,* 1983, 19(1), 58-73; Masters, W. & Johnson, V. *Homosexuality in Perspective.* Boston: Little, Brown, 1979.

Other studies report lower levels of sexual activity among lesbians. Burch, B. Psychological merger in lesbian couples: A joint ego psychological and systems approach. *Family Therapy,* 1982, 9(3), 201-208; Blumstein, P. & Schwartz, P. *American Couples: Money, Work, Sex.* New York: William Morrow, 1983; Decker, B. Counseling gay and lesbian couples. *Journal of Social Work and Human Sexuality,* 1984, 2(2/3), 39-52; Kaufman, P., Harrison, E., & Hyde, M. Distancing for intimacy in lesbian relationships. *American Journal of Psychiatry,* 1984, 14, 530-533; Nichols, M. Relationships between sexual behavior, erotic arousal, romantic attraction, and self-labeled sexual orientation. Paper presented at the SSSS Conference, San Diego, 1985; Roth, S. Psychotherapy with lesbian couples: Individual issues, female socialization, and the social context. *Journal of Marital and Family Therapy,* 1985, 11(3), 273-286; Schreiner-Engle, P. *Clinical aspects of female sexuality.* Paper presented at the meeting of the International Academy of Sex Research, Amsterdam, the Netherlands. September 20, 1986.

42. Doll and her colleagues found 11 percent of their sample of homosexually identified men were celibate. Masters and Johnson report treating a sample of 57 such men. Doll, L. S., Petersen, L. R., White, C. R., Johnson, E. S., Ward, J. W.,

& the Blood Donor Study Group. Homosexually and nonhomosexually identified men who have sex with men: A behavioral comparison. *The Journal of Sex Research*, 1992, 29(1), 1-14; Masters, W. & Johnson, V. *Homosexuality in Perspective*. Boston: Little, Brown, 1979, p. 275.

43. Leif, H. I. Evaluation of inhibited sexual desire: Relationship aspects. In H. S. Kaplan (Ed.), *Comprehensive Evaluation of Disorders of Sexual Desire*. Washington, DC: American Psychiatric Press, 1985; LoPiccollo, L. Low sexual desire. In S. R. Lieblum & L. A. Pervin (eds.), *Principles and Practice of Sex Therapy*. New York: Guilford, 1980; Schover, L. LoPiccollo, J. Effectiveness of treatment for dysfunction of sexual desire. *Journal of Sex and Marital Therapy*, 1982, 8, 179-197; Hawton, K., Catalan, J., Martin, P., & Fagg, J. Prognostic factors in sex therapy. *Behavior Research and Therapy*, 1986, 24, 377-385.

44. Kurdek, L. A. & Schmitt, J. P. Relationship quality of partners in heterosexual married, heterosexual cohabiting, gay, and lesbian relationships. *Journal of Personality and Social Psychology*, 1986, 51, 711-720.

45. De Cecco, J. P. & Shively, M.G. (Eds.), *Bisexual and Homosexual Identities, Critical Theoretical Issues. Origins of Sexuality and Homosexuality*. Binghamton, NY: Harrington Park Press, 1984.

46. The exact definition of homosexual sex in a survey rests upon the particular wording in the relevant questions. For example, a survey that asked a subject, "Have you had sex with another person of your gender to the point of orgasm?" and labeled the people who said "yes" homosexual, would be defining "homosexual" differently from a study that asked, "Have you had sex with another person of your gender in which either you or the other person had an orgasm?" There are obviously, many permutations of possibility here and each could produce different numbers.

47. For example, one study asked subjects, "Now, thinking about the time since your 18th birthday (including the past 12 months), how many male partners have you ever had sex with?" Smith, T. W. Adult sexual behavior in 1989: Number of partners, frequency of intercourse, and risk of AIDS. *Family Planning Perspectives*, 1991, 23(3), 102-107.

48. We are not using the Guttmacher study here because that study (reporting only one percent homosexual activity) required oral or anal intercourse. The review that reports an average of 6 percent reporting homosexual activity in a variety of studies is Rogers, S. M. & Turner, C. F. Male-male sexual contact in the U.S.A.: Findings from five sample surveys, 1970-1990. *The Journal of Sex Research*, 1991, 28(4), 491-519; The Guttmacher study is: Billy, J. O. G., Tanfer, K., Grady, W. R., & Klepinger, D. The sexual behavior of men in the United States. *Family Planning Perspectives*, 1993, 25(2), 52-60; Tanfer, K. National survey of men: Design and execution. *Family Planning Perspectives*, 1993, 25(2), 83-86.

49. For example, in their review of five sample surveys from 1970 through 1990, Rogers and and Turner concluded:

> Given the history of social intolerance of same-gender sexual contact in American (and many other) societies, it is reasonable to expect that our estimates contain a negative bias of unknown magnitude. That is to say, it

> is likely that more men in our surveys will have concealed same-gender sexual experiences they have had than will report experiences they have not had.

Similar statements can be found in other studies. Rogers, S. M. & Turner, C. F. Male-male sexual contact in the U.S.A.: Findings from five sample surveys, 1970-1990. *The Journal of Sex Research*, 1991, 28(4), 491-519, quote from p. 516; See: Lever, J., Kanouse, D. E., Rogers, W. H., Carson, S., & Hertz, R. Behavior patterns and sexual identity of bisexual males. *The Journal of Sex Research*, 1992, 29(2), 141-167; Fay, R. E., Turner, C. F., Klassen, A. D., & Gagnon, J. H. Prevalence and patterns of same-gender contact among men. *Science*, 1989, 243, 338-348; Warren, C. A. B. *Identity and Community in the Gay World*. New York: John Wiley and Sons, 1974.

The best available evidence, which is still quite questionable, indicates that perhaps half the people who have had homosexual sex lie to avoid disclosing it. Clark, J. P. & Tifft, L. L. Polygraph and interview validation of self-reported deviant behavior. *American Sociological Review*, 1966, 31, 516-523.

50. There is, of course, a range in the nonresponse rate between the different studies. The Guttmacher's 1 percent study (Billy et al., 1993.) reported only 70 percent. The one study with a very high response rate (i.e., 88 percent) also had a much higher proportion of reported homosexual behavior. This study estimated that the percentage of men with adult homosexual activity in the last 11 years was 8.1 percent. Billy, J. O. G., Tanfer, K., Grady, W. R., & Klepinger, D. The sexual behavior of men in the United States. *Family Planning Perspectives*, 1993, 25(2), 52-60; Tanfer, K. National survey of men: Design and execution. *Family Planning Perspectives*, 1993, 25(2), 83-86.

51. Groves, R. M., Cialdini, R. B. & Couper, M. P. Understanding the decision to participate in a survey. *Public Opinion Quarterly*, 1992, 56, 477-494.

52. Turner, C. F., Miller, H. G., & Moses, L. E. (Eds.). *AIDS: Sexual Behavior and Intravenous Drug Use*. Washington, DC: National Academy Press, 1989. Miller, H. G., Turner, C. F., & Moses, L. E. (Eds.). *AIDS: The Second Decade*. Washington, DC: National Academy Press, 1990, 369-375.

53. Ford, K. & Norris, A. Methodological considerations for survey research on sexual behavior: Urban African-American and Hispanic youth. *Journal of Sex Research*, 1991, 28(4), 539-555.

54. Pilot study of a household survey to determine HIV seroprevalence. *Morbidity and Mortality Weekly Report,* January 11, 1991, 40(1), 1-5.

55. Kane, E. W. & Macaulay, L. J. Interviewer gender and gender attitudes. *Public Opinion Quarterly*, 1993, 57, 1-28.

56. In a study in 1966, five of 45 male college students indicated on a questionnaire that they had experienced homosexual sex as an adult. When these students were threatened with a lie detector test, two indicated that they had lied when they said they had and six indicated that they had lied when they said they had not had homosexual sex.

The RAND review, done for the Secretary of Defense in 1993, referred to a study reported by Clark and Tifft (1966) in which they found that although only

7.5 percent of male subjects reported that they had had sexual experience with a man in a questionnaire, once they were confronted with the possibility of a polygraph test of their truthfulness many confessed to such behavior, and although some who had said they had had such behavior on the questionnaire changed their mind with the polygraph. The final percentage who admitted such behavior was 22.5 percent. National Defense Research Institute, *Sexual Orientation and U. S. Military Personnel Policy: Options and Assessment*, Prepared for the Office of the Secretary of Defense, MR-OSD, RAND, 1993; Clark, J. P.; & Tifft, L. L. Polygraph and interview validation of self-reported deviant behavior. *American Sociological Review*, 1966, 31, 516-523.

57. This is somewhat less than Kinsey's calculation of 37 percent in 1948, but then, as we have seen, Kinsey's sample is somewhat biased in favor of prisoners who seem to have more homosexual contact than other groups.

58. The RAND review done for the Secretary of Defense in 1993 referred to the study used here, Clark and Tifft, 1966 to estimate the proportion of subjects who lie in a study on homosexual activity. The RAND group estimated on this basis that the proportion of men who had homosexual sex was 22.5 percent. However, they used the base rate of admitted homosexuality reported in the Clark and Tifft study which was 7.5 percent. This base rate is not as reliable as the base rate reported in the Roger and Turner review cited above which was reported to be 6 percent. National Defense Research Institute, *Sexual Orientation and U.S. Military Personnel Policy: Options and Assessment*, Prepared for the Office of the Secretary of Defense, MR-323-OSD, RAND, 1993; Clark, J. P. & Tifft, L. L. Polygraph and interview validation of self-reported deviant behavior. *American Sociological Review*, 1966, 31, 516-523.

59. Numerous observers have talked about the way in which female sexuality is less orgasmically measured than men's. See, for example, Kinsey's report on female sexuality. Kinsey, A., Pomeroy, W. B., Martin, C. E., & Gebhard, C. E. *Sexual Behavior in the Human Female*. Philadelphia: W. B. Saunders Co., 1953, pp. 454. Also see Hite. Hite, S. *The Hite Report: A Nationwide Study of Female Sexuality*. New York: Macmillan, 1976, 265-269.

60. The data reported by Klassen, Williams, and Levitt was collected in 1970 although the book in which it appeared was published in 1989. The figures (see page 415) from which it is concluded here that women had about half the homosexual experience that men had in 1970 was based on lifetime homosexual experience, not just adult homosexual experience. Klassen, A. D., Williams, C. J., & Levitt, E. E. *Sex and Morality in the United States: An Empirical Inquiry under the Auspices of the Kinsey Institute*. Middletown, CT: Wesleyan Unversity Press, 1989.

61. The Hite report is based on a 1972 national sample of 1,844 subjects who responded to a questionnaire in a variety of sources. It is a cross between a representative sample and a convenience sample. She reported that 8 percent said they "preferred sex with women" and another 9 percent who had had experience with women did not state their preference. This gives us an estimated base rate of 17

percent of women having experienced sex with women. Hite, S. *The Hite Report: A Nationwide Study of Female Sexuality.* New York: Macmillan, 1976, p. 261.

62. Smith reported on 1988-1989 data that indicated an increase in reported female homosexuality. In the 1988 data, there were fewer women than men engaging in homosexuality, but in the 1989 data there were equal proportions. Nancy Friday concluded from her nonrandom sample that there is far more interest in lesbianism today. Smith, T. W. Adult sexual behavior in 1989: Number of partners, frequency of intercourse and risk of AIDS. *Family Planning Perspectives*, 1991, 23(3), 102-107; Friday, N. *Women on Top: How Real Life Has Changed Women's Sexual Fantasies*. New York: Simon & Schuster, 1991, p. 201.

63. This point was also made by National Defense Analyst David F. Burrelli who says, "The Department of Defense has outlined specific definitions as a part of its policy (of banning homosexuals). Since this definition is likely to be different from others in use, it is unlikely that there will be agreement on the proportion of military personnel who are homosexual." Burrelli, D. F. Homosexuals and U.S. military personnel policy. *CRS Congressional Report Service Report for Congress*, January 14, 1993, p. CRS-13.

64. The legal and administrative policy evolved during this 75-five year period through many different versions.

65. Department of Defense (DoD Directive) 1332.14.

66. The Uniform Code of Military Justice (UCMJ), Article 125.

67. Kathleen Gilberd, a legal expert on the issue of homosexual discharge from the military, interpreted the 1994 guidelines in this way, "The regulations published in 1994 define a homosexual act to include not only any bodily contact for the purpose of satisfying sexual desire, but also any bodily contact that a reasonable person would understand to demonstrate a propensity or intent to engage in acts to satisfy sexual desire. In the latter definition, no homosexual orientation or interest is required." 01/08/93.

68. In Roger and Turner's review of five studies, four asked if there was a relationship between having been in the military and having had a homosexual experience. Those men who had served in the military were consistently more likely to have had homosexual experience. The average study showed that about 4.8 percent of nonvets had had homosexual sex whereas 7.3 percent of vets had had homosexual sex. Rogers, S. M. & Turner, C. F. Male-male sexual contact in the U.S.A.: Findings from five sample surveys, 1970-1990. *The Journal of Sex Research*, 1991, 28(4), 491-519.

69. Harry reported that 57 percent of homosexuals and 60 percent of heterosexual males in his samples had served in the military. Although Williams and Weinberg report that 47 percent of the homosexuals in their sample had served in the military. McWhirter and Mattison found 53 percent of their sample of homosexual couples had served in the military. Harry, Joseph. Homosexual men and women who served their country. In J. De Cecco (Ed.), *Bashers, Baiters, and Bigots: Homophobia in American Society.* Binghamton, NY: Harrington Park Press, 1985; Williams, C. & Weinberg, M. *Homosexuals and the Military.* New York: Harper & Row, 1971; McWhirter, D. P. & Mattison, A. M. *The Male Cou-*

ple: How Relationships Develop. Englewood Cliffs, NJ, Prentice-Hall, Inc., 1984, 149. Rogers and Miller found that 7.6 percent of the men that had reported military service also reported engaging in same-gender contact whereas only 5.1 percent of other men reported same-gender contact. Rogers, S. M. & Turner, C. F. Male-male sexual contact in the U.S.A.: Findings from five sample surveys, 1970-1990. *The Journal of Sex Research*, 1991, 28(4), 491-519.

70. These figures are calculations made using the data published by the United States General Accounting Office. *Defense Force Management: Statistics Related to DoD's Policy on Homosexuality.* Report to Congressional Requesters, June, 1992. The figures below are the average yearly population and average yearly discharges for homosexuals for the years 1980 through 1990.

	Av. Yearly Pop.	Av. Yearly Disch.
ARMY	769,749	385
NAVY	562,783	785
AIR FORCE	577,605	272
MARINES	195,633	96

Total population – 2,105,770
Total homosexual discharges – 1,538

The proportion discharged for homosexuality is .0007303, which is about 1 per 1,300 soldiers discharged for homosexuality. If we figure that 6 percent of the soldiers have a homosexual interest then there were an average of 126,346 such soldiers during this period, only a little over 1 percent of which were discharged for homosexuality.

71. Richardson said:

> Perhaps the pendulum has swung rather far, though elderly critics of the sexual license enjoyed by the young should make sure that their hearts are purged of any secret envy of the freedoms which were not available, or not enjoyed, in their own youth. Prophets of doom, pointing to historical examples when sexual license was a symptom of national decadence, are apt to pick on homosexuality. With homosexual men flaunting their preferences and insisting on their right not to be discriminated against, this is no longer a matter of secretiveness. In my pamphlet I wrote:
> Homosexuality occasionally becomes a disciplinary problem, but far more often remains a personal one and may be a source of deep unhappiness to more of our men than we suspect.

Richardson, F. M. *Fighting Spirit: A Study of Psychological Factors in War.* New York: Crane, Russak & Company, Inc, 1978, p. 132.

CHAPTER 7

1. In 1983, when the All Volunteer Force was 10 years old, Gus Lee, who had served as a special assistant for the All Volunteer Force and director of manpower requirements and utilization, wrote, "It is easy to forget the widespread skepticism concerning the feasibility of the volunteer force that prevailed in the Pentagon building in 1970. I used to say that there weren't a dozen people in the Pentagon at the time who were convinced the volunteer force would work. . . . As late as 1969, 62 percent of the respondents in public opinion polls favored continuance of the draft over the volunteer force. By arguing the feasibility and desirability of a volunteer force the Gates report helped to change opinion both in the press and among the general public." Lee, Gus C. Commentary. In W. Bowman, R. Little, & G. T. Sicilia (Eds.), *The All Volunteer Force after a Decade: Retrospect and Prospect.* Washington: Pergamon-Brassey's, 1986, p. 104.

2. See Pulwers, Jack E. The information and education programs of the armed forces: An administrative and social history, 1940-1945; Unpublished Doctoral Dissertation, 1983. Catholic University of America, DAI 4404; Muson, Edward Lyman. *The Management of Men: A Handbook on the Systematic Development of Morale and the Control of Human Behavior.* New York: H. Holt and Company, 1921, pp. 8,9,10.

Baynes points out that prior to the twentieth century, the brutal system of discipline was not unique to the military. "Even in the early twentieth century, obedience was enforced by the accepted means of physical dicipline. Men in authority in all walks of life were expected to enforce discipline strictly. This applied to schoolmasters, employers of labor, foremen, parents, policemen, and every type of person one can think of with the least vestige of authority, as much as to officers and N.C.O.s of the Army. And there were few doubts about how to enforce discipline. The schoolmaster told a boy to learn something, and if the boy did not know the answer the next day the master beat him; the foreman ordered a man to do a job, and if it was not done the man was sacked; in the Army an N.C.O. gave an order, and the private who failed to obey was doubled off to the guardroom and put in close arrest." Baynes, J. *Morale: A Study of Men and Courage.* New York: Frederick Praeger, 1967, 185-186.

3. Janowitz, M. *The Professional Soldier: A Social and Political Portrait.* New York: The Free Press, 1960, p. 38.

4. Pulwers reports a mobilization document dated October 21, 1939, which created a Morale Division in the Office of the Adjutant General. Pulwers, Jack E. The information and education programs of the armed forces: An administrative and social history, 1940-1945. Unpublished Doctoral Dissertation, 1983, Catholic University of America, DAI 4404. (see page 283).

5. Over the next four years it was known as the Special Services Division and then the Information and Education Division. Stouffer, S. A. et al. *The American Soldier: Adjustment During Army Life.* Princeton, NJ: Princeton University Press, 1949, Vol. I, p. 12.

6. Americans in World War II felt that it was important to give the soldier entertainment and recreation. A popular article in the *Readers Digest* in that era reflects that common sentiment:

"During the early fighting in North Africa I saw a soldier start to light a fire with the tattered remnants of a month-old newspaper. He was nearly mobbed. 'Hey!' yelled one of his buddies. 'There's 50 men haven't read that yet!'

"Things are better now–thanks to the Army's Special Service Division, whose task is to fight the soldier's worst enemy, boredom. . . . ."

He goes on to describe that the Special Service Office graduates a class of 400 every four weeks, one of which was assigned to each regiment and saw to it "that every soldier in the front-line area receives free each week cigarettes, matches, candy, soap, and a copy of *Stars and Stripes*, official newspaper of the North African theater."

Then there were A-kits: footballs, baseballs, bats, gloves, badminton sets, and volleyballs, B-kits: books, Victrolas, radios, small games such as cards, chess, and checkers as well as envelopes, pencils, and pens. In one month, movie performances were given at 700 places in North Africa to an attendance of 2,251,695. "There were shows as close as 25 miles to the firing line. . . ."

The person who directed Special Services was Brigadier General Ben Sawbridge. Painton, Frederick C. Fun behind the front. *Readers Digest*, October 1943, 99-102.

7. Jenkins describes how the military became involved in a dramatics program for military service personnel during World War II. Initially it was done to enhance morale. Later it was understood as a possible propaganda tool. This program, however, was eliminated at the end of World War II. Jenkins, D. J. Soldier theatricals: 1940-1945 (Special Services, World War II). Unpublished Doctoral Dissertation, 1992, Bowling Green State University, DAI 5312.

8. Pulwers, Jack E. The information and education programs of the armed forces: An administrative and social history, 1940-1945. Unpublished Doctoral Dissertation, 1983, Catholic University of America, DAI 4404. (see page 85).

9. Pulwers, Jack E. The information and education programs of the armed forces: An administrative and social history, 1940-1945. Unpublished Doctoral Dissertation, 1983, Catholic University of America, DAI 4404. (see page 86).

10. Pulwers, Jack E. The information and education programs of the armed forces: An administrative and social history, 1940-1945. Unpublished Doctoral Dissertation, 1983, Catholic University of America, DAI 4404. (see page 88).

11. Pulwers, Jack E. The information and education programs of the armed forces: An administrative and social history, 1940-1945. Unpublished Doctoral Dissertation, 1983, Catholic University of America, DAI 4404. (see page 99).

12. Things get confused with the old concept of morale when cohesion also is used to imply that the soldiers stick together in a way that supports the military leadership. The concept of cohesion was suggested in a very influential article by Shils and Janowitz immediately after WWII which suggested that we replace the simple concept of "morale" with concepts that discriminated between different elements of morale. "Cohesion" or the bonding of the individual service mem-

bers, was one of those elements. Nevertheless, the concept inches back toward the concept of morale as authors (e.g., Johns et al., 1984; Henderson, 1985) notice that some "cohesion," or closeness among the soldiers, may actually result in their resistance to military authority. Shils, E. A. & Janowitz, M. Cohesion and disintegration in the Wehrmacht in World War II. *Public Opinion Quarterly*, 1948, 12, 281; Johns, J. H. et al., *Cohesion in the U.S. Military*. Washington, DC: National Defense University Press, 1984, p. 9; Henderson, W. D. *Cohesion: The Human Element in Combat*. Washington, DC: National Defense University Press, 1985, p. 4; Kellett, A. *Combat Motivation: The Behavior of Soldiers in Battle*. Boston: Kluver & Nijhoff Publishing, 1982, p. 319.

13. Shils, E. A. & Janowitz, M. Cohesion and disintegration in the Wehrmacht in World War II. *Public Opinion Quarterly*, 1948, 12, 280-315, p. 284.

14. Shils, E. A. & Janowitz, M. Cohesion and disintegration in the Wehrmacht in World War II. *Public Opinion Quarterly*, 1948, 12, 280-315. quote from p. 285.

15. The scholarly sources of this conclusion are as follows: Stouffer, S. A. et al., *The American Soldier*. Princeton, NJ: Princeton University Press, 1949, Vols. I and II; Shils, E. A. & Janowitz, M. Cohesion and disintegration in the Wehrmacht in World War II. *Public Opinion Quarterly*, 1948, 12, 280-315; Homan, George C. The small warship. *American Sociological Review*, 1946, 11, 294-300; Lazarfeld, Paul F. *Quarterly*, 1949, 13, 377-404; Shils, E. A. Primary groups in the American army. In Robert K. Merton & Paul F. Lazarsfeld (Eds.), *Continuities in Social Research: Studies in the Scope and Method of the American Soldier*. New York: Free Press, 1950, 16-39; Mandelbaum, D. G. *Soldiers Groups and Negro Soldiers*. Berkeley and Los Angeles: University of California Press, 1959, 5-87; Hilmar, N. A. The dynamics of military group behavior. In Charles H. Coates & Roland J. Pellegrin (Eds.), *Military Sociology*. University Park, MD: Social Science Press, 1965, 311-335; Grinker, R. R. & Spiegel, J. P. *Men under Stress*. New York: McGraw-Hill, Inc., 1963, 443-460.

16. Shemella, P. The military does not look like America. *Army*, July 1993, 44. Captain Paul Shemella, U.S. Navy, serves as chief of the policy, strategy, and doctrine division at the U.S. Special Operations Command, Tampa, Florida.

17. The quotation is from Dwight Eisenhower's testimony made before the Senate Armed Services committee. He was arguing against integrating "Negroes" into the military. Quotation was taken from: Bass, G. J. Their words: Discrimination, 1948 and 1993. *New Republic*, Feb. 22, 1993, 208(8), 15.

18. The most recent and thorough analysis of the existing data on cohesion was reported by Mullen & Cooper (1993). Evans and Dion (1991) report a review of 16 field studies and an average correlation of .36. Also see Oliver, L. W. *Cohesion Research: Conceptual and Methodological Issues*. Alexandria, VA: U.S. Army Research Institute for the Behavioral and Social Sciences, 1990; Mullen, B. & Cooper, C. *The Relation between Group Cohesiveness and Performance: An Integration*, Unpublished manuscript, Department of Psychology, Syracuse University, 1993, cited in the RAND Report; National Defense Research Institute, *Sexual Orientation and U.S. Military Personnel Policy: Options and Assessment*, Prepared for the Office of the Secretary of Defense, MR-323-OSD, RAND, 1993; Evans, N. J. &

Dion, K. L. Group cohesion and performance: A meta-analysis. *Small Group Research*, 1991, 22, 175-186.

19. This conclusion is primarily drawn from Mullen and Cooper. However, Lott and Lott also provide evidence that success promotes cohesion rather than cohesion promoting success. Mullen, B. & Cooper, C. The relation between group cohesiveness and performance: An integration. Unpublished manuscript, Department of Psychology, Syracuse University, 1993. Cited in MacCoun, R. What is known about unit cohesion and military performance. National Defense Research Institute, *Sexual Orientation and U.S. Military Personnel Policy: Options and Assessment*, Prepared for the Office of the Secretary of Defense, MR-323-OSD, RAND, 1993; Lott, A. J. & Lott, B. E. Group cohesiveness, communication level and conformity. *Journal of Abnormal and Social Psychology*, 1961, 62, 408-412.

20. The studies cited here are meta-analyses (meaning that they review a number of other studies). In reviewing nonmilitary literature, Evans and Dion found that among 16 studies, the average correlation between performance and cohesion was .36. Oliver reviewed 14 army studies and found an average correlation of .32. Mullen and Cooper reviewed 49 studies under contract with the Army Research institute and found an average correlation of .25, although only a correlation of .20 for military groups. Evans, N. J. & Dion, K. L. Group cohesion and performance: A meta-analysis. *Small Group Research*, 1991, 22, 175-186; Oliver, L. W., *The Relationship of Group Cohesion to Group Performance: A Research Integration Attempt.* Alexandria, VA: U.S. Army Research Institute for the Behavioral and Social Sciences, 1988. Cited in MacCoun, R. What is known about unit cohesion and military performance. National Defense Research Institute, *Sexual Orientation and U.S. Military Personnel Policy: Options and Assessment*, Prepared for the Office of the Secretary of Defense, MR-323-OSD, RAND, 1993; Mullen, B. & Cooper, C. *The relationship between group cohesiveness and performance: An integration*, Unpublished manuscript, Department of Psychology, Syracuse University, 1993. Cited in MacCoun, R. What is known about unit cohesion and military performance. National Defense Research Institute, *Sexual Orientation and U.S. Military Personnel Policy: Options and Assessment*, Prepared for the Office of the Secretary of Defense, MR-323-OSD, RAND, 1993.

21. Wesbrook, S. D. The potential for military disintegration. In S. C. Sarkesian (Ed.), *Combat Effectiveness: Cohesion, Stress, and the Volunteer Military.* Beverly Hills, CA: Sage, 1980, 244-278; Savage, P. L. & Gabriel, R. A. Cohesion and disintegration in the American army: An alternative perspective, *Armed Forces and Society*, 1976, 2, 340-376; Ingraham, L. H. *The Boys in the Barracks: Observations on American Military Life.* Philadelphia: ISHI, 1984.

22. Vaitkus & Griffith (1990) compared the unit replacement technique with the individual replacement technique for creating units with good morale and cohesion. They tested the morale and cohesion at three separate times afterwards, found a significant improvement in time one. It deteriorated by time two but was still significant, and it deteriorated more by time three and was not significant ex-

cept for one variable, the tendency to socialize with members of their own unit after hours. This was, however, considered an important variable since it served to predict willingess to fight. Vaitkus, Mark & Griffith, J. An evaluation of unit replacment on unit cohesion and individual morale in the U.S. Army All-Volunteer Force. *Military Psychology*, 1990, 2, 221-239.

23. Meerloo, J. A. M. *Mental Seduction and Menticide*. London: Jonathan Cape, 1957.

24. Bednar, R. L. & Battersby, C. P. The effects of specific cognitive structure on early group development. *Journal of Applied Behavioral Science*, 1976, 12, 513-522; Stockton, R., Rohde, R. I., & Haughey, J. The effects of structured group exercises on cohesion, engagement, avoidance, and conflict. *Small Group Research*, 1992, 23(2), 155-168.

25. In spite of the lack of evidence, military leaders sometimes argue that traditional military indoctrination in manly warrior virtues actually improves personal relationships. See, for example, Richardson, F. M. *Fighting Spirit: A Study of Psychological Factors in War*. New York: Crane, Russak & Co., Inc., 1978, p. 4.

26. Darryl Henderson is a major spokesman for the ban against homosexuals, and someone who writes extensively about the importance of cohesion to motivate soldiers in combat. See especially, Henderson, W. D. *Cohesion: The Human Element in Combat*. Washington, DC: National Defense University Press, 1985.

27. Henderson, W. D. Analysis of the Report on the Canadian Forces Internal Survey on Homosexual Issues. (An addendum to *Impact of Cohesion on the Combat Performance of Military Units, August 1990.*), August 1991, p. 6.

28. Henderson, W. D. Analysis of the Report on the Canadian Forces Internal Survey on Homosexual Issues. (An addendum to *Impact of Cohesion on the Combat Performance of Military Units, August 1990.*), August 1991, p. 7.

29. Benecke, M. M. & Dodge, K. S. Lesbian baiting as sexual harassment: Women in the military. Warren Blumenfeld (Ed.), *Homophobia: How We All Pay the Price*. Boston: Beacon Press, 1992; Benecke, M. M. & Dodge, K. S. Military women in nontraditional job fields: Casualties of the armed forces' War on Homosexuals. *Harvard Women's Law Journal*, 1990, 13, 215-250; Hudson, V. *Remarks Regarding Sexual Harassment during the Gulf War*. Presented April 29, 1992 at the Annual Conference of the Defense Advisory Committee on Women in the Services.

30. Salzman, L. "Latent" homosexuality. In Judd Marmor (Ed.), *Sexual Inversion: The Multiple Roots of Homosexuality*. New York: Basic Books, 1965; Fasteau, M. F. *The Male Machine*. New York: McGraw Hill, 1972, p. 15; Clark, D. Homosexual encounter in all-male groups, In L. Solomon & B. Berzon (Eds.), *New Perspectives on Encounter Groups*. San Francisco: Jossey-Bass: 1972, pp. 376-377; Goldberg, H. *The New Male*. New York: New American Library, 1980; David, D. S. & Brannon, R. The male sex role: Our culture's blueprint of manhood, and what it's done for us lately. In D. S. David & R. Brannon (Eds.), *The Forty-Nine Percent Majority: The Male Sex Role*. Reading, MA: Addison-Wesley Pub., 1976; Farrell, W. *The Liberated Man: Beyond Masculinity*. New York: Random House, 1974; Morin, S. F. & Garfinkle, E. M. Male homophobia. *Journal of Social Issues*, 1978, 34,

29-47; Pleck, J. H. The male sex role: Definitions, problems, and sources of change. *Journal of Social Issues*, 1976, 32, 155-164; Rubin, L. *Just Friends: The Role of Friendship in Our Lives.* New York: Harper & Row, 1985; Woods, S. M. Some dynamics of male chauvinism. *Archives of General Psychiatry*, 1976, 33, 63-65.

31. Schmitt, J. P. & Kurdek, L. A. Age and gender differences in and personality correlates of loneliness in different relationships. *Journal of Personality Assessment,* 1985, 49(5), 485-496; Williams, D. G. Gender, masculinity-femininity, and emotional intimacy in same-sex friendship. *Sex Roles*, 1985, 12(5-6), 587-600; Wright, Paul H. & Scanlon, Mary B. Gender role orientations and friendship: Some attenuation, but gender differences abound. *Sex Roles*, 1991 May, 24 (9-10), 551-566.

32. Levinson, D. *The Seasons of a Man's Life.* New York: Ballantine, 1978.

33. Grigsby, J. P. & Weatherley, D. Gender and sex-role differences in intimacy of self-disclosure. *Psychological Reports*, 1983, 53, 891-897; Narus, L. R. & Fischer, J. L. Strong but not silent: A re-examination of expressivity in the relationships of men. *Sex Roles*, 1982, 8, 159-168.

34. Devlin, P. K. & Cowan, G. A. Homophobia, perceived fathering, and male intimate relationships. *Journal of Personality Assessment*, 1985, 49(5), 467-473; Leonard, H. E. Homophobia and self-disclosure: The result of sex role socialization. Unpublished Doctoral Dissertation, 1981, California School of Professional Psychology, San Diego, DAI 4205. Okum, M. E. Personal space as a reaction to the threat of an interaction with a homosexual. Unpublished Doctoral Dissertation, Catholic University of America, 1975; McRoy, D. T. Gay and heterosexual men's friendships: The relationships between homophobia, anti-femininity and intimacy, Unpublished Doctoral Dissertation, 1990, California School of Professional Psychology, Los Angeles, DAI 5112.

35. In a study reported in Derlega et al. subjects were asked to bring a friend to the laboratory and then they were photographed demonstrating the way they would act if they greeted that friend at the airport. Men almost invariably shook hands whereas women almost invariably hugged (study 1). In another study in this series (study 2) subjects were shown pictures of men and women approaching each other, greeting, and walking away. In some pictures they greeted by hugging, in others they merely shook hands. And in some pictures they walked away side by side, and in some pictures they had their arms around each other's waist. The data was clear. Men who hugged, or put their arm around each other's waist, were much more likely to be seen as homosexually involved than women who did the same thing, especially when men made the judgment. In Derlega, V. J., Lewis, R. J., Harrison, S., Winstead, B. A., & Costanza, R. Gender differences in the initiation and attribution of tactile intimacy. *Journal of Nonverbal Behavior*, 1989, 13(2), 83-96.

36. Monsour, M. Meanings of intimacy in cross- and same-sex friendships. *Journal of Social and Personal Relationships*, 1992, 9, 277-295.

37. Booth, A. Sex and social participation. *American Sociological Review*, 1972, 37, 183-192; Booth, A. & Hess, E. Cross-sex friendship. *Journal of Marriage and the Family*, 1974, 36, 38-47; Hill, C. T., & Stull, D. E. Sex differences

in effects of social and value similarity in same-sex friendship. *Journal of Personality and Social Psychology*, 1981, 41, 488-505; Jourard, S. *The Transparent Self*. New York: D. Van Nostrand, 1971; Lewis, R. Emotional intimacy among men. *Journal of Social Issues*, 1978, 34, 109-121; Weiss, L. & Lowenthal, M. F. Life course perspective on friendship. In M. Thurnher & D. Chiriboga (Eds.), *Four Stages of Life*. San Francisco: Jossey-Bass, 1975.

38. Grigsby, J. P. & Weatherley, D. Gender and sex-role differences in intimacy of self-disclosure. *Psychological Reports*, 1983, 53, 891-897; Narus, L. R. & Fischer, J. L. Strong but not silent: A re-examination of expressivity in the relationships of men. *Sex Roles*, 1982, 8, 159-168.

39. Jones, D. C. Friendship satisfaction and gender: An examination of sex differences in contributors to friendship satisfaction. *Journal of Social and Personal Relationships*, 1991, 8, 167-185; Monsour, M. Meanings of intimacy in cross- and same-sex friendships. *Journal of Social and Personal Relationships*, 1992, 9, 277-295; Wheeler, L., Reiss, H., & Nezlek, J. Loneliness, social interaction and sex roles. *Journal of Personality and Social Psychology*, 1983, 45, 943-953.

40. For reviews of studies showing that both males and females find women more emotionally supportive see: Hays, R. B. Friendship. In S. W. Duck (Ed.), *Handbook of Personal Relationships*, Chichester, England: Wiley, 1988, 391-408; Winstead, B. A. Sex differences in same-sex friendships. In V. J. Derlega & B. A. Winstead (Eds.), *Friendship and Social Interaction*. New York: Springer-Verlag, 1986.

41. Wright, P. H. & Scanlon, M. B. Gender role orientations and friendship: Some attenuation, but gender differences abound. *Sex Roles*, 1991, 24(9/10), 551-566.

42. The military report on homosexuals given to Secretary Aspin, July 1993, suggested that the legal policy of foreign countries accepting homosexuals is made workable because in these countries "few service members openly declare their homosexuality due to fears of baiting, bashing, and negative effects to their careers." "Recommended DoD Homosexual Policy Outline." Office of the Secretary of Defense Working Group Memorandum, 8 June, 1993.

43. Colonel Ronald E. Everett, U.S. Army Reserve retired, North Olmstead, Ohio. Letter to the editor. *Army*, June 1993, p. 4.

44. Eighteen percent of women and 9 percent of men know a male homosexual. Twenty seven percent of women and 14 percent of men know a lesbian. Specifically, 16 percent of men who did not know a homosexual were favored about lifting the ban, whereas 22 percent who were acquainted with a homosexual thought the ban should be lifted. Among women, the comparable figure was 40 percent and 52 percent. Although these data were obtained without random sampling, the comparison between men and women and between those who know and do not know a homosexual, supports general findings reported on civilians elsewhere. Males feel more negative about male homosexuals than they do about lesbians or than women feel about either gay men or lesbians. Also, studies of civilian groups show that those who know a homosexual are more likely to

accept homosexuality. Miller, L. Moskos/Miller. 1992 Sociological Survey of the Army. Report to the RAND Corporation on Soldier Attitudes toward Gays and Lesbians in the Military, Northwestern University, May 1993. National Defense Research Institute, *Sexual Orientation and U.S. Military Personnel Policy: Options and Assessment*, Prepared for the Office of the Secretary of Defense, MR-323-OSD, RAND, 1993, p. 217.

45. Fred described how tight and intimate this setting is. He said,

> The sleeping area is very close. Each bunk is only about 2 1/2 feet high, 3 feet wide, 6 feet long. There were 3 bunks on top of each other, and 4 hallways of racks. I didn't have much problem getting used to it. Most people try to keep quiet, respect each other's space. Each individual had a curtain. If your curtain was closed, people wouldn't bother you. Everyone was low key. I would go to sleep thinking about my boyfriend, not the guys around me. I just wouldn't be interested in somebody that was heterosexual.

46. The author met Bob over Compuserve in the latter part of 1993. He agreed to be interviewed and introduced the author to two friends of his, one homosexual (but not a lover) and one heterosexual. Bob is 42 years old and has lived in a monogamous relationship with another man for the last 19 years.

47. This quote is taken from Bob's account of the letter he received. When Frank wrote the author explaining his reaction to Bob's revelation he said,

> Bob and I corresponded frequently during my last year in the army, while I was stationed at Army Security Agency headquarters in Arlington, Virgina. I shared an apartment in nearby Alexandria with a friend and fellow soldier, and recall him bringing the mail up one afternoon and handing me a bulging envelope. I immediately knew it was from Bob because of its thickness–our letters sometimes ran to 30 pages–so I sat down at our dinette, which doubled as a desk, and began reading, expecting the customary flow on various topics. This letter, however, was devoted to Bob's revelation that he was a homosexual. As I recall, he expressed his full acceptance of this portion of his makeup and his hope that it would not interfere with our friendship. I was not shocked, but was admittedly surprised because it had never occurred to me that he was gay. I got out my pad of lined paper, took pen in hand, and wrote back that same day, assuring Bob that his homosexuality was not of any particular significance to me and would in no way alter our friendship. This exchange of letters took place in late 1971 or early 1972, and Bob and I remain close friends to this day.

48. *Meinhold v. U.S. Department of Defense,* 808 F. Supplement 1455.

49. Cited in Dewey, K. M. Conduct unconstitutional. *California Lawyer,* 1993, July, 36-40, 84.

50. Henderson, W. D. Analysis of the Report on the Canadian Forces Internal Survey on Homosexual Issues. (An addendum to *Impact of Cohesion on the Combat Performance of Military Units, August 1990.*), August 1991.

51. For example, Darryl Henderson has been a major expert on behalf of the ban in both the United States and Canada. He argued in the Canadian case that their own research indicated heterosexuals would not accept homosexuals. He pointed to one of their surveys that showed that over 60 percent of Canadian forces were negative toward male homosexuals.

> The June 1991 report by Urban Dimensions Inc., on homosexual issues in the Canadian Forces provides much data that indicates values widely held among current members of the Canadian Forces could significantly disrupt and hinder cohesion in Canadian military units if a policy of accepting homosexuals into the Canadian military were adopted. Over 60% of the Canadian Forces are very or mostly negative toward male homosexuals. Moreover, a majority of the survey respondents viewed homosexuality as unacceptable to most segments of Canadian Society. These data indicate the potential for major cleavages within the Canadian Forces should homosexuals be enrolled and retained.

Henderson, W. D. Analysis of the Report on the Canadian Forces Internal Survey on Homosexual Issues. (An addendum to *Impact of Cohesion on the Combat Performance of Military Units, August 1990.*), August 1991, p. 3.

In spite of Henderson's warning, however, homosexuals did not disrupt cohesion. The ban was lifted in October of 1992. And, in the ten months since that time, there has been no evidence of disruption. This conclusion is based on the author's conversation with several key people who monitor personnel policy for the Canadian military. It is based in part on a conversation on 06/18/93 with Ron Dickenson, Acting Director of Personnel–Policy 2 at the National Defense Headquarters in Ottawa, Canada. Dickenson indicated that no one has asked to resign from the military because of homosexuals, or submitted a grievance saying they do not want to be in the service because of the removal of the ban against homosexuals, or in any other way that can be detected, caused a disruption in the smooth running of the military. This information was also confirmed by George Logan, the official whom Ron Dickenson replaced in June of 1993. On August 17, 1993, it was confirmed by Frank Pinch, PhD, is the recently retired Director General Personnel Policy Division, who indicated he was still in contact with those members of the Canadian forces who would know if there was any disruption due to the new policy which dropped the ban against homosexuals in the Canadian military. As of August 17, 1993, therefore, the lifting of the ban against homosexuals in the Canadian military had lasted approximately ten months without a disruptive incident.

52. Miller, L. Moskos/Miller, 1992, Sociological Survey of the Army. Report to the RAND Corporation on Soldier Attitudes toward Gays and Lesbians in the Military, Northwestern University, May 1993.

53. National Defense Research Institute, *Sexual Orientation and U.S. Military Personnel Policy: Options and Assessment.* Prepared for the Office of the Secretary of Defense, MR-323-OSD, RAND, 1993. p. 422.

54. National Defense Research Institute, *Sexual Orientation and U.S. Military Personnel Policy: Options and Assessment.* Prepared for the Office of the Secretary of Defense, MR-323-OSD, RAND, 1993. p. 422.

55. National Defense Research Institute, *Sexual Orientation and U.S. Military Personnel Policy: Options and Assessment.* Prepared for the Office of the Secretary of Defense, MR-323-OSD, RAND, 1993. p. 104.

56. Schlossman, S., Mershon, S., Livers, A., Jacobson, T., & Haggerty, T. Potential insights from analogous situations: Integrating blacks into the U.S. military. National Defense Research Institute, *Sexual Orientation and U.S. Military Personnel Policy: Options and Assessment.* Prepared for the Office of the Secretary of Defense, MR-323-OSD, RAND, 1993. pp. 158-190.

57. At least one major jurist has explained that because the argument predicted a disaster that did not materialize with the integration of blacks and women, it will not be a compelling argument in the case of homosexuals (Posner, 1992). Posner, R. A. *Sex and Reason.* Cambridge, MA: Harvard University Press, 1992.

58. Fox, R. E. Proceedings of the American Psychological Association, Inc., for the Year 1991: Minutes of the Annual Meeting of the Council of Representatives. *American Psychologist,* 47, 927; American Psychiatric Association Fact Sheet, Gay and Lesbian Issues, April, 1993.

CHAPTER 8

1. Even the most conservative estimate would place the number of homosexuals in the military today at over 50,000. Since only 1,000 were discharged each year in recent years, this means that not more than one in every 50 homosexuals gets discharged. If we were to define the term homosexual to include everyone the military would count as homosexual, for the military defines the term very broadly, indeed, then it is probably more accurate to say that one in every 1,000 or even one in every 1,500 gets discharged for homosexuality. This varies, of course, by the year and by the service.

2. The figures vary, of course, from year to year and from service to service, but according to the U.S. General Accounting Analysis of homosexual discharge statistics, a woman in any military service between 1980 and 1990 was at least two or three times more likely than a man to be discharged for homosexuality, and in the Marines at least six times more likely. United States General Accounting Office. *Defense Force Management: DoD's Policy on Homosexuality.* Report to Congressional Requesters, June 1992, 4; Shilts, R. *Conduct Unbecoming.* New York: St. Martin's Press, 1993, 595.

3. The following case was constructed as a plausible example illustrating the way such confessions are obtained. It was written with the assistance of an agent who conducted such investigations. This agent, Linda Gautney, worked for the NIS for five years and during this time interrogated subjects for homosexuality.

4. NIS stands for Naval Investigative Service.

5. Gudjonsson, G. H. The relationship of intelligence and memory to interrogative suggestibility: The importance of range effects. *British Journal of Clinical*

Psychology, 1988, 27(2), 185-187; Singh, K. K. & Gudjonsson, G. H. Interrogative suggestibility among adolescent boys and its relationship with intelligence, memory and cognitive set. *Journal of Adolescence*, 1992, 15(2), 155-161; Coid, J. Suggestibility, low intelligence and a confession to crime. *British Journal of Psychiatry*, 1981, 139, 436-438.

6. Sharrock, R. & Gudjonsson, G. H. Intelligence, previous convictions and interrogative suggestibility: A path analysis of alleged false confession cases. *British Journal of Clinical Psychology*, 1993, 32(2), 169-175; Carroll, C. J. Self-implication and the Miranda rights: Handicapped versus nonhandicapped inviduals. Unpublished Doctoral Dissertation, 1991, University of Alabama, DAI 5205.

7. Register, P. A. & Kihstrom, J. F. Hypnosis and interrogative suggestability. *Personality & Individual Differences*, 1988, 9(3), 549-558.

8. We know that younger people, and people who are more neurotic and guilt prone, tend to confess more readily in interrogations. Gudjonsson, G. H. & Petursson, H. Custodial interrogation: Why do suspects confess and how does it relate to their crime attitude and personality? *Personality and Individual Differences*, 1991, 12(3), 295-306.

9. Belle, O. S. Confession and punishment in authoritarian relationships. *Corrective Psychiatry & Journal of Social Therapy*, 1970, 16(1-4), 69-73.

10. Ofshe, R. J. Inadvertent hypnosis during interrogation: False confession due to dissociative state: Misidentified multiple personality and the satanic cult hypothesis. *International Journal of Clinical & Experimental Hypnosis*, 1992, 40(4), 125-156.

11. Gudjonsson, G. H. The effects of suspiciousness and anger on suggestibility. *Medicine, Science and the Law*, 1989, 29(3), 229-232.

12. The names of all the characters in Karen's life are pseudonyms.

13. This story was verified with an independent interview with the woman who is being called Charlotte here. Charlotte is not her real name. She confirmed the narration, and expressed concern for Karen. Charlotte expressed a great deal of care and tenderness for Karen, comparing her feelings to those she might have for a man who was attracted to her but whose feelings she did not reciprocate.

14. Taken from the "Personal Statement of My Reasons for Resignation" that Karen Stupski attached to her resignation.

15. This is based on a December 7, 1993 interview with Vaughn Taylor. Taylor was the attorney who defended Laura Hinkley.

16. $18,000 paid to her civilian attorney. (Shilts, R. *Conduct Unbecoming: Gays and Lesbians in the U.S. Military: Vietnam to the Persian Gulf.* New York: St. Martin's Press, 1993, p. 326.)

17. (Shilts, R. *Conduct Unbecoming: Gays and Lesbians in the U.S. Military: Vietnam to the Persian Gulf.* New York: St. Martin's Press, 1993, p. 106 and p. 326.)

18. Richardson, J. T., Mavromatis, A., Mindel, T., & Owens, A. C. Individual differences in hypnagogic and hypnopompic imagery. *Journal of Mental Imagery*, 1981, 5(2), 91-96.

19. Ahsen, A. Hypnagogic and hynopompic imagery transformations. *Journal of Mental Imagery*, 1988, 12(2), 1-50. Hypnopompic hallucinations are more likely to occur when the subject is taking certain kinds of medications, but we do not know if Jack's accuser was taking these medications. Albala, A. A., Weinberg, N., & Allen, S. M. Maprotiline-induced hypnopompic hallucinations. *Journal of Clinical Psychiatry*, 1983, 44(4), 149-150; Hemmingsen, R., & Rafaelsen, O. J. Hypnagogic and hypnopompic hallucinations during amitriptyline treatment. *Acta Psychiatrica Scandinavica*, 1980, October, 62(4), 364-368.

20. Polygraphs are not allowed in a court of law as evidence. Although Congress has considered the evidence for and against the validity of polygraphs on numerous occasions, it has, each time, determined that its validity is still in question. Katkin tells of the congressional evaluation of polygraphs in 1965, 1976, and 1983. In each case Congress decided that the technique was insufficiently reliable to use in courts as evidence. Katkin, E. S. Polygraph testing, psychological research, and public policy: An introductory note. *American Psychologist*, 1985, March 40 (3), 346-347.

21. Laura Gautney, the ex-NIS agent who later identified as a lesbian and who assisted in writing portions of this chapter, believed that it would be a violation of the polygrapher's ethics to dishonestly inform the accused that the polygraph detected a lie in order to get a confession. Nevertheless, attorney Vaughn Taylor, December 7, 1993, described a case that he won in a federal court in which the verdict declared that a polygraph was probably described dishonestly so as to convict the accused. Moreover, we found from Laura Gautney's description of what happened during interrogations that it was not considered unethical for the interrogator to lie by saying that there was other incriminating evidence when in fact evidence did not exist. It seems reasonable to speculate, therefore, that the polygrapher lied to Jack when he told him he had not passed the test in order to secure a confession from Jack.

22. Sharrock, R. & Gudjonsson, G. H. Intelligence, previous convictions and interrogative suggestibility: A path analysis of alleged false confession cases. *British Journal of Clinical Psychology*, 1993, 32(2), 169-175; Carroll, C. J. Self-implication and the Miranda rights: Handicapped versus nonhandicapped invididuals. Unpublished Doctoral Dissertation, 1991, University of Alabama, DAI 5205.

CHAPTER 9

1. These figures were taken from ABC *Nightline*, 12/10/93. Their cited source documents were from the Department of Defense.

2. Not only the military, but all the programs that contracted with the military to provide defense are at stake. Veggeberg, S. In hot pursuit of post-cold war survival, weapons labs see industrial partnership. *The Scientist*, 7(12), June 14, 1993.

3. Nye, J. S. Jr. Review of *An Insider Explores the Astonishing Realities of America's Defense Establishment* by Richard Stubbing. *New York Times Book Review*, September 28, 1986, p. 9.

4. Borosage, R. L. All dollars no sense: The cold war is over, but the Pentagon is still spending like there's no tomorrow. *Mother Jones,* September/October, 1993, 18 (5), 41-46. Gansler talks of the difficulties of converting the military industrial complex and says, "The spector of a rapidly shrinking defense budget is in many ways more menacing than any challenge the U.S. military has recently faced on the battlefield." Gansler, J. S. Forging an integrated industrial complex. *Technology Review*, July 1993, 96 (5), 24-28.

5. Martin, L. Peacekeeping as a growth industry. *The National Interest*, Summer, 1993, 3-11.

6. There is a flood of articles in the professional and popular literature on the legal and moral dilemma of whether the international community should compromise the soveign rights of nations in order to pursue humanitarian goals. See, for example, Roberts, A. Humanitarian war: Military intervention and human rights. *International Affairs*, 1993, 69(3), 429-449; Martin, L. Peacekeeping as a growth industry. *The National Interest*, Summer 1993, 3-11; Shields, P. M. A new paradigm for military policy: Socioeconomics. *Armed Forces and Society*, Summer 1993, 511-531; Pease, K. K. & Forsythe, D. P. Human rights, humanitarian intervention, and world politics. *Human Rights Quarterly*, 1993, 15, 290-314; Falk, R. Intervention revisited: Hard choices and tragic dilemmas. *The Nation*, December 20, 1993, 755-764.

7. Pease, K. K. & Forsythe, D. P. Human rights, humanitarian intervention, and world politics. *Human Rights Quarterly*, 1993, 15, 290-314.

8. Pease, K. K. & Forsythe, D. P. Human rights, humanitarian intervention, and world politics. *Human Rights Quarterly*, 1993, 15, 290-314.

9. The Soviet Union did not collapse until August of 1991, but the Cold War was declared over several years before that. The percentage of Americans who perceived the Soviet Union as posing a serious threat to the U.S. dropped from 60 percent in June 1988 to 43 percent in December 1988 to 40 percent in July 1989. West, P. Thaw in Cold War offers Democrats a chance against Republicans. *The Baltimore Sun*, Friday, December 1, 1989. Cited in Luz, George A. Military civic action in the 1990s: A forecast. John W. De Pauw & George A. Luz (Eds.), *Winning the Peace: The Strategic Implications of Military Civic Action*. New York: Praeger, 1993.

Weidenbaum felt that we knew that the Cold War was over in March 1, 1990 listening to the testimony of William Webster, the director of the Central Intelligence Agency. Webster reported that, "There is little chance that Soviet hegemony could be restored in Eastern Europe." The underlying idea is that any hardline successor to the present Soviet leadership would face the same severe economic and political pressures and would be deterred from engaging in a major military buildup or from taking a confrontational stance toward the United States. Webster went on to state that Marxist-Leninist ideology is now bankrupt and that Communist parties will continue "to lose legitimacy and strength." That now widely held view, bolstered by events in the Soviet Union since then, underscores the weakness of the Soviet system. Yet we should not be carried away by enthusiastic prognostications of the prospects for democratic, market-oriented societies to emerge quickly in what has been the Soviet sphere of influence. Quotes are from: Bush is reported willing to accept big cuts in military budget. *The New York Times*, March 18, 1990, p. 20.

10. For an account of how the United Nations' vision of Peacekeeping has evolved to include humanitarian interventions see Goulding. Goulding listed several types of Peacekeeping, and although what he calls "Type five," which has only recently emerged, it constitutes what in other contexts is called "Humanitarian intervention." "It requires an integrated program including humanitarian relief, a ceasefire, demobilization of troops, a political process of national reconciliation, the rebuilding of political and administrative structures, economic rehabilitation and so on. . . . The new United Nations force in Somalia will have the same task (as in the Congo) and, like its predecessor in the Congo, is likely to have to use force to achieve it." Also see the recent statement by Boutros Boutros-Ghali. Goulding, M. The evolution of United Nations peacekeeping. *International Affairs*, 1993, 69(3), 451-464; Boutros Boutros-Ghali. An agenda for peace: Preventive diplomacy, peacemaking and peacekeeping. *U.N. Document*, A/47/277 of 17 June, 1992, para. 20. (Also published as a booklet by U.N. Department of Information, New York, 1992).

For an account of NATO's thinking on humanitarian intervention, see Martin, L. Peacekeeping as a growth industry. *The National Interest*, Summer, 1993, 3-11.

11. Since 1991, and particularly since the end of the Persian Gulf War in March 1991, American armed forces have been involved in a long list of non-traditional military missions: Operation Sea Angel for flood relief in Bangladesh, in the rescue of civilians following the volcano eruptions of Mount Pinatubo in the Philippines and of Mount Etna in Italy, in drug interdiction along U.S. borders as well as in Latin America, in a domestic mission to restore order after the Los Angeles riot, and in disaster relief following hurricanes in Florida and Hawaii. In addition, the U.S. has joined other nations in missions for rescuing foreign nationals in Zaire and has participated in Operation Hope in Somalia.

12. Interview with Captain Kevin Green, Department of Democracy and Peacekeeping in the Pentagon, 12/14/93.

13. President Clinton's address to the 48th Session of the United Nations General Assembly, 09/27/93, The United Nations, New York, New York.

14. Moskos, C. Mandating inclusion: The military as a social lab. *Current,* July-August, 1993, 354, 20-27.

15. Charles Moskos makes the point in a recent article that African Americans and women were accepted in the military because there was a manpower need for them, not because it was the morally right thing to do. Moskos, Charles. Mandating inclusion: The military as a social lab. *Current*, July-August, 1993, 354, 20-27.

16. This is the quotation by Colin Powell, taken from ABC News *Nightline* transcript for show No. 2867 (p. 1) which was aired on May 19, 1992. According to transcript commentary, Powell made the statement on February 5, 1992.

> Skin color is a benign, non-behavioral characteristic. Sexual orientation is perhaps the most profound of human behavioral characteristics. Comparison of the two is a convenient but invalid argument. I believe the privacy rights of all Americans in uniform have to be considered, especially since those rights are often infringed upon by conditions of military service.

17. There are several reasons for believing that homosexuals will not disclose their identity casually. (1) They have not done so in other militaries when the ban has been lifted. (2) Most homosexuals typically keep their identities hidden in this culture, especially in contexts that they judge to be hostile toward them.

18. We can expect homosexuals to disclose in a way that engenders respect because it is the case that when heterosexuals do learn that one of their acquaintances is homosexual they typically find themselves being less condemning of homosexuals.

19. The reasons for thinking that lifting the ban will improve morale has been outlined in Chapter 7. It has to do with the fact that the ban makes many heterosexuals nervous about being called homosexual or thought to be homosexual even when they are not. Lifting the ban will decrease this measure of divisiveness, over the long run, and should make it more possible for heterosexuals to discuss issues of intimacy between them without worrying that they will be thought homosexual.

20. In Chapters 2 and 3 we talked about the way bodily modesty is part of the heterosexual culture in America, serving more to enhance heterosexual excitement than to diminish it. In most cultures, and in the United States as well, sexual excitement is diminished in situations of undress by conforming to an etiquette of disregard.

References

Addison, W. E. Beardedness as a factor in perceived masculinity. *Perceptual & Motor Skills*, June, 1989, 68 (3, Pt 1), 921-922.

Aguero, J. E. & Bloch, L. President Clinton spends too much time on gay rights say a majority of Americans in a *U.S. News & World Report* poll. *U.S. News & World Report Press Release*. Saturday, June 26, 1993.

Ahsen, A. Hypnagogic and hynopompic imagery transformations. *Journal of Mental Imagery*, 1988, 12(2), 1-50.

Akers, R. L., Hayner, N. S., & Gruninger, W. Homosexual and drug behavior in different types of prisons. In E. Segarin & D. E. MacNamara. *Corrections: Problems of Punishment and Rehabilitation*. New York: Praeger, 1972, 70-79.

Akin, S. R. & Gallagher, J. Class struggle. *Advocate*, March 9, 1993, 624, 44.

Albala, A. A., Weinberg, N., & Allen, S. M. Maprotiline-induced hypnopompic hallucinations. *Journal of Clinical Psychiatry*, 1983, 44(4), 149-150.

Aldridge, R. G. Sexuality and incarceration, *Corrective and Social Psychiatry and Journal of Behavior Technology, Methods and Therapy*, 1983, 29(3), 74-77.

Alexander, K. & McCullough, J. Women's preference for gynecological examiners: Sex versus role. *Women and Health*, 1981, 6, 123.

Allgeier, A. R. & Allgeier, E. R. *Sexual Interactions* (2nd ed.). Lexington, MA: Heath, 1988.

Altman, I. *The Environment and Social Behavior*. Monterey, CA: Brooks-Cole, 1975.

Altman, I. Privacy: A conceptual analysis. *Environment and Behavior*, 1976, 8, 7-29.

Altman, I. Privacy regulation: Culturally universal or culturally specific? *Journal of Social Issues*, 1977, 33(3) 66-84.

Altman, I. & Chemers, M. M. *Culture and Environment*. Monterey, CA: Brooks-Cole, 1980.

Altman, I. & Taylor, D. A. *Social Penetration: The Development of Interpersonal Relationships*. New York: Holt, 1973.

Altman, I., Vinsel, A., & Brinn, B. B. Dialectical conceptions in social psychology: An application to social penetration and privacy regulation. *Advances in Experimental Social Psychology*, 1981, 14, 107-159.

American Psychiatric Association Fact Sheet, Gay and Lesbian Issues, April 1993.

Anderson, C. W. & Smith, R. Sigma and honor: Gay, lesbian, and bisexual people in the U.S. Military. In L. Daimant (Ed.), *Homosexual Issues in the Workplace*. Washington, DC: Taylor & Francis, 1993.

Anderson, L. T. Desensitization in vivo for men unable to urinate in a public facility. *Journal of Behavior Therapy and Experimental Psychiatry*, 1977, 8, 105-106.

Anonymous. A case of imperforate vagina which terminated fatally. *The New England Journal of Medicine and Surgery*, January, 1820, 9(1), 243-244.

Antoun, R. T. On the modesty of women in Arab Muslim villages: A study of the accommodation of traditions. *American Anthropologist*, 1968, 70(4), 671-697.

Appointment in Somalia. (Editorial). *National Review*, December 28, 1992, 44(25), 10-12.

Armstrong, R. O. *Education and Manners: Self-Culture*, 1898, 8, 241-242.

Asayama, S. Sexual behavior in Japanese students: Comparisons for 1974, 1960, and 1952. *Archives of Sexual Behavior*, 1976, 5(5), 371-390.

Ashley, B. M. Compassion and sexual orientation. In Jeannine Gramick & Pat Furey (Eds.), *The Vatican and Homosexuality*. New York: Crossroad, 1988, 105-111.

Barbach, L. G. *For Yourself: The Fulfillment of Female Sexuality*. Garden City, NY: Doubleday, 1975, p. 79.

Barry, J. The collapse of Les Aspin. *Newsweek*, December 27, 1993, 122(26), 23-25.

Bass, G. J. Their words: Discrimination, 1948 and 1993. *New Republic*, February 22, 1993, 208(8), 15.

Bayer, R. *Homosexuality and American Psychiatry: The Politics of Diagnosis*. New York: Basic Books, 1981.

Baynes, J. *Morale: A Study of Men and Courage*. New York: Frederick Praeger, 1967.

Beane, J. Choiceful sex, intimacy and relationships for gay and bisexual men. In Franklin Abbot (Ed.), *Men & Intimacy: Personal Accounts Exploring the Dilemmas of Modern Male Sexuality*. Freedom, CA: The Crossing Press, 1990.

Bednar, R. L. & Battersby, C. P. The effects of specific cognitive structure on early group development. *Journal of Applied Behavioral Science*, 1976, 12, 513-522.

Belkin, B. M. Homophobia in women, Unpublished Doctoral Dissertation, 1982, Adelphi University, DAI 4205.

Bell, A. P. & Weinberg, M. S. *Homosexualities: A Study of Diversity among Men and Women*. New York: Simon & Schuster, 1978.

Bell, J. J. Public manifestation of personal morality: Limitations on the use of solicitation statutes to control homosexual cruising. *Journal of Homosexuality*, 1979-1980, 5(1), 97-114.

Belle, O. S. Confession and punishment in authoritarian relationships. *Corrective Psychiatry & Journal of Social Therapy*, 1970, 16(1-4), 69-73.

Benecke, M. M. & Dodge, K. S. Military women in nontraditional job fields: Casualties of the armed forces' war on homosexuals. *Harvard Women's Law Journal*, 1990, 13, 215-250.

Benecke, M. M. & Dodge, K. S. Lesbian baiting as sexual harassment: Women in the military. In Warren Blumenfeld (Ed.), *Homophobia: How We All Pay the Price*. Boston: Beacon Press, 1992.

Berger, G., Hank, L., Rauzi, T., & Simkins, L. Detection of sexual orientation by heterosexuals and homosexuals. *Journal of Homosexuality*, 1987, 13(4), 83-100.

Bérubé, A. *Coming Out under Fire: The History of Gay Men and Women in World War Two*. New York: The Free Press, 1990.

Bhugra, D. Doctors' attitudes to male homosexuality: A survey. *Sexual & Marital Therapy*, 1990, 5(2):167-174.

Bieber, I., Dain, H., Dince, P., Drellich, M., Grand, H., Gundlach, T. H., Kremer, M., Rifkin, A., Wilbur, C., & Bieber, T. *Homosexuality:*

A Psychoanalytic Study of Male Homosexuals. New York: Basic Books, 1962.

Bigner, J. J. & Jacobsen, R. B. Parenting behaviors of homosexual and heterosexual fathers. *Journal of Homosexuality*, 1989, 18(1-2), 173-186.

Billy, J. O. G., Tanfer, K., Grady, W. R., Klepinger, D. The sexual behavior of men in the United States. *Family Planning Perspectives*, 1993, 25(2), 52-60.

Black, K. N. & Stevenson, M. R. The relationship of self-reported sex-role characteristics and attitudes toward homosexuality. In John P. De Cecco (Ed.) *Bashers, Baiters & Bigots: Homophobia in American Society*. Binghamton, NY: Harrington Park Press, 1985, 83-93.

Blumenfeld, W. (Ed.) *Homophobia: How We All Pay the Price*. Boston: Beacon Press, 1992.

Blumstein, P. W. & Schwartz, P. Lesbianism and bisexuality. In Erich Goode (Ed.), *Sexual Deviance and Sexual Deviants*. New York: Morrow, 1974, 278-295.

Blumstein, P. W. & Schwartz, P. Bisexuality in men. *Urban Life*, 1976, 5, 339-358.

Blumstein, P. W. & Schwartz, P. Bisexuality: Some psychological issues. *Journal of Social Issues*, 1977, 33, 30-45.

Blumstein, P. W. & Schwartz, P. *American Couples: Money, Work, Sex*. New York: William Morrow, 1983.

Booth, A. Sex and social participation. *American Sociological Review*, 1972, 37, 183-192.

Booth, A. & Hess, E. Cross-sex friendship. *Journal of Marriage and the Family*, 1974, 36, 38-47.

Borosage, R. L. All dollars no sense: The Cold War is over, but the Pentagon is still spending like there's no tomorrow. *Mother Jones,* 18 (5), September-October, 1993: 41-46.

Boswell, J. *Christianity, Social Tolerance, and Homosexuality*. Chicago: University of Chicago Press, 1980.

Boutros-Ghali, B. An agenda for peace: Preventive diplomacy, peacemaking and peacekeeping, *U.N. Document*, A/47/277 of 17 June 1992, para. 20. (Also published as a booklet by U.N. Department of Information, New York, 1992).

Bowker, L. H. *Prison Victimization*. New York: Elsevier, 1980.

Britton, D. M. Homophobia and homosexuality: An analysis of boundary maintenance. *The Sociological Quarterly*, 31(3), 423-439.

Bryan, W. J. The effective use of nudity in treating sexual problems. *Journal of the American Institute of Hypnosis*, 1972, 13(2), 71-73, 76-78.

Burch, B. Psychological merger in lesbian couples: A joint ego psychological and systems approach. *Family Therapy*, 1982, 9(3), 201-208.

Burrelli, D. F. Homosexuals and U.S. military personnel policy. *CRS Congressional Report*, January 14, 1993.

Bush is reported willing to accept big cuts in military budget, *The New York Times*, March 18, 1990, p. 20.

Buss, A. H. *Self-Consciousness and Social Anxiety*. San Francisco: W. H. Freeman, 1980.

Buss, A. H., Iscoe, I. & Buss, E. H. The development of embarrassment. *The Journal of Psychology*, 1979, 103, 227-230.

Cain, R. Relational contexts and information management among gay men. *Families in Society*, 1991, 72(6), 344-352.

Carrier, J. M. & Magna, J. R. Mexican and Mexican-American male sexual behavior and spread of AIDS in California. *The Journal of Sex Research*, 1991, 28, 425-441.

Carroll, C. J. Self-implication and the Miranda rights: Handicapped versus nonhandicapped individuals. Unpublished Doctoral Dissertation, 1991, University of Alabama, DAI 5205.

Casler, L. Nudist camps. *Medical Aspects of Human Sexuality*, May 1971, 92-98.

Cass, V. C. Homosexual identity formation: Testing a theoretical model. *Journal of Sex Research*, May 1984, 20 (2):143-167.

Chandler, R. *The Times* poll: Americans like Pope but challenge doctrine. *Los Angeles Times*, 23 August 1987, p. 20. Cited in Gramick, J. Rome speaks, the Church responds. In Jeannine Gramick & Pat Furey (Eds.), *The Vatican and Homosexuality*. New York: Crossroad, 1988.

Chapman, A. H. Psychogenic urinary retention in women: A report of a case. *Psychosomatic Medicine*, 1959, 21(2), 119-122.

Chapman, B. E. & Brannock, J. C. Proposed model of lesbian identity development: An empirical examination. *Journal of Homosexuality*, 1987, 14, 69-80.

Chilune, G. J. Self-disclosure and its relationship to marital intimacy. *Journal of Counseling and Clinical Psychology*, 40 (1), 1984, 216-219.

Chitwood, K. L. The relation of attitudes toward the male role, attitudes toward homosexuality and sex typed characteristics to traditionality of occupational choice among college men. Unpublished Doctoral Dissertation, 1980, New York University, DAI 4207.

Clark, D. Homosexual encounter in all-male groups. In L. Solomon & B. Berzon (Eds.), *New Perspectives on Encounter Groups*. San Francisco: Jossey-Bass, 1972, pp. 376-377.

Clark, D. *Loving Someone Gay*. New York: Signet, 1977.

Clark, J. P. & Tifft, L. L. Polygraph and interview validation of self-reported deviant behavior. *American Sociological Review*, 1966, 31, 516-523.

Coben, S. *Rebellion against Victorianism: The Impetus for Cultural Change in 1920s America*. New York: Oxford University Press, 1991.

Coid, J. Suggestibility, low intelligence and a confession to crime. *British Journal of Psychiatry*, 1981, 139, 436-438.

Coleman, E. The married lesbian. *Marriage and Family Review*, 1989, 14, 3-4, 119-126.

Coleman, E. & Edwards, B. *Body Liberation: Freeing Your Body for Greater Self-Acceptance, Health, and Sexual Satisfaction*. Los Angeles, CA: J. P. Tarcher, 1977.

Coleman, E., Hoon, P., & Hoon, E. Arousability and sexual satisfaction in lesbian and heterosexual women. *Journal of Sex Research*, 1983, 19(1), 58-73.

Connell, R. W. Very straight gay: Masculinity, homosexual experience, and the dynamics of gender. *American Sociological Review*, 1992, 57(6), 735-751.

Cooper, A. No longer invisible: Gay and lesbian Jews build a movement. In R. Hasbany (Ed.), *Homosexuality and Religion*. Binghamton, NY: Harrington Park Press, 1989.

Cornelius, D. L. An application of a rules-based theory of interpersonal communication: The rules of taboo communication within a "gay community." Unpublished Doctoral Dissertation, 1980, Florida State University, DAI 4103.

Cozby, P. C. Self-disclosure, a literature review. *Psychological Bulletin*, 1973, 79, 73-91.

Craig Smith, D. *The Naked Child: The Long-Range Effects of Family and Social Nudity.* Palo Alto, CA: R & E Research Associates, Inc., 1981.

Crawley, E. Nudity and dress. In M. E. Roach & J. B. Eicher (Eds.), *Dress, Adornment, and the Social Order.* New York: John Wiley & Sons, 1965, 46-49.

Daimant, L. (Ed.) *Homosexual Issues in the Workplace.* Washington, DC: Taylor & Francis, 1993.

Dank, B. M. Coming out in the gay world. *Psychiatry*, 1971, 34, 180-195.

Dank, B. M. Why homosexuals marry women. *Medical Aspects of Human Sexuality*, 1972, 15-23.

D'Augelli, A. & Rose, M. L. Homophobia in a university community: Attitudes and experiences of heterosexual freshmen. *Journal of College Student Development*, 1990, 31(6), 484-491.

David, D. S. & Brannon, R. The male sex role: Our culture's blueprint of manhood, and what it's done for us lately. In D. S. David & R. Brannon (Eds.), *The Forty-Nine Percent Majority: The Male Sex Role*. Reading, MA: Addison-Wesley Pub., 1976.

Davis, Alan. Sexual assaults in the Philadelphia prison system. In David Petersen & Charles Thomas (Eds.), *Corrections: Problems and Prospects.* Englewood Cliffs, NJ: Prentice Hall, 1975.

De Cecco, J. P. & Shively, M. From sexual identity to sexual relationships: A contextual shift. In J. P. De Cecco & M. G. Shively (Eds.), *Bisexual and Homosexual Identities, Critical Theoretical Issues: Origins of Sexuality and Homosexuality.* Binghamton, NY: Harrington Park Press, 1984.

De Cecco, J. P. Obligation versus aspiration. In J. P. De Cecco (Ed.), *Gay Relationships.* Binghamton, NY: Harrington Park Press, 1987.

Decker, B. Counseling gay and lesbian couples. *Journal of Social Work and Human Sexuality*, 1984, 2(2/3), 39-52.

D'Emilio, J. & Freedman, E. B. *Intimate Matters: A History of Sexuality in America.* New York: Harper & Row, 1988.

deMonteflores, C. & Schultz, S. J. Coming out: Similarities and differences for lesbians and gay men. *Journal of Social Issues,* 1978, 34(3), 59-72.

Derlega, V. J., Lewis, R. J., Harrison, S., Winstead, B. A., & Costanza, R. Gender differences in the initiation and attribution of tactile intimacy. *Journal of Nonverbal Behavior,* 1989, 13(2), 83-96.

Devlin, P. K. & Cowan, G. A. Homophobia, perceived fathering, and male intimate relationships. *Journal of Personality Assessment,* 1985, 49(5), 467-473.

Dewey, K. M. Conduct unconstitutional. *California Lawyer,* 1993, July, 36-40, 84.

Ditzion, S. *Marriage, Morals, and Sex in America.* New York: W. W. Norton, 1969.

Doll, L. S., Petersen, L. R., White, C. R., Johnson, E. S., Ward, J. W., & the Blood Donor Study Group. Homosexually and nonhomosexually identified men who have sex with men: A behavioral comparison. *The Journal of Sex Research,* 1992, 29(1), 1-14.

Domar, A. D. Psychological aspects of the pelvic exam: Individual needs and physician involvement. *Women & Health,* 1985-86, 10(4), 75-90.

Donald, R. R. Masculinity and machismo in Hollywood's war films. In Steve Craig (Ed.), *Men, Masculinity, and the Media,* Steve Craig (Ed.), Newbury Park, CA: Sage Publications, 1992.

Donovan, J. M. Homosexual, gay, and lesbian: Defining the words and sampling the populations. *Journal of Homosexuality,* 1992, 24(1/2), 27-47.

Down, J. F. Nudity in Japanese visual media: A cross-cultural observation. *Archives of Sexual Behavior,* 1990, 19(6), 583-594.

Druss, R. G. Cases of suspected homosexuality seen at an army mental hygiene consultation service. *Psychiatric Quarterly,* 1967, 41(1), 62-70.

Dunbar, J., Brown, M., & Amoroso, D. Some correlates of attitudes toward homosexuality. *Journal of Social Psychology,* 1973, 89, 271-279.

Dunkle, J. H. & Francis, P. L. The role of facial masculinity/femininity in the attribution of homosexuality. *Sex Roles*, 1990, 23(3-4), 157-167.

Earl, W. L. Married men and same-sex activity: A field study on HIV risk among men who do not identify as gay or bisexual. *Journal of Sex and Marital Therapy*, 1990, 16(4), 251-257.

Edwards, G. R. A critique of creationist homophobia. In Richard Hasbany (Ed.), *Homosexuality and Religion*. Binghamton, NY: The Haworth Press, 1989, 95-118.

Ehrlich, H. J. & Graeven, D. B. Reciprocal self-disclosure in a dyad. *Journal of Experimental Social Psychology*, 1971, 7, 389-400.

Eichberg, R. *Coming Out: An Act of Love*. New York: Dutton, 1990.

Elias, N. *The Court Society*. Edmund Jephcott (trans). New York: Pantheon Books, 1983.

Elliot, R. A case of inhibition of micturition: Unsystematic desensitization. *The Psychological Record*, 1967, 17, 525-530.

Ellis, H. Sexual inversion. *Studies in the Psychology of Sex, Vol. I.*, New York: Random House, 1905. Westphal's work is listed only as published in the *Archiv für Psychiatrie*, 1870.

Ellis, H. *Studies in the Psychology of Sex*. New York: Random House, 1942.

Ellis, L., Hoffman, H., & Burke, D. M. Sex, sexual orientation and criminal and violent behavior. *Personality & Individual Differences*, 1990, 11(12), 1207-1212.

Ellsworth, P. & Ross, L. Intimacy in response to direct gaze, *Journal of Experimental Social Psychology*, 1975, 11, 592-613.

Emerson, J. P. Behavior in private places: Sustaining definitions of reality in gynecological examinations. *Recent Sociology*, 1970, 2, 74-97.

Evans, N. J., & Dion, K. L. Group cohesion and performance: A meta-analysis. *Small Group Research*, 1991, 22, 175-186.

Everett, R. E. Colonel, U.S. Army Reserve, retired. Letter to the editor, *Army*, June, 1993,

Faderman, L. *Surpassing the Love of Men: Romantic Friendship and Love between Women from the Renaissance to the Present.* New York: William Morrow, 1981.

Falk, R. Intervention revisited: Hard choices and tragic dilemmas. *The Nation*, December 20, 1993, 755-764.

Farrell, W. *The Liberated Man: Beyond Masculinity*. New York: Random House, 1974.

Farylo, B. & Paludi, M. A. Research with the Draw-A-Person Test: Conceptual and methodological issues. *Journal of Psychology*, 1985, 119(6), 575-580.

Fasteau, M. F. *The Male Machine*. New York: McGraw Hill, 1972.

Fay, R. E., Turner, C. F., Klassen, A. D., & Gagnon, J. H. Prevalence and patterns of same-gender contact among men. *Science*, 1989, 243, 338-348.

Felding, W. J. *Strange Customs of Courtship and Marriage*. New York: Garden City Publishing, 1942.

Ficarrotto, T. J. Racism, sexism, and erotophobia: Attitudes of heterosexuals towards homosexuals. *Journal of Homosexuality*, 1990, 19(1), 111-116.

Finlay, B. & Scheltema, K. E. The relation of gender and sexual orientation to measures of masculinity, femininity and androgyny: A further analysis. *Journal of Homosexuality*, 1991, 21(3), 71-85.

Firestone, I., Lictman, C. M. & Evans, J. R. Privacy and solidarity: Effects of nursing home accommodation on environmental perception and sociability preferences. *International Journal of Aging and Human Development*, 1980, 11(3), 229-241.

Fisher, L. Armed and gay. *Maclean's*, May 24, 1993, 106(21), 14-16.

Fisher, P. *The Gay Mystique: The Myth and Reality of Male Homosexuality*. New York: Stein and Day, 1972.

Fling, S. & Manosevitz, M. Sex typing in nursery school children's play interest. *Developmental Psychology*, 1972, 7, 146-152.

Ford, C. S. & Beach, F. A. *Patterns of Sexual Behavior*. New York: Harper and Brothers, 1951.

Ford, K. & Norris, A. Methodological considerations for survey research on sexual behavior: Urban African-American and Hispanic youth. *Journal of Sex Research*, 1991, 28(4), 539-555.

Fox, R. E. Proceedings of the American Psychological Association, Inc., for the Year 1991: Minutes of the Annual Meeting of the Council of Representatives. *American Psychologist*, 1992, 47, 927.

Franke, R. & Leary, M. R. Disclosure of sexual orientation by lesbians and gay men: A comparison of private and public processes. *Journal of Social and Clinical Psychology*, 1991, 10(3), 262-269.

Freud, S. Three essays on the theory of sexuality (Originally published in 1905). In J. Strachey (Ed.), *The Standard Edition of the Complete Psychological Works of Sigmund Freud.* New York: Macmillan, 1953.

Friday, N. *Women on Top: How Real Life Has Changed Women's Sexual Fantasies*. New York: Simon & Schuster, 1991.

Furnham, A. & Taylor, L. Lay theories of homosexuality: Etiology, behaviors and "cures." *British Journal of Social Psychology*, 1990, 29(2), 135-147.

Gadpaille, W. J. Homosexuality in adolescent males. *Journal of the American Academy of Psychoanalysis*, 1975, 3(4), 361-371.

Gagnon, J. H. & Simon, W. The social meaning of prison homosexuality. In Robert Carter & Daniel Glaser (Eds.), *Correctional Institutions*. Philadelphia: Lippincott, 1972, p. 225.

Gansler, J. S. Forging an integrated industrial complex. *Technology Review*, 1993, 96(5), 24-28.

Gebhard, P. & Johnson, A. *The Kinsey Data*. Philadelphia: W. B. Saunders, 1979.

Gebhard, P. H., Gagnon, J. H., Pomeroy, W. B., & Christenson, C. V. *Sex Offenders: An Analysis of Types*. New York: Harper & Row, 1965.

Gentry, C. S. Social distance regarding male and female homosexuals. *Journal of Social Psychology*, 1987, 127, 199-208.

Glassner, B. & Owen, C. Variation in attitudes toward homosexuality. *Cornell Journal of Social Relations*, 1976, 11, 161-176.

Goffman, E. Attitudes and rationalizations regarding body exposure. In M. E. Roach and J. Eiocher (Eds.), *Dress, Adornment, and the Social Order*. New York: John Wiley, 1965, 50-52.

Goffman, E. *The Presentation of Self.* Garden City, NY: Doubleday, 1959, 188-189.

Goldberg, H. *The New Male.* New York: New American Library, 1980.

Goldman, R. J. & Goldman, J. D. Children's perceptions of clothes and nakedness: A cross-national study. *Genetic Psychology Monographs*, 1981, 104(2)9, 163-185.

Gonsiorek, J. C. Results of psychological testing on homosexual populations. *American Behavioral Scientist*, 1982, 25, 385-396.

Gonsiorek, J. C. The empirical basis for the demise of the illness model of homosexuality. In J. Gonsiorek & J. Weinrich (Eds.), *Homosexuality: Research Implications for Public Policy*, 115-136. Newbury Park, CA: Sage, 1991.

Goode, E. & Troiden, R. R. Correlates and accompaniments of promiscuous sex among male homosexuals. *Psychiatry*, 1980, 43(1), 51-59.

Goulding, M. The evolution of United Nations peacekeeping. *International Affairs*, 1993, 69(3), 451-464.

Gramick, J. Rome speaks, the Church responds. In Jeannine Gramick & Pat Furey (Eds.), *The Vatican and Homosexuality*. New York: Crossroad, 1988.

Green, R. *The Sissy Boy Syndrome, and the Development of Homosexuality*. New Haven: Yale University Press, 1987.

Grigsby, J. P. & Weatherley, D. Gender and sex-role differences in intimacy of self-disclosure. *Psychological Reports*, 1983, 53, 891-897.

Grinker, R. R. & Spiegel, J. P. *Men under Stress*. New York: McGraw-Hill, Inc., 1963, 443-460.

Gross, A. E., Green, S. K., Storek, J. T., & Vanyr, J. M. Disclosure of sexual orientation and impressions of male and female homosexuals. *Personality and Social Psychology Bulletin*, 1980, 6(2), 307-314.

Groves, R. M., Cialdini, R. B. & Couper, M. P.. Understanding the decision to participate in a survey. *Public Opinion Quarterly*, 1992, 56, 477-494.

Gudjonsson, G. H. The relationship of intelligence and memory to interrogative suggestibility: The importance of range effects. *British Journal of Clinical Psychology*, 1988, 27(2), 185-187.

Gudjonsson, G. H. The effects of suspiciousness and anger on suggestibility. *Medicine, Science and the Law*, 1989, 29(3), 229-232.

Gudjonsson, G. H. & Petursson, H., Custodial interrogation: Why do suspects confess and how does it relate to their crime, attitude, and personality? *Personality and Individual Differences*, 1991, 12(3), 295-306.

Gurwitz, S. & Marcus, M. Effects of anticipated interaction, sex and homosexual stereotypes on first impressions. *Journal of Applied Social Psychology*, 1978, 8(1), 47-56.

Gutstadt, J. P. Male pseudoheterosexuality and minimal sexual dysfunction. *Journal of Sex and Marital Therapy*, 1976, 2(4), 297-302.

Haar, E., Halitsky, V., & Stricker, G. Factors related to the preference for a female gynecologist. *Medical Care*, 1975, 13(9), 782-790.

Haar, E., Halitsky, V., & Stricker, G. Patients' attitudes toward gynecologic examination and to gynecologists. *Medical Care*, 1977, 15(9), 787-795.

Haines, T. L. & Yaggy, L. W. *The Royal Path of Life: Aims and Aids to Success and Happiness*. Chicago: Western Publishing House, 1882.

Hammersmith, S. K. & Weinberg. M. S. Homosexual identity: Commitment, adjustment, and significant others. *Sociometry*, March 1973, 36(1), 56-79.

Hanslin, J. & Briggs, M. Dramaturgical desexualization: The sociology of the vaginal examination. In J. Henslin (Ed.), *Studies in the Sociology of Sex*. New York: Appleton-Century Crofts, 1971.

Harris, B. *Beyond Her Sphere: Women and the Professions in American History*. Westport, CT: Greenwood Press, 1978.

Harry, J. Gay male and lesbian family relationships. In E. Macklin (Ed.), *Contemporary Families and Alternative Lifestyles: Handbook on Research and Theory*. Beverly Hills, CA: Sage, 1983.

Harry, J. *Gay Couples*, 1984, New York: Praeger.

Harry, J. Homosexual men and women who served their country. In J. De Cecco (Ed.), *Bashers, Baiters, and Bigots: Homophobia in American Society*. New York: Harrington Park Press, 1985.

Harry, J. & DeVall, W. *The Social Organization of Gay Males*. New York: Praeger, 1978.

Hart, M., Roback, H., Tittler, B., Weitz, L., Walston B., & McKee, E. Psychological adjustment of nonpatient homosexuals: Critical review of the research literature. *Journal of Clinical Psychiatry*, 1981, 39, 604-608.

Hartley, R. E. Sex role pressures and the socialization of the male child. *Psychological Reports*, 1959, 5, 457-468.

Hartman, W. E. & Fithian, M. A. *Treatment of Sexual Dysfunction*. Long Beach, CA: Center for Marital and Sexual Studies, 1972.

Hatfield, L. D. Gay life is getting better. *San Francisco Examiner*, June 30, 1989, A15.

Hawton, K., Catalan, J., Martin, P., & Fagg, J. Prognostic factors in sex therapy. *Behavior Research and Therapy*, 1986, 24, 377-385.

Hayes, S. C. & Leonard, S. R. Sex-related motor behavior: Effects on social impression and social cooperation. *Archives of Sexual Behavior*, 1983, 12, 415-426.

Hays, R. B. Friendship. In Duck, S. (Ed.), *Handbook of Personal Relationships*, 391-408. Chichester, England: Wiley, 1988, 391-408.

Hedblom, J. H. Dimensions of lesbian sexual experience. *Archives of Sexual Behavior*, 1973, 2, 329-341.

Hemmingsen, R. & Rafaelsen, O. J. Hypnagogic and hypnopompic hallucinations during amitriptyline treatment. *Acta Psychiatrica Scandinavica*, 1980, October, 62(4), 364-368.

Hencken, J. D. Conceptualizations of homosexual behavior which preclude homosexual self-labeling. Special Issue: Bisexual and Homosexual Identities: Critical Clinical Issues. *Journal of Homosexuality*, 1984, 9(4) 53-63.

Hencken, J. D. Conceptualizations of homosexual behavior which preclude homosexual self-labeling. In John De Cecco (Ed.), *Gay Personality and Sexual Labeling*. Binghamton, NY: The Haworth Press, 1985.

Henderson, W. D. *Cohesion: The Human Element in Combat*. Washington, DC: National Defense University Press, 1985.

Henderson, W. D. Analysis of the Report on the Canadian Forces Internal Survey on Homosexual Issues. (An addendum to *Impact of Cohesion on the Combat Performance of Military Units, August. 1990*), August, 1991.

Henkin, J. The sociology of the secret: Techniques for the neutralization of stigma among male homosexuals. Unpublished Doctoral Dissertation, 1984, City University of New York, DAI 4501.

Henry, III, William. A mindset under siege. *Time*, November 30, 1992.

Henslin, J. & Briggs, M. Dramaturgical desexualization: The sociology of the vaginal examination. In J. Henslin (Ed.), *Studies in in the Sociology of Sex*. New York: Appleton-Century Crofts, 1971, 243-277.

Herdt, G. & Boxer, A. Introduction: Culture, history, and life course of gay men. In G. Herdt (Ed.), *Gay Culture in America*. Boston: Beacon, 1992.

Herek, G. M. Beyond "homophobia": A social psychological perspective on attitudes toward lesbians and gay men. *Journal of Homosexuality*, 1984, 10, 1-21.

Herek, G. M. Heterosexuals' attitudes toward lesbians and gay men: Correlates and gender differences. *Journal of Sex Research*, 1988, 25 (4), 451-477.

Herek, G. M. Stigma, prejudice, and violence against lesbians and gay men. In J. C. Gonsiorek & J. D. Weinrich (Eds.), *Homosexuality: Research Implications for Public Policy*. Newbury Park, CA: Sage, 1991.

Herek, G. M. Capitanio, J. P., Glunt, E. K. *Intergroup contact predicts heterosexuals' attitudes toward gay men*. Paper presented at the meeting of the American Psychological Society, San Diego, CA, 1992.

Heron, A. (Ed.) *Towards a Quaker View of Sex*. London: Friends Home Service Committee, 1963.

Hetrick, E. & Martin, A. Developmental issues and their resolution for gay and lesbian adolescents. Special Issue: Psychotherapy with Homosexual Men and Women: Integrated Identity Approaches for Clinical Practice. *Journal of Homosexuality*, 1987, 14 (1-2):25-43.

Hill, C. T. & Stull, D. E. Sex differences in effects of social and value similarity in same-sex friendship. *Journal of Personality and Social Psychology*, 1981, 41, 488-505.

Hilmar, N. A. The dynamics of military group behavior. In Charles H. Coates & Roland J. Pellegrin (Eds.), *Military Sociology*. University Park, MD: Social Science Press, 1965, 311-335.

Historical notes: A letter from Freud. *American Journal of Psychiatry*, 1951, 786.

Hite, S. *The Hite Report: A Nationwide Study of Female Sexuality*. New York: Macmillan, 1976.

Homan, G. C. The small warship, *American Sociological Review*, 1946, 11, 294-300.

Hooker, M. A. The adjustment of the male overt homosexual. *Journal of Projective Techniques*, 1957, 21, 17-31.

Hudson, V. *Remarks Regarding Sexual Harassment During the Gulf War.* Presented April 29, 1992, at the Annual Conference of the Defense Advisory Committee on Women in the Services.

Humphrey, M. A. *My Country, My Right to Serve*. New York: Harper Collins, 1988, 139-143.

Humphreys, L. *Tearoom Trade*. Chicago: Aldine, 1970.

Ingraham, L. H., *The Boys in the Barracks: Observations on American Military Life*. Philadelphia, PA: ISHI, 1984.

Janowitz, M. *The Professional Soldier: A Social and Political Portrait.* New York: The Free Press, 1960.

Janzen, W. B. & Coe, W. C. Clinical and sign prediction: The Draw-A-Person and female homosexuality. *Journal of Clinical Psychology*, 1975, 31(4), 757-765.

Jeffreys, S. *The Spinster and Her Enemies: Feminism and Sexuality, 1880-1930.* London: Pandora, 1985.

Jenkins, D. J. Soldier theatricals: 1940-1945 (Special Services, World War II). Unpublished Doctoral Dissertation, 1992, Bowling Green State University, DAI 5312.

Jesser, C. & Donovan, L. Nudity in the art training process: An essay with reference to a pilot study. *Sociological Quarterly*, 1969, 10, 355-371.

Johns, J. H. & Defense Management Study Group on Military Cohesion. *Cohesion in the U.S. Military.* Washington, DC: National Defense University Press, 1984.

Jones, D. C. Friendship satisfaction and gender: An examination of sex differences in contributors to friendship satisfaction. *Journal of Social and Personal Relationships*, 1991, 8, 167-185.

Jones, H. K. *Toward a Christian Understanding of the Homosexual*. New York: Associated Press, 1966.

Jones, R. W. & De Cecco, J. P. The femininity and masculinity of partners of heterosexual and homosexual relationships. *Journal of Homosexuality*, 1982, 8(2), 37-44.

Jourard, S. M. Some psychological aspects of privacy. *Law and Contemporary Problems*, 1966, 31(2), 307-318.

Jourard, S. *The Transparent Self.* New York: D. Van Nostrand, 1971.

Jourard, S. M. *Self-Disclosure: An Experimental Analysis of the Transparent Self.* New York: Wiley, 1971.

Kahill, S. Human figure drawing in adults: An update of the empirical evidence 1967-1982. *Canadian Psychology,* 1984, 25(4), 269-292.

Kane, E. W. & Macaulay, L. J. Interviewer gender and gender attitudes. *Public Opinion Quarterly,* 1993, 57, 1-28.

Kaplan, F. S. Preview, privacy, and political process: Some thoughts on bathroom graffiti and group identity. In Henry Kellerman (Ed.), *Group Cohesion: Theoretical and Clinical Perspectives.* New York: Grune & Stratton, 1981.

Kardiner, A. The flight from masculinity. In H. M. Ruitenbeck (Ed.), *The Problem of Homosexuality in Modern Society.* New York: E. P. Dutton, 1963.

Katkin, E. S. Polygraph testing, psychological research, and public policy: An introductory note. *American Psychologist,* 1985, 40(3), 346-347.

Kaufman, P., Harrison, E., & Hyde, M. Distancing for intimacy in lesbian relationships. *American Journal of Psychiatry,* 1984, 14, 530-533.

Keisler, C. A., Collins, B. E. & Miller, N. *Attitude Change: A Critical Analysis of Theoretical Approaches.* New York: John Wiley & Sons, 1969.

Kellerman, H. (Ed.) *Group Cohesion: Theoretical and Clinical Perspectives.* New York: Grune & Stratton, 1981.

Kellett, A. *Combat Motivation: The Behavior of Soldiers in Battle.* Boston: Kluver & Nijhoff Publishing, 1982.

Khan, B. Not-so-gay life in Karachi: A view of a Pakistani living in Toronto. In Arno Schmitt & Jehoda Sofer (Eds.), *Sexuality and Eroticism Among Males in Moslem Societies.* Binghamton, NY: The Haworth Press, 1992, 93-104.

Kinsey, A. C., Pomeroy, W. B., & Martin, C. *Sexual Behavior in the Human Male.* Philadelphia: W. B. Saunders & Co., 1948.

Kinsey, A., Pomeroy, W. B., Martin, C. E., & Gebhard, C. E. *Sexual Behavior in the Human Female.* Philadelphia: W. B. Saunders Co., 1953.

Kirkham, G. L. Homosexuality in prison. In J. M. Henslin (Ed.), *Studies in the Sociology of Sex*. New York: Appleton-Century Crofts, 1971.

Klassen, A. D., Williams, C. J. & Levitt, E. E. *Sex and Morality in the United States: An Empirical Enquiry under the Auspices of the Kinsey Institute*. Middletown, CT: Wesleyan University Press, 1989.

Koocher, G. Bathroom behavior and human dignity. *Journal of Personality and Social Psychology*, 1977, 35(2), 120-121.

Krafft-Ebing, R. von. *Psychopathia Sexualis: A Medico-Forensic Study*. New York: Pioneer Publications, Inc., 1939.

Krafft-Ebing, R. von. *Aberrations of Sexual Life, After the Psychopathia Sexualis. A Medico-Legal Study for Doctors and Lawyers*. Arthur Viv Burbury (trans.), Springfield, IL: Thomas Inc. 1959.

Kramer, M. Don't settle for hypocrisy. *Time*, 1993, 142(4), 41.

Kurdek, L. A. & Schmitt, J. P. Relationship quality of partners in heterosexual married, heterosexual cohabiting, gay, and lesbian relationships. *Journal of Personality and Social Psychology*, 1986, 51, 711-720.

Lamontagne, Y. & Marks, I. M. Psychogenic urinary retention: Treatment by prolonged exposure. *Behavior Therapy*, 1973, 4, 581-585.

Laner, M. R. Permanent partner priorities: Gay and straight. In J. P. De Cecco (Ed.), *Gay Relationships*. Binghamton, NY: Harrington Park Press, 1987.

Lansky, L. M. The family structure also affects the model: Sex-role attitudes in parents of preschool children. *Merrill-Palmer Quarterly*, 1967, 13, 139-150.

Larsen, P., Reed, M., & Hoffman, S. Attitudes of heterosexuals toward homosexuals: A Likert-type scale and construct validity. *The Journal of Sex Research*, 1980, 16, 245-257.

Larson, P. C. Gay male relationships. In W. Paul & J. D. Weinrich (Eds.), *Homosexuality as a Social Issue*. Beverly Hills, CA: Sage, 1982.

Laslett, B. The family as a public and private institution: An historical perspective. *Journal of Marriage and the Family*, 1973, 35, 480-492.

LaTorre, R. A., & Wendenburg, K. Psychological characteristics of bisexual, heterosexual, and homosexual women. *Journal of Homosexuality*, 1983, 9(1), 87-97.

Lawler, J. A social construction of the body: Nurses' experiences. Unpublished Doctoral Dissertation, 1990, University of New South Wales, Australia, DAI 5110.

Lee, G. C. Commentary. In W. Bowman, R. Little & G. T. Sicilia (Eds.) *The All Volunteer Force after a Decade: Retrospect and Prospect*. Washington: Pergamon-Brassey's, 1986.

Leif, H. I. Evaluation of inhibited sexual desire: Relationship aspects. In H. S. Kaplan (Ed.), *Comprehensive Evaluation of Disorders of Sexual Desire*. Washington, DC: American Psychiatric Press, 1985.

Leonard, H. E. Homophobia and self-disclosure: The result of sex role socialization. Unpublished Doctoral Dissertation, 1981, California School of Professional Psychology, DAI 4205.

Lever, J., Kanouse, D. E., Rogers, W. H., Carson, S., & Hertz, R. Behavior patterns and sexual identity of bisexual males. *The Journal of Sex Research*, 1992, 29(2), 141-167.

Levinson, D. *The Seasons of a Man's Life*. New York: Ballantine, 1978.

Levitt, E. & Klassen, A. Public attitudes toward homosexuality: Part of the 1970 national survey by the Institute for Sex Research. *Journal of Homosexuality*, 1974, 1(1), 29-43.

Lewis, L. The coming-out process for lesbians: Integrating a stable Identity. *Social Work*, 1984, 29(5), 464-469.

Lewis, R. Emotional intimacy among men. *Journal of Social Issues*, 1978, 34, 109-121.

Liebman, M. *Coming Out Conservative*. San Francisco: Chronicle Books, 1992.

Lief, H. & Fox, R. Training for detached concern. In H. I. Lief, V. F. Lief, & N. R. Lief. (Eds.), *The Psychological Basis of Medical Practice*. New York: Hoeber Medical Division, Harper & Row, 1963.

Lochhead, C. Raucous house hearing on military's gay ban. *San Francisco Chronicle*, May 6, 1993, A1, A19.

LoPiccollo, L. Low sexual desire. In S. R. Lieblum & L.A. Pervin (Eds.), *Principles and Practice of Sex Therapy*. New York: Guilford, 1980.

Lott, A. J. & Lott, B, E. Group cohesiveness, communication level and conformity. *Journal of Abnormal and Social Psychology*, 1961, 62, 408-412.

Loulan, J. Research on the sex practices of 1,566 lesbians and the clinical applications. *Women and Therapy*, 1988, 7, 221-234.

Loulan, J. Preliminary report on survey of lesbian sex practices. Unpublished manuscript. Cited in Falco, K. L. *Psychotherapy with Lesbian Clients*. New York: Brunner/Mazel, 1991, p. 144.

Luz, G. A. Military civic action in the 1990's: A forecast. John W. DePauw & G. A. Luz (Eds.), *Winning the Peace: The Strategic Implications of Military Civic Action.* New York: Praeger, 1993.

Maccoby, E. & Jacklin, C. *The Psychology of Sex Differences*. Stanford, CA: Stanford University Press, 1974.

MacCoun, R. What is known about unit cohesion and military performance. National Defense Research Institute, *Sexual Orientation and U.S. Military Personnel Policy: Options and Assessment*, Prepared for the Office of the Secretary of Defense, MR-323-OSD, RAND, 1993.

Maginnis, R. L. A case against lifting the ban on homosexuals. *Army*, January 1993, 43(1) 37-40.

Malchow, C. W. *The Sexual Life*. St. Louis: C.V. Mosby Co., 1923, 60-61.

Mandelbaum, D. G. *Soldier Groups and Negro Soldiers.* Berkeley, CA: University of California Press, 1959, 5-87.

Manzella, D. B. Nude in the classroom. *American Journal of Art Therapy*, 1973, 12(3), 165-182.

Marcus, S. *The Other Victorians: A Study of Sexuality and Pornography in Mid-Nineteenth-Century England.* New York: Basic Books, 1966.

Markee, N. L., Carey, I. L., & Pedersen, E. L. Body cathexis and clothed body cathexis: Is there a difference? *Perceptual & Motor Skills*, 1990, 70(3, Pt 2) 1239-1244.

Marquart, J.W. Prison guards and the use of physical coercion as a mechanism of prisoner control. *Criminology*, 1986, 24(2), 347-367.

Martin, A. D. Learning to hide: The socialization of the gay adolescent. *Adolescent Psychiatry*, 1982, 10, 52-65.

Martin, L. Peacekeeping as a growth industry. *The National Interest*, Summer, 1993, 3-11.

Masters, W. & Johnson, V. *Homosexuality in Perspective*. Boston: Little, Brown, 1979.

McDonald, G. J. & Moore, R. J. Sex-role self-concepts of homosexual men and their attitudes toward women and male homosexuality. *Journal of Homosexuality*, 1978, 4(1), 3-14.

McNeil, J. *The Church and the Homosexual*. Kansas City, MO: Sheed, Andrews, and McMeel, 1976.

McRoy, D. T. Gay and heterosexual men's friendships: The relationships between homophobia, anti-femininity and intimacy, Unpublished Doctoral Dissertation, 1990, California School of Professional Psychology, Los Angeles, DAI 5112.

McWhirter, D. P. & Mattison, A. M. *The Male Couple: How Relationships Develop*. Englewood Cliffs, NJ: Prentice-Hall, Inc. 1984.

Meerloo, J. A. M. *Mental Seduction and Menticide*. London: Jonathan Cape, 1957.

Meinhold v. U.S. Department of Defense, 808 F. Supplement, 1455.

Middlemist R. D., Matter, C. F., & Knowles, E. Personal space invasions in the lavatory: Suggestive evidence for arousal. *Journal of Personality and Social Psychology*, 1976, 33(5), 541-546.

Miles, R. *Love, Sex, Death, and the Making of the Male*. New York: Summit Books, 1991.

Milham, J., San Miguel, C. C., & Kellogg, R. A. Factor analytic conceptualization of attitudes toward male and female homosexuals. *Journal of Homosexuality*, 1976, 2 (1), 3-10.

Miller, G.R. & Steinberg, M. *Between People: A New Analysis of Interpersonal Communication*. Palo Alto, CA: Science Research Associates, 1975.

Miller, H. G., Turner, C. F., & Moses, L. E. (Eds.). *AIDS: The Second Decade.* Washington, DC: National Academy Press, 1990, 369-375.

Miller, L. Moskos/Miller. 1992 Sociological Survey of the Army. Report to the RAND Corporation on Soldier Attitudes toward Gays and Lesbians in the Military, Northwestern University, May

1993. Cited in the National Defense Research Institute, Sexual Orientation and U.S. Military Personnel Policy: Options and Assessment, Prepared for the Office of the Secretary of Defense, MR-323-OSD, RAND, 1993.

Millstein, S. G., Adler, N. E., Irwin, C. E. Sources of anxiety about pelvic examinations among adolescent females. *Journal of Adolescent Health Care*, 1984, 5(2), 106-111.

Minnegerode, F. A. Attitudes toward homosexuality: Feminist attitudes and sexual conservatism. *Sex Roles*, 1976, 2, 347-352.

Minton, H. L. & McDonald, G. J. Homosexual identity formation as a developmental process. In J. P. De Cecco & M. G. Shively (Eds.), *Bisexual and Homosexual Identities, Critical Theoretical Issues: Origins of Sexuality and Homosexuality*. Binghamton, NY: Harrington Park Press, 1984.

Monsour, M. Meanings of intimacy in cross- and same-sex friendships. *Journal of Social and Personal Relationships*, 1992, 9, 277-295.

Moore, B. *Privacy, Studies in Social and Cultural History*. Armonk, NY: M. E. Sharpe, Inc., 1984.

Morin, S. F. & Garfinkle, E. M. Male homophobia. *Journal of Social Issues*, 1978, 34, 29-47.

Morton, T.L. Intimacy and reciprocity of exchange: A comparison of spouses and strangers. *Journal of Personal and Social Psychology*, 1978, 36, 72-81.

Moskos, C. (Ed.) *The Military–More Than Just a Job?* Washington: Pergamon-Brassey's, 1988.

Moskos, C. Why banning homosexuals still makes sense. *Navy Times*, March 30, 1992.

Moskos, C. Mandating inclusion: The military as a social lab. *Current*, July-August, 1993, 354, 20-27.

Muir, F. *An Irreverent and Almost Complete Social History of the Bathroom*. New York: Stein & Day, 1983.

Mullen, B. & Cooper, C. *The relation between group cohesiveness and performance: An integration.* Unpublished manuscript, Department of Psychology, Syracuse University, 1993. Cited in the National Defense Research Institute, *Sexual Orientation and U.S. Military Personnel Policy: Options and Assessment*, Prepared for the Office of the Secretary of Defense, MR-323-OSD, RAND, 1993.

Muson, E. L. *The Management of Men: A Handbook on the Systematic Development of Morale and the Control of Human Behavior.* New York: H. Holt and Company, 1921.

Nacci, P. L. & Kane, T. R. Sex and sexual aggression in federal prisons: Inmate involvement and employee impact. *Federal Probation*, 1984, 48(1), 46-53.

Narus, L. R. & Fischer, J. L. Strong but not silent: A re-examination of expressivity in the relationships of men. *Sex Roles*, 1982, 8, 159-168.

National Defense Research Institute. *Sexual Orientation and U.S. Military Personnel Policy: Options and Assessment*, Prepared for the Office of the Secretary of Defense, MR-323-OSD, RAND, 1993.

Naval operations: Sexual harassment. *Economist*, July 4, 1992, 324(7766), A29.

Navy secretary quits in 1991 convention sex-abuse furor. *Facts on File*, July 2, 1992, 52(2693), 484.

Necef, M. U. Turkey on the brink of modernity: A guide for Scandinavian gays. In Arno Schmitt & Jehoda Sofer (Eds.), *Sexuality and Eroticism Among Males in Moslem Societies*. Binghamton, NY: The Haworth Press, 1992, 71-75.

Nemeyer, L. Coming out: Identity congruence and the attainment of adult female sexuality. Unpublished Doctoral Dissertation, 1980, Boston University School of Education, DAI 4105.

Newman, B. S. Development of heterosexual attitudes toward lesbians. Unpublished Doctoral Dissertation, 1985, University of Pittsburgh, DAI 4705.

Newson, J. & Newson, E. *Four years old in an Urban Community.* London: Allen & Unwin, 1968.

Nichols, M. The treatment of inhibited sexual desire (ISD) in lesbian couples. *Women and Therapy*, 1982, 1(4), 49-66.

Nichols, M. Relationships between sexual behavior, erotic arousal, romantic attraction, and self-labeled sexual orientation. Paper presented at the SSSS Conference, San Diego, 1985.

Norman A. H. The Dynamics of Military Group Behavior. In Charles H. Coates and Roland J. Pellegrin (Eds.), *Military Sociology*. University Park, MD: Social Science Press, 1965.

Nugent, R. & Gramick, J. Homosexuality: Protestant, Catholic, and Jewish Issues: A fishbone tale. In Hasbany, R. (Ed.), *Homosexuality and Religion*. Binghamton, NY: Harrington Park Press, 1989.

Nunngesser, L. G. *Homosexual Acts, Actors, and Identities*, New York: Praeger, 1983.

Nyberg, K. L. & Alston, J. P. Homosexual labeling by university youths. *Adolescence*, 1977, 12(48), 541-556.

Nye, J. S. Jr. Review of *An Insider Explores the Astonishing Realities of America's Defense Establishment* by Richard Stubbing. *New York Times Book Review*, September 28, 1986.

Oberstone, A. K. & Sukonek, H. Psychological adjustment and lifestyle of single lesbians and single heterosexual women. *Psychology of Women Quarterly*, 1976, 1(2), 172-188.

Ofshe, R. J. Inadvertent hypnosis during interrogation: False confession due to dissociative state: Misidentified multiple personality and the satanic cult hypothesis. *International Journal of Clinical & Experimental Hypnosis*, 1992, 40(4), 125-156.

Okum, M. E. Personal space as a reaction to the threat of an interaction with a homosexual. Unpublished Doctoral Dissertation, 1975, Catholic University of America, DAI 3604.

Oldham, S., Farnill, D., & Ball, I. Sex-role identity of female homosexuals. *Journal of Homosexuality*, 1982, 8(1), 41-46.

Oliver, L. W. *The Relationship of Group Cohesion to Group Performance: A Research Integration Attempt*. Alexandria, VA: U.S. Army Research Institute for the Behavioral and Social Sciences, 1988. Cited in the National Defense Research Institute, Sexual Orientation and U.S. Military Personnel Policy: Options and Assessment, Prepared for the Office of the Secretary of Defense, MR-323-OSD, RAND, 1993.

Oliver, L. W., *Cohesion Research: Conceptual and Methodological Issues*. Alexandria, VA: U.S. Army Research Institute for the Behavioral and Social Sciences, 1990.

Orwin, A. Treatment of a situational phobia: A case for running. *British Journal of Psychiatry*, 1974, 125, 95-98.

Otjen, J. P., DaVitte, W. B., Miller, G. L., Redd, J. S., & Loy, J. M. (The Office of the Secretary of Defense Working Group), *Memo-*

randum for the Secretary of Defense (Recommended DoD Homosexual Policy), June 8, 1993.

Painton, F. C. Fun behind the front. *Readers Digest*, October 1943, 99-102.

Panton, P. & Toufexis, A. The shrinking ten percent. *Time*, April 26, 1993, 141(17), 27.

Parke, R. D. & Sawin, D. B. Children's privacy in the home: Developmental, ecological and child-rearing determinants. *Environment and Behavior*, 1979, 11(1), 87-104.

Paul, J. P. The bisexual identity: An idea without social recognition. In J. P. De Cecco & M. Shively (Eds.), *Origins of Sexuality and Homosexuality*, Binghamton, NY: Harrington Park Press, 1984.

Pease, K. K. & Forsythe, D. P. Human rights, humanitarian intervention, and world politics. *Human Rights Quarterly*, 1993, 15, 290-314.

Peplau, L. A. What homosexuals want in relationships. *Psychology Today*, March, 1981, 28-38.

Peplau, L. A. Research on homosexual couples: An overview. In J. P. De Cecco *Gay Relationships*. New York: Harrington Park Press, 1987.

Peplau, L. A., & Gordon, S. L. The intimate relationships of lesbians and gay men. In E. R. Allgeier & N. B. McCormick (Eds.), *Gender Roles and Sexual Behavior*. Palo Alto, CA: Mayfield, 1982.

Perin, N. *Dr. Bowdler's Legacy. A History of Expurgated Books in England & America*. New York: Atheneum, 1969.

Peterson, J. & Marin, G. Issues in the prevention of AIDS among Black and Hispanic men. *American Psychologist*, 1988, 43, 871-877.

Pilot study of a household survey to determine HIV seroprevalence. *Morbidity and Mortality Weekly Report*, January 11, 1991, 40(1), 1-5.

Pleck, J. H. The male sex role: Definitions, problems, and sources of change. *Journal of Social Issues*, 1976, 32, 155-164.

Ponse, B. Lesbians and their worlds. In J. Marmor (Ed.), *Homosexual Behavior: A Modern Appraisal*. New York: Basic Books, 1980, 157-175.

Posner, R. A. *Sex and Reason.* Cambridge, MA: Harvard University Press, 1992.

President Clinton's address to the 48th Session of the United Nations General Assembly, September 27, 1993, The United Nations, New York, New York.

President Clinton spends too much time on gay rights say a majority of Americans in a *U.S. News & World Report* poll. *U.S. News & World Report Press Release*, June 26, 1993.

Price, J. H. High school students' attitudes toward homosexuality. *The Journal of School Health*, 1982, 52(8), 469-473.

Price, V. & Hsu, M. L. Public opinion about AIDS policies: The role of misinformation and attitudes toward homosexuals. *Public Opinion Quarterly*, 1992, 56, 29-52.

Pulwers, J. E. The information and education programs of the armed forces: An administrative and social history, 1940-1945. Unpublished Doctoral Dissertation, 1983, Catholic University of America, DAI 4404.

Rado, S. *Psychoanalysis of Behavior II.* New York: Grune & Stratton, 1962.

Reback, C. J. The Social Construction of Sexualities: A Study of Redefining Identity. Unpublished Doctoral Dissertation, 1986, University of California, Santa Cruz, DAI 4706.

"Recommended DoD Homosexual Policy Outline." Office of the Secretary of Defense Working Group Memorandum, 8 June, 1993.

Rees, B. & Leach, D. The social inhibition of micturition(paruresis): Sex similarities and differences. *Journal of American College Health Association*, 1975, 203-205.

Register, P. A. & Kihstrom, J. F. Hypnosis and interrogative suggestibility. *Personality & Individual Differences*, 1988, 9(3), 549-558.

Reid, E. & Novak, P. Personal space: An unobtrusive measures study. *Bulletin of the Psychonomic Society*, 1975, 5(3), 265-266.

Reiss, B. F. Psychological tests in homosexuality. In J. Marmor (Ed.), *Homosexual Behavior: A Modern Reappraisal.* New York: Basic Books, 1965.

Report details abuses at '91 naval aviators' convention. *Facts on File,* April 29, 1993, 53(2735), 305.

Richardson, D. & Hart, J. The development and maintenance of a homosexual identity. In John Hart and Diane Richardson (Eds.), *The Theory and Practice of Homosexuality*. London: Routledge & Kegan Paul, 1981.

Richardson, F. M. *Fighting Spirit: A Study of Psychological Factors in War*. New York: Crane, Russak & Co., Inc., 1978.

Richardson, J. T., Mavromatis, A., Mindel, T., & Owens, A. C. Individual differences in hypnagogic and hypnopompic imagery. *Journal of Mental Imagery*, 1981, 5(2), 91-96.

Roback, H. B., Langevin, R., & Zajac, Y. Sex of free choice figure drawings by homosexual and heterosexual subjects. *Journal of Personality Assessment*, 1974, 38(2), 154-155.

Roberts, A. Humanitarian war: Military intervention and human rights. *International Affairs*, 1993, 69(3), 429-449.

Robertson, G. Parent-child relationships and homosexuality. *British Journal of Psychiatry*, 1972, 121(564), 525-528.

Robinson, W. J. *Woman: Her Sex and Love Life*. New York: J. J. Little and Ives, Co., 1917, 273-274.

Rogers, S. M. & Turner, C. F. Male-male sexual contact in the U.S.A.: Findings from five sample surveys, 1970-1990. *The Journal of Sex Research*, 1991, 28(4), 491-519.

Rosenfeld, A., Siegel-Gorelick, B., Haavik, D., Duryea, M., Wenegrat, A., Martin, J., & Bailey, R. Parental perceptions of children's modesty: A cross-sectional survey of ages two to ten years. *Psychiatry*, 1984, 47, 351-365.

Ross, M. W. *The Married Homosexual Man: A Psychological Study*. Boston: Routledge and Kegan Paul, 1983.

Ross, M. W. & Arrindell, W. A. Perceived parental rearing patterns of homosexual and heterosexual men. *Journal of Sex Research*, 1988, 24, 275-281.

Roth, S. Psychotherapy with lesbian couples: Individual issues, female socialization, and the social context. *Journal of Marital and Family Therapy*, 1985, 11(3), 273-286.

Rothblum, E. D. & Brehony, K. A. The Boston marriage today: Romantic but asexual relationships among lesbians. In Charles Silverstein (Ed.), *Gays, Lesbians, and Their Therapists: Studies in Psychotherapy*. New York: W. W. Norton, 1991.

Rothenberg, D. Sexual behavior in an abnormal setting. *Corrective and Social Psychiatry and Journal of Behavior Technology, Methods and Therapy*, 1983, 29(3), 78-81.

Rubin, L. *Just Friends: The Role of Friendship in Our Lives*, New York: Harper & Row, 1985.

Rugoff, M. *Prudery and Passion: Sexuality in Victorian America*. New York: G.P. Putnam's Sons, 1971.

Ruitenbeek, H. M. (Ed.) *The Problem of Homosexuality in Modern Society*. New York: E. P. Dutton, 1963.

Russell, P. & Gray, C. D. Prejudice against a progay man in an everyday situation: A scenario study. *Journal of Applied Social Psychology*, 1992, 22(21), 1676-1687.

Rust, P. C. The politics of sexual identity: Sexual attraction and behavior among lesbian and bisexual women. *Social Problems*, 1992, 39(4), 366-386.

Rust, P. C. "Coming out" in the age of social constructionism. *Gender & Society*, 1993, 7(1), 50-77.

Saad, L. & McAneny, L. Americans deeply split over ban on gays in military. *The Gallup Poll Monthly*, February 1993, 6-12.

Saghir, M. T., & Robins, E. *Male and Female Homosexuality: A Comprehensive Investigation*. Baltimore: Williams & Wilkins, 1973.

Salzman, L. "Latent" homosexuality. In Judd Marmor (Ed.), *Sexual Inversion: The Multiple Roots of Homosexuality*. New York: Basic Books, Inc., 1965.

Savage, P. L. & Gabriel, R. A., Cohesion and disintegration in the American army: An alternative perspective. *Armed Forces and Society*, 1976, 2, 340-376.

Scacco, A. M. *Rape in Prison*. Springfield, IL: C.C. Thomas, 1975.

Scacco, A. M. *Male Rape: A Casebook of Sexual Aggressions*. New York: AMS Press, 1982.

Scanzoni, L. *Is the Homosexual My Neighbor? Another Christian View*. San Francisco: Harper & Row, 1978.

Schlossman, S., Mershon, S., Livers, A., Jacobson, T., & Haggerty, T. Potential insights from analogous situations: Integrating blacks into the U.S. military. National Defense Research Institute, *Sexual Orientation and U.S. Military Personnel Policy:*

Options and Assessment, Prepared for the Office of the Secretary of Defense, MR-323-OSD, RAND, 1993.

Schmitt, J. P. & Kurdek, L. A. Age and gender differences in and personality correlates of loneliness in different relationships. *Journal of Personality Assessment*, 1985, 49(5), 485-496.

Schneider, B. E. Coming out at work: Bridging the private/public gap. *Work and Occupations*, 1986, 13(4), 463-487.

Schneider, W. & Lewis, I. A. The straight story on homosexuality and gay rights. *Public Opinion*, February/March, 1984, 7, 16-20, 59-60.

Schover, L. & LoPiccollo, J. Effectiveness of treatment for dysfunction of sexual desire. *Journal of Sex and Marital Therapy*, 1982, 8, 179-197.

Schreiner-Engle, P. *Clinical aspects of female sexuality*. Paper presented at the meeting of the International Academy of Sex Research, Amsterdam, the Netherlands, September 20, 1986.

Sears, R., Maccoby, E., & Levin, H. *Patterns of Child Rearing*. Evanston, IL: Row, Peterson, 1957.

Sedgwick, E. K. *Epistemology of the Closet*. Berkeley: University of California Press, 1990.

Segal, J. & Segal, Z. "Standards on Nudity." *Parents Magazine*, May 1990, 65(5), p. 211.

Segarin, E. Prison homosexuality and its effects on post-prison sexual behavior. *Psychiatry*, 1976, 245-257.

Seifert, R. Constructions of masculinity–The military as a discursive power. *Argument*, 1992, November-December 34(6), 859-872.

Sepekoff, B. The development of an instrument to measure homophobia among heterosexual males. Unpublished Doctoral Dissertation, 1985, New York University, DAI 4701.

Seyfried, B. A. & Hendrick, C. When do opposites attract? When they are opposite in sex and sex-role attitudes. *Journal of Personality and Social Psychology*, 1973, 25, 15-20.

Seymore, C., DuRant, R. H., Jay, M. S., Freeman, D., Gomez, L., Sharp, C., & Linder, C. W. Influence of the position during the examination and the sex of the examiner on patient anxiety during pelvic examination. *Journal of Pediatrics*, February, 1986, 108(2), 312-317.

Sharrock, R. & Gudjonsson, G. H. Intelligence, previous convictions and interrogative suggestibility: A path analysis of alleged false confession cases. *British Journal of Clinical Psychology*, 1993, 32(2), 169-175.

Shawver, Lois. Research variables in psychology and the logic of their creation. *Psychiatry*, 1977, 40 (1), 1-16.

Shawver, Lois & Kurdys, Douglas. Shall we employ women guards in male prisons? *Journal of Psychiatry and Law*, 1987, 15(2), 277-295.

Shemella, P. The military does not look like America. *Army*, July, 1993, 44.

Sherif, C. W., Sherif, M., & Nebergall, R. E. *Attitude and Attitude Change; The Social Judgment Involvement Approach*. Philadelphia, PA: W. B. Saunders Co., 1965.

Shields, P. M. A new paradigm for military policy: Socioeconomics. *Armed Forces and Society*, Summer 1993, 511-531.

Shields, S. A. & Harriman, Robert E. Fear of male homosexuality: Cardiac responses of low and high homonegative males. In John P. De Cecco (Ed.), *Bashers, Baiters & Bigots: Homophobia in American Society*. Binghamton, NY: Harrington Park Press, 1985, 53-68.

Shils, E. A. Primary groups in the American army. In Robert K. Merton and Paul F. Lazarsfeld (Eds.), *Continuities in Social Research: Studies in the Scope and Method of "The American Soldier."* New York: Free Press, 1950, 16-39.

Shils, E. A. & Janowitz, M. Cohesion and Disintegration in the Wehrmacht in World War II. *Public Opinion Quarterly*, 1948, 12, 280-315.

Shils, E. B. Privacy: Its constitution and vicissitudes. *Law and Contemporary Problems*, 1966, 31, 281-306.

Shilts, R. *Conduct Unbecoming*. New York: St. Martin's Press, 1993.

Shilts, R. What's fair in love and war. *Newsweek*, 1993, 121(5).

Sigelman, C. K., Howell, J. L., Cornell, D. P., Cutright, J. D., Dewey, J. C. Courtesy stigma: The social implications of associating with a gay person. *The Journal of Social Psychology*, 1991, 131(1), 45-56.

Sinclair, K. & Ross, M. W. Consequences of decriminalization of homosexuality: A study of two Australian states. *Journal of Homosexuality*, 1985, 12(1), 119-127.

Singh, K. K. & Gudjonsson, G. H. Interrogative suggestibility among adolescent boys and its relationship with intelligence, memory, and cognitive set. *Journal of Adolescence*, 1992, 15(2), 155-161.

Smith, H. A modest test of cross-cultural differences in sexual modesty, embarrassment and self-disclosure. *Qualitative Sociology*, 1980, 3(3), 223-241.

Smith, T. W. Adult sexual behavior in 1989: Number of partners, frequency of intercourse and risk of AIDS. *Family Planning Perspectives*, 1991, 23(3), 102-107.

Socarides, C. W. *The Overt Homosexual*. New York: Grune & Stratton, 1968.

Sokolov, E. *Perception and the Conditioned Reflex*. New York: Macmillan, 1963.

Soloff, P. H. Pseudohomosexual psychosis in basic military training. *Archives of Sexual Behavior*, 1978, 7(5), 503-510.

Solomon, G. F. & Solomon, J. C. Shyness and sex, *Medical Aspects of Human Sexuality*, 1971, 5(5), 10-19.

Steffan v. Cheney, Civil action No. 88-3669-Og, U.S. District Court, District of Columbia, Dec. 09, 1991.

Steffensmeier, D. & Steffensmeier, R. Sex differences in reactions to homosexuals: Research continuities and further developments. *The Journal of Sex Research*, 1974, 10, 52-67.

Stephens, W. N. *A Cross-Cultural Study of Modesty and Obscenity and Pornography*. Vol. 3. Washington, DC: U.S. Printing Office, 1971.

Stockton, R., Rohde, R. I., & Haughey, J. The effects of structured group exercises on cohesion, engagement, avoidance, and conflict. *Small Group Research*, 1992, 23(2), 155-168.

Stokes, K., Kilmann, P. R., & Wanlass, R. L. Sexual orientation and sex role conformity. *Archives of Sexual Behavior*, 1983, 12(5), 427-433.

Stone, L. *The Family, Sex, and Marriage in England, 1500-1800: The Abridged Edition*, New York: Harper Torchbooks, 1979.

Storms, M. O. Theories of sexual orientation. *Journal of Personality and Social Psychology*, 1980, 38(5), 763-792.

Story, M. D. A comparison of social nudists and non-nudists on experience with various sexual outlets. *Journal of Sex Research*, 1987, 23(2), 197-211.

Stouffer, S. A., Lumsdaine, A. A., Lumsdaine, M. H., Williams, Jr., R. M., Smith, M. B., Janis, I. L., Star, S. A., & Cottrell. L. S. *The American Soldier: Adjustment During Army Life.* Vol. I, p. 12 and *The American Soldier: Combat and Its Aftermath,* Vol. II. Princeton: Princeton University Press, 1949.

Tanfer, K. National survey of men: Design and execution. *Family Planning Perspectives*, 1993, 25(2), 83-86.

Thompson, E. H., Grisanti, C., & Pleck, J. H. Attitudes toward the male role and their correlates. *Sex Roles*, 1985, 13(7-8) 413-427.

Thompson, G. H. & Fishburn, W. R. Attitudes toward homosexuality among graduate counseling students. *Counselor Education and Supervision*, 1977, December, 121-130.

Topfree, bottomfree. *Economist*, 1992, August 15, 324(7772), A19.

Towell, P. Military dismissals. *Congressional Quarterly Weekly Report*, February 6, 1993, 51(6), 274.

Town, J. P. & Harvey, J. H. Self-disclosure, attribution and social interaction. *Social Psychology Quarterly*, 1981, 44(4), 291-300.

Trevor-Roper, H. R. *The Age of Louis XIV and Other Selected Writings*. New York: Washington Square Press, 1963.

Troiden, R. R. Homosexual identity development. *Journal of Adolescent Health Care*, March 1988, 9(2), 105-113.

Turnbull, D. & Brown, M. Attitudes toward homosexuality and male and female reactions to homosexual and heterosexual slides. *Canadian Journal of Behavioral Science*, 1977, 9(1), 68-80.

Turner, B. & Support Staff. Gays under fire. *Newsweek*, September 14, 1992, 35-40.

Turner, C. F., Miller, H. G., & Moses, L. E. (Eds.), *AIDS: Sexual Behavior and Intravenous Drug Use*. Washington, DC: National Academy Press, 1989.

United States General Accounting Office. *Defense Force Management: Statistics Related to DoD's Policy on Homosexuality.* Report to Congressional Requesters, June 1992, 4.

Vaitkus, M. & Griffith, J. An evaluation of unit replacement on unit cohesion and individual morale in the U.S. Army All-Volunteer Force. *Military Psychology*, 1990, 2, 221-239.

Veggeberg, S. In hot pursuit of post-cold war survival, weapons labs see industrial partnership. *The Scientist*, 7(12), June 14, 1993, p.1.

Vivona, C. & Gomillion, M. Situation morality of bathroom nudity. *Journal of Sex Research*, 1972, 8 (2), 128-135.

Wahl, C. W. & Golden, J. Psychogenic urinary retention. Report of 6 cases. *Psychosomatic Medicine*, 1963, 25(6), 543-555.

Walters, R. G. *Primers for Prudery: Sexual Advice to Victorian America*. Englewood Cliffs, NJ: Prentice-Hall, 1974.

Waring, E. M. & Chelune, G. J. Marital intimacy and self-disclosure. *Journal of Clinical Psychology*, 1983, 39, 183-190.

Warren, C. A. B. *Identity and Community in the Gay World*. New York: John Wiley and Sons, 1974.

Warwick, H.M. & Salkovskis, P.M. Unwanted erections in obsessive-compulsive disorder. *British Journal of Psychiatry*, December 1990, 157, 919-921.

Weaver, G. S. *The Heart of the World or Home and Its Wide Work*, 18th edition. Chicago: Elder Publishing Co., 1882.

Weinberg, G. Becoming a nudist. *Psychiatry*, February 1966, 15-24.

Weinberg, G. *Society and the Healthy Homosexual*. New York: St. Martin's Press, 1972.

Weinberg, M. Sexual modesty, social meanings, and the nudist camp. *Social Problems*, 1964, 12, 311-318.

Weinberg, M. S. & Williams, C. J. *Male Homosexuals*. New York: Oxford University Press, 1974.

Weis, C. B. & Dain, R. N. Ego development and sex attitudes in heterosexual and homosexual men and women. *Archives of Sexual Behavior*, 1979, 8(4), 341-355.

Weiss, L. & Lowenthal, M. F. Life course perspective on friendship. In M. Thurnher & D. Chiriboga (Eds.), *Four Stages of Life*. San Francisco: Jossey-Bass, 1975.

Wells, J. W. & Kline, W. B. Self-disclosure of homosexual orientation. *Journal of Social Psychology*, 1987, 127(2), 191-197.

Wells, J. W. Teaching about gay and lesbian sexual and affectional orientation using explicit films to reduce homophobia. *Journal of Humanistic Education and Development*, 1989, 28(1), 18-34.

Wesbrook, S. D. The potential for military disintegration, In S. C. Sarkesian (Ed.), *Combat Effectiveness: Cohesion, Stress, and the Volunteer Military*. Beverly Hills, CA: Sage, 1980.

West, P. Thaw in Cold War offers Democrats a chance against Republicans. *The Baltimore Sun*, Friday, December 1, 1989.

Wheeler, L., Reiss, H. & Nezlek, J. Loneliness, social interaction, and sex roles. *Journal of Personality and Social Psychology*, 1983, 45, 943-953.

Whitam, F. L., & Mathy, R. M. *Male Homosexuality in Four Societies: Brazil, Guatemala, the Philippines, and the United States*. New York: Praeger, 1986.

Whiting, J. W. M. & Child, I. L. *Child Training and Personality: A Cross-Cultural Study*. New Haven: Yale University Press, 1953.

Whitley, B. E., Jr. The relationship of heterosexuals' attributions for the causes of homosexuality to attitudes toward lesbians and gay men. *Personality and Social Psychology Bulletin*, 1990, 16(2), 369-377.

Wilcox, D. *Ethical Marriage*. Michigan, 1900. Cited without a publisher in Haller, J. S. & Haller, R. M. *The Physician and Sexuality in Victorian America*. Urbana: University of Illinois Press, 1974.

Williams, C. & Weinberg, M. *Homosexuals and the Military*. New York: Harper & Row, 1971.

Williams, D. G. Gender, masculinity-femininity, and emotional intimacy in same-sex friendship. *Sex Roles*, 1985, 12(5-6), 587-600.

Williams, G. E. & Johnson, A. M. Recurrent urinary retention due to emotional factors: A case report. *Psychosomatic Medicine*, 1956, 18(1), 77-80.

Williams, G. W. & Degenhardt, E. T. Paruresis: A survey of a disorder of micturition. *The Journal of General Psychology*, 1954, 51, 19-29.

Winstead, B. A. Sex differences in same-sex friendships. In V. J. Derlega & B. A. Winstead (Eds.), *Friendship and Social Interaction*. New York: Springer-Verlag, 1986.

Wood-Allen, Mary, M.D. *What a Young Woman Ought to Know.* Philadelphia: The Vir Publishing Co., 1905.

Wooden, W. S. & Parker, J. *Men Behind Bars: Sexual Exploitation in Prison.* New York: Plenum Press, 1982.

Woods, S. M. Some dynamics of male chauvinism. *Archives of General Psychiatry,* 1976, 33, 63-65.

Wright, P. H. & Scanlon, M. B. Gender role orientations and friendship: Some attenuation, but gender differences abound. *Sex Roles,* 1991, 24(9/10), 551-566.

Yeazell, R. B. *Fictions of Modesty: Women and Courtship in the English Novel.* Chicago: University of Chicago Press, 1991.

Zarit, J. Intimate look of the Iranian male. In Arno Schmitt & Jehoda Sofer (Eds.), *Sexuality and Eroticism Among Males in Moslem Societies.* Binghamton, NY: The Haworth Press, 1992, 55-60.

Zgourides, G. D. Paruresis: Overview and implications for treatment. *Psychological Reports,* 1987, 60(3, pt. 2), 1171-1176.

Subject Index

Name Index